LYMINGTON
An Illustrated History

Following pages
A view of Lymington from Green Lane, now Monument Lane, on the
east side of the river, engraved in 1832.
The quay is clearly visible on the left, and the High Street climbs westward in the
centre towards the twelfth century parish church of St Thomas.

THE DOVECOTE PRESS

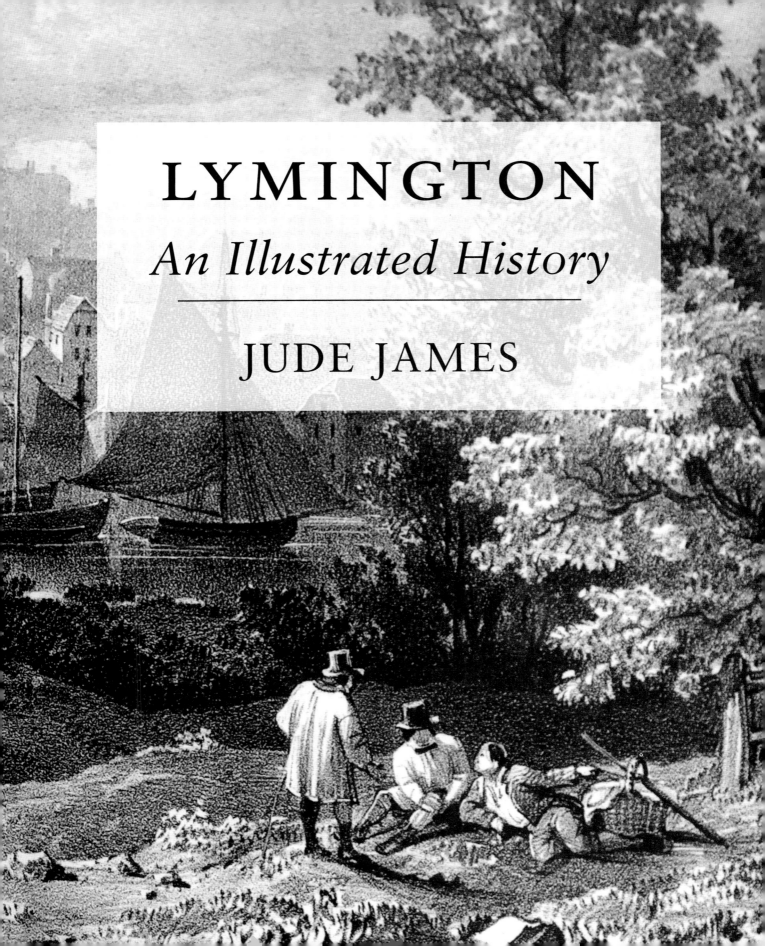

LYMINGTON

An Illustrated History

JUDE JAMES

"But I shall let the little I have learnt go forth into the day in order that someone better than I may guess the truth, and in his work may prove and rebuke my error. At this I shall rejoice that I was yet the means whereby this truth has come to light."
Albrecht Dürer (1471-1528)

"Perhaps if a copy of this work may survive for a century, some antiquarian, yet unborn, may follow up our plan . . . "
Edward King (1821-85) in *Old Times Revisited in Lymington*

The Town Hall of 1710, which stood in the High Street
until it was demolished in 1858.

First published in 2007 by The Dovecote Press Ltd
Wimborne Minster, Dorset, BH21 4JD

ISBN 978-1-904-34953-2

© Jude James 2007

Designed and produced by The Dovecote Press Ltd
Printed and bound in Singapore

All papers used in books produced by The Dovecote Press
are natural, recyclable products made from wood grown in
sustainable, well-managed forests.

A CIP catalogue record for this book is available
from the British Library

Contents

Foreword

ANY HISTORY needs to be selective in the choice of sources used and, once chosen, the manner of interpreting them and integrating the results into the narrative is in the hands of the writer. It must be said that some things which one historian would put in another would leave out.

With this history my aim has been to try to select from the voluminous quantities of surviving records those that contain evidence which seemed to me most reflective and descriptive of the town's development over about a thousand years. By so doing I have tried to present a coherent story of a market town and small port with a strong emphasis on its social, political and economic life.

To make the result both intelligible and manageable the history has been restricted geographically to the manor and parish of Lymington with greatest emphasis on the area of the town or borough. Space has precluded the inclusion of more than incidental references to the places beyond Lymington except where these are wholly relevant. The extension of the borough in 1832 and again a century later has necessitated incorporating something of the history of those places which were subsumed by the boundary changes.

My interpretations, sometimes at variance with those already in print and popularly accepted, are founded, so far as possible, on a wide-ranging and dispassionate examination of the original sources. Some fresh ideas and interpretations have emerged because a larger quantity of records is now available for research and because it has been possible to re-evaluate some of the previously published accounts on the basis of new evidence.

Details and anecdotes are used throughout, not merely for their own sake, but because in some ways they more fully reveal the nature of the people and the times in which they were living.

All approaches to telling a history have inherent problems. The one I have chosen is essentially a chronological narrative, but on occasion it has seemed more sensible to allow particular themes to be developed and analysed outside the constraints of a strict chronology.

The Footnotes and Bibliography will enable interested readers to explore much more fully some of those aspects, which I may have done no more than touch upon.

CASH EQUIVALENTS

There is no precise way in which historic monetary values can be accurately related to present day prices. Many factors concerned with types and availability of commodities at different times make precise equivalents impossible. For example, the retail price index will vary significantly from that of average earnings and in turn, will differ from per capita GDP. However, readers would no doubt like some kind of guidance and an abstract formulation based on the retail price index (RPI) can be given.

If money value is taken to be what could be purchased for £100 in 2005 one would only have needed 4s. 3d. in 1264 and by 1550, even after early Tudor inflation, one would only need 8s. 10d. By 1650 the sum required had increased to £1 4s. 5d. and in 1800 it was £2 1s. 4d but by 1900 had dropped to £1 7s. 9d. By 1950 it was £6 9s 9d and, following the high inflationary pressures of the last part of the 20th century, the sum had risen to £88.69 by the year 2000. [For these figures I would like to acknowledge, Lawrence H. Officer, "Purchasing Power of British Pounds from 1264 to 2005", MeasuringWorth.com 2006.]

All money values are shown in the currency form of their time, i.e. sterling (£ s. d.) up to 1971 and decimal thereafter. Sometimes medieval values have been transcribed as shillings and pence instead of just pence, e.g. 20d. is shown as 1s. 8d. The medieval 'mark' (13s. 4d.) is usually translated into its shillings and pence equivalent. Up to the seventeenth century money values were almost always written in small Roman numerals (viij^d), in the text these have been mostly transcribed in Arabic numerals (8d.).

DATES AND DATING

All dates appear as in the original documents or sources with the exception of the year which, before 1752, has been amended to begin on 1 January instead of 25 March. In quoting dates no account has been taken of the eleven 'lost' days in September 1752 when the Julian calendar was superseded by the Gregorian. Regnal years (e.g. 47 Hen. III or 13 Eliz. I), even where the style is retained, are transcribed also as calendar dates (e.g. 1262 or 1570).

FOREIGN WORDS AND PHRASES

All foreign words appear in italics and are either translated or explained. Occasionally Latin words are shown in brackets where a precise translation is not possible or is dubious.

PERSONAL AND PLACE-NAMES

Personal names were often spelt in a variety of ways until the standardization of the nineteenth century. In the middle ages they were frequently given Latin forms (e.g. *Mercator* = Merchant, *Cymentarius* = Mason, *Faber* = Smith, and so forth). Often the spellings varied within a single document: particularly to be noted is William Lytecane whose name was spelled in a number of quite different forms, e.g. Lytecave, Lyteknave, Littlecane, Littlecave, etc.

In the book, in order to avoid confusion, the practice has been to use either the name form as it first appears or the form that has become customary or most generally accepted as correct. The use of '*le*' (the) or '*de*' (of) is also variable, for example we find in Henry le Chaundelir (Chandeler, Chaundler, Chandler = Candlemaker or Candleseller) appearing both with and without '*le*'; the same is true of '*de*', early records note the later earls of Devon as 'de Courtenay' (Courteney, Courtney) but later just as 'Courtenay'.

Spelling of place-names is just as variable, e.g. 'Bolra', or 'Bolder' for modern Boldre and Lymington itself has about twenty different forms.

QUOTED TEXTS OR PHRASES

All contemporary historic quotations are shown either within single inverted commas or indented. Spelling and the use of capitals is transcribed as in the original document but punctuation is inserted to improve sense.

Acknowledgements

MY GREATEST debt is to the *real* historian of Lymington, Arthur Lloyd, whose painstaking researches and uses of source material has been an inspiration. His encouragement and kindness have been unflagging. Other assiduous workers on the town's history have provided me, through discussion and more especially in their published works, with a most valuable resource without which much of what I have written would have been far less informed. The first of these is the late Edward King of Lymington who generously allowed me to use sources in his home and on one occasion permitted me to take precious original material home. Equally, my indebtedness to the late Robert 'Bob' Coles, who has opened all our eyes to many facets of Lymington's past that few had touched upon before, is very great. His splendid brief *The Story of Lymington* has been a useful guide to the general picture. My thanks go to the late Brian Down who through his varied books and booklets and his contributions, as reporter, to the *Advertiser and Times,* has provided much material on which I have freely drawn.

The Friends of the St Barbe Museum, Lymington, especially the honorary curator, Dr Joanna Close-Brooks, FSA, have helped very greatly and I extend my warm thanks to them all. The Lymington and Pennington Town Council generously allowed me to photograph the bushel measure and the model of the old Town Hall now deposited in the museum collections. They also permitted an archaeological excavation in Grove Gardens which provided a tentative insight to the borough's medieval morphology.

I am grateful to the following for allowing the reproduction of illustrations in their possession or for which they hold the copyright: St Barbe Museum, Dr Joanna Close-Brooks, Mrs Janet Irvine, the Bridgeman Art Library, London, for *Before the Magistrate* by George Elgar Hicks, and Hampshire County Council Museums Service and Gill Arnott for the fine painting on the front cover, *Lymington Harbour* by J. Miles Gilbert.

Of much value have been the varied contributions made by many individuals, amongst them Ann Coles for access to her late husband's collections, the late Ted Marsh, Mrs Janet Irvine (née King), Mrs Jackie Stone, the late Jack Bradbury and the late Bill Klitz; Richard Reeves for several important medieval references and David Eels for additional information on the de Redvers family. David Hill kindly allowed access to the only surviving salt works buildings. I owe each of them a debt of thanks. Charles Curry, MBE, editor of the *Advertiser and Times,* as always, has been most helpful in permitting access to the newspaper files. The librarians at the University Library, Southampton, the Lymington Branch Library, the British Library and, more especially, the archivists and staff at the Hampshire and Dorset Record Offices have been unfailingly helpful. Steven Marshall, curator of the St Barbe Museum, has generously assisted whenever requested.

I have been fortunate to benefit from the careful advice and editing of David Burnett, my publisher, to whom I owe a considerable debt.

I am particularly indebted to the forbearance of Peggy, my wife, who constantly and constructively criticised the manuscript as it progressed and offered much practical advice. Thankfully, she also nourished the author!

Any errors or misinterpretations that may remain after all the help and advice I have received are my sole responsibility.

JUDE JAMES
Hordle
2007

Prologue

For two centuries Lymington has been renowned as a centre for yachting and if, today, it has national or, indeed, international fame it is largely because of this maritime role. However, the visitor to present day Lymington will quickly learn that the town has an importance in local affairs extending far beyond its vital and valuable connection with the river, upon whose rising westward bank it is built.

For the sake of introduction let us imagine coming to Lymington early on a sunny Saturday morning in late spring. Whether arriving from the west or the north we find the approaches are suburban but even so the town itself can be readily bypassed by following the loop of the A337 road. A deliberate turn must be made to enter the urban heart of Lymington. Apart from the ubiquitous motor vehicles it might at first be thought that one was entering a backwater. But such an impression will soon be dispelled, for the visitor will find the street already busy and, as the church is approached, with its grey stone-battlemented tower crowned by a delightful domed cupola containing a solitary bell, the activity gives the appearance of chaos. It is market day. Stall-holders jostle and mill around their pitches as the booths are erected and all the paraphernalia of trade and commerce is placed on portable tables for the delectation of the would be customer.

At this early hour the wan morning sun sends shafts like stage limelight along the street into the visitor's eyes. Pause to see the hurly-burly compose itself into an attractive scene as the canopied stalls, some colourfully bedecked, are aligned in two ranks on either side of the wide street, in counterpoint to the kaleidoscope of the brick and tiled façades of shops rising behind their temporary competitors. The traffic builds as the magnetic appeal of the

Saturday market day in the High Street.

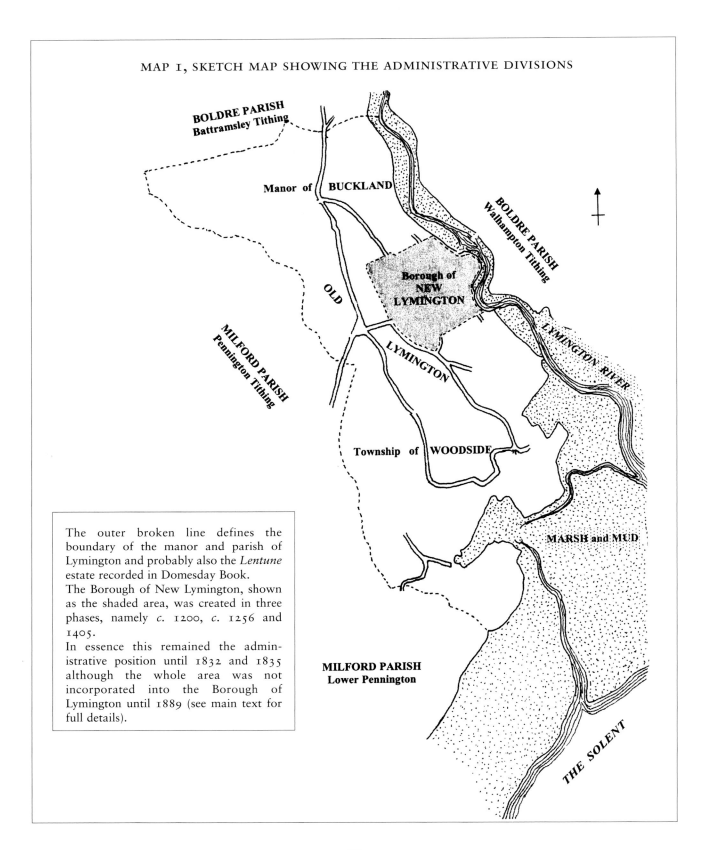

BOLDRE PARISH
Battramsley Tithing

Manor of BUCKLAND

BOLDRE PARISH
Walhampton Tithing

OLD

Borough of
NEW
LYMINGTON

MILFORD PARISH
Pennington Tithing

LYMINGTON

LYMINGTON RIVER

Township of WOODSIDE

MARSH and MUD

The outer broken line defines the boundary of the manor and parish of Lymington and probably also the *Lentune* estate recorded in Domesday Book.

The Borough of New Lymington, shown as the shaded area, was created in three phases, namely *c.* 1200, *c.* 1256 and 1405.

In essence this remained the administrative position until 1832 and 1835 although the whole area was not incorporated into the Borough of Lymington until 1889 (see main text for full details).

MILFORD PARISH
Lower Pennington

THE SOLENT

Lymington Quay in about 1947.

Saturday market draws its customers from the town and the surrounding hinterland. Uniformed policemen guide the growing traffic through the now narrowed street between the stalls. The town's car parks quickly fill, as on every other Saturday throughout the year.

Pavements are soon thronged with bustling crowds of shoppers and bargain-hunters. The cries of vendors, with fabulous offers, encourage purchasers from among the mêlée – a scene full of colour, life and movement. This is Lymington on show, continuing and sustaining a tradition established many centuries before of serving the native townsfolk and the country-dwellers drawn from the New Forest villages. Such a day is a time to trade, a time to gossip and renew old acquaintances, to seek for bargains, to buy too much and, perhaps, spend too much – markets were ever the same!

People of all stations and ages are there; the elderly supported by sticks competing for pavement room with infants propelled in pushchairs, the housewife and the businessman, the holidaymaker and the yachtsman, many laden with cheap and colourful plastic bags bulging ever greater as the produce is piled in. Here bric-a-brac vies with locally grown vegetables; handbags with sweet stalls; clothing with fresh fish; and permeating the air the aroma of 'fast foods' from stall-holders seeking to tempt and nourish the hungry: hot snacks and drinks in plastic cups soon to be discarded to augment the ever growing piles of refuse that before the day is done will form unsightly heaps along the gutters. Visitors and locals alike may seek refreshments in the more comfortable pubs and cafés that lie conveniently spaced along the High Street. After a suitable snack a brisk walk down the steeply dipping street, past the last group of stalls, leads to the cobbled and still picturesque Quay Street, guiding the visitor towards the quay and riverside.

At the quay the broad undulating waters of the Lymington River reflect the hulls and masts of hundreds of boats and yachts. Across the water, on the far side, the large white and blue Wightlink ferries are moored: one loading vehicles and passengers for the journey to Yarmouth on the Isle of Wight, just four miles distant across the Solent. This ferry route maintains a link, established in the middle ages, when both Lymington and the Isle of Wight belonged to the same landowning family, the de Redvers.

Such might be the impressions of a visitor. At a superficial level all the key elements in the life of the town are, at least, glimpsed in a journey from church to quay. But, of course, there is much more to Lymington that can be sensed from such a casual visit, as this book hopefully reveals.

ONE
From Farmstead to Borough

As with many English towns, Lymington's precise origins are difficult to discover. The early evidence has been diluted or swept away with the passing of the centuries. All dynamic urban communities change, expand and modify and in so doing frequently obscure the detail of their earlier history. Thus a description of origins is often speculative, but one fact is clear. Lymington is first mentioned in that early account of places and land ownership called Domesday Book. In that record, compiled at Winchester in 1086, it states:

> The Earl [Roger of Shrewsbury] holds 1 hide in LENTUNE and Fulcuin [holds it] of him. Leuing held it in paragio [i.e. as his own manor]. [It was] then assessed for 1 hide; now for half a hide, because the woodland is in the Forest. [There is] land for 2 ploughs. There 1 villein, 2 serfs and 3 bordars have 1 plough and [there is] 4 acres of meadow. In the time of King Edward the Confessor [i.e. 1066] it was valued at 20s; later and now at 15s.

This bald and solitary entry[1] raises a number of queries. The first concerns the name 'Lentune' and whether it is correct to interpret this as Lymington? Place-name scholars cogently suggest that the scribe entering the Lymington details in the Domesday Book had inadvertently abridged the name so that the middle element was omitted. This can be shown when Lymington is named as both **Lemynton** and **Limenton** in the reign of Henry I, only a matter of about thirty or forty years later. Accepting that to be the case we should now consider what the name means. It was once widely accepted that *Lemen* was a Celtic word meaning *elm tree* and that it became attached to the river, that is, *Elm (tree) River*, possibly meaning a river which had elm trees growing along its banks. Subsequently the settlement or *ton* near its estuary became defined by the river name. However, more recently it has been suggested that the *Lemen* element is derived from *Lemana* meaning *marsh*. So the most recent interpretation suggests that Lymington originally meant *Marsh Settlement (or village)* that is to say, settlement or village by the marsh.[2]

Whichever interpretation is preferred it nevertheless remains true that the overwhelming probability is that the *Lentune* of *Domesday* is the place later called Lymington. But what does the entry mean? What is described is a small agricultural settlement, tenanted by a man named Leuing or Leving, with a tiny resident population comprising the six recorded individuals, of whom one is a substantial farmer (the villein), three who may be described as smallholders (the bordars) and two slaves (serfs). If all had families we may perhaps

The entry for Lymington (Lentune) as it appears in Domesday Book.

estimate a population of about thirty.

That is hardly the description of a settlement of sufficient stature to form the basis of a significant, though small, market town and harbour. It is of course possible that those responsible for compiling the *Domesday* account failed to enter the details of some larger manor: there are examples of this happening elsewhere.3 However, deductions can only be made on the basis of what is known and recorded and in the *Domesday* account we have clear documentary proof of the existence of a tiny agricultural hamlet from which the later town of Lymington developed.

It should also be noticed that the tax assessment for *Lentune* was reduced from 20s. to 15s. because the woodland belonging to the manor became subject to Forest Law within the freshly created royal hunting preserve known as the New Forest (in *Domesday Book*: 'Nova foresta'). This kind of reduction in value happened to many manors in the area.4 The reason for this was that woodland abutting or close to the designated forest was subject to occupation by the beasts of the chase and, as such, would be of less value than when exclusively part of the manor. The taxable assessment for Lymington (*Lentune*) was set at one hide. By the 1080s the hide no longer represented a precise area of land, as undoubtedly it originally had, but referred solely to the tax or rate due on each manor. What it does indicate is a measure of wealth for any particular community and an assessment of one hide indicates a low value.

Where precisely was this manor of *Lentune* situated? Today it is not readily recognised that there is a small stream, the Stanford rivulet, running north-south to the west of Lymington which marked its former boundary with Pennington in the parish of Milford (see Map 1). It is now little more than a culvert, but in late Anglo-Saxon and Norman times it may well have assumed far greater importance. The road into Lymington from the west had to cross it via a ford whose name has survived into present times, namely, Stanford or, in its original meaning, Stone-ford. It seems highly probable that the original *Domesday* settlement lay on the gently rising ground and plateau to the east of this stream, the area occupied today by the modern Rowans Park housing estate, Waitrose supermarket and the St Thomas Street area. With its arable, this would have provided a workable agricultural unit on the level plateau for two plough teams, with its associated meadow lying alongside the stream. The much larger Lymington River would have defined the eastern boundary of the manor, but the steep slope down to the river may well have discouraged its exploitation as arable by oxen-drawn ploughs and it would merely have been pasture or even scrub.

Of course, folk had been living in and around the Lymington area long before recorded history. The region of Wessex, within which Lymington lies, had been settled by prehistoric peoples since very remote times. Evidence of human activity in the form of flint hand-axes has been found in the gravel deposits throughout the surrounding area and this takes us back to the Palaeolithic or Old Stone Age period about 25,000 BC or even earlier. These peoples were tribal and nomadic, living by hunting and gathering wild foods, so we cannot speak of them as having established settlements in the sense of towns and villages that can be equated with those of historic times. In around 4000 BC the first farmers of the Neolithic or New Stone Age arrived, but, they seem to have left little evidence of their presence in the area. Later new racial and cultural groups arrived, such as the so-called Beaker Folk and the metal-using Bronze Age peoples. Both groups, during a period of over a thousand years, left artefacts, tools and evidence of their occupation in Lymore, Sway and on the forest heathlands.

Buckland Rings, a magnificent embanked and ditched earthen fortress, about one mile north of Lymington was constructed in the Iron Age, the period lasting from about 600 BC up to the time of the Roman occupation of Britain in the first century AD. It has not been possible to date the fort precisely but it may have been built as early as the third or fourth century BC.5 It clearly shows the Celtic people of that time were farming along the fertile valley of the Lymington River a few hundred yards above its effective tidal limit. Of their lives and circumstances we know very little, and we cannot show any direct connection with the later establishment of the agricultural community

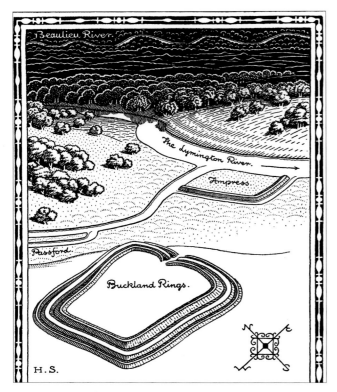

A conjectural drawing by Heywood Sumner showing a bird's eye view of the Iron Age fort at Buckland Rings. Passford Water on the left marks the parish boundary.

Interestingly, there are twenty-two settlements along the coastal margin utilising the better quality land south of the New Forest, whose names end in the Saxon word *tun* (. . . ton), meaning farmstead or village, and one of these is Lymington. Of that early settlement we have no knowledge except through the already quoted *Domesday* entry.

Thus Lymington first emerges into the faint gleam of early recorded history as a small agricultural community, yet one apparently with sufficient potential to grow into an important market town with a harbour and an industry based on the extraction of salt from sea water. It is a curious and unexplained fact that *Domesday* omits any mention of salt pans *(salinae)* at Lymington, yet records six at Hordle lying only three or four miles to the west. Does this omission provide, perhaps, a further reason for suspecting a missing reference to another manor at Lymington? This we are unlikely ever to discover.

In the interval between the end of the eleventh century and about 1200 little detail of Lymington's story emerges from the surviving annals. In the time of *Domesday* Lymington was part of the extensive estates of Roger Bêlleme, Earl of Shrewsbury, but when, at the death of William Rufus in the New Forest in August 1100, Robert, the then Earl of Shrewsbury (son of Roger), backed Robert Curthose, William the Conqueror's eldest son, in his claim for the English kingdom, he made what proved to be an injudicious alliance, for it was Henry Beauclerc, Robert's younger brother, who was successful in gaining the throne to become Henry I. The new king, anxious to reward those who had supported his cause and punish those who opposed him, dispossessed supporters of Robert by confiscating their lands in order to grant them to his own allies.

So it was that Lymington together with Christchurch, Breamore, the Isle of Wight and other lands were granted, in about 1102, to Richard de Redvers (died 1107) who had loyally supported Henry's cause both in Normandy and England. Richard de Redvers was the head of a Norman noble family (see de Redvers pedigree chart in the Appendices). It was his son, Baldwin (died 1155), who, on being raised to the peerage in 1141, took

described in *Domesday*. It seems therefore wrong to describe these Iron Age farmers and warriors as precursors of historic Lymington. Their society and the manner in which it was organised has no demonstrable link with that emerging about 1,000 years later. Although the Romans occupied the area, evidence for any settlement in the vicinity of Lymington itself is totally lacking. The few Roman coins of Claudius (died AD54) found in the eighteenth century near Buckland Rings do not constitute evidence of Roman settlement.[6]

The real antecedent of historic Lymington lies in the arrival of the Anglo-Saxons during the sixth and seventh centuries. The Venerable Bede[7] refers to them thus:

These new-comers were from the three most formidable races of Germany, the Saxons, Angles and Jutes. From the Jutes are descended the people of Kent and the Isle of Wight and *those in the province of the West Saxons opposite the Isle of Wight who are called Jutes to this day* (AD 730).

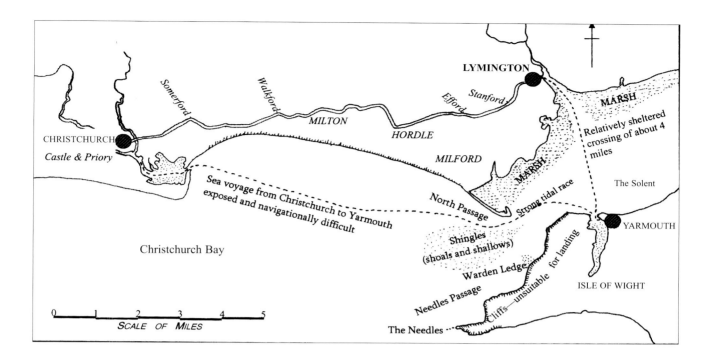

The map contains the following labels: LYMINGTON; Somerford; Walkford; Stanford; Efford; MARSH; Relatively sheltered crossing of about 4 miles; MILTON; HORDLE; CHRISTCHURCH; Castle & Priory; MILFORD; MARSH; The Solent; Sea voyage from Christchurch to Yarmouth exposed and navigationally difficult; North Passage; Strong tidal race; YARMOUTH; Christchurch Bay; Shingles (shoals and shallows); unsuitable for landing; Warden Ledge; ISLE OF WIGHT; Needles Passage; Cliffs—unsuitable for landing; The Needles; 0 1 2 3 4 5; SCALE OF MILES

Map 2. The routes between Christchurch and the Isle of Wight, showing how the land passage to Lymington was preferable to the hazardous sea route.

the title Earl of Devon from the huge estates he was granted in that county.[8]

In those feudal times the great landowning magnates were keen to maximise the resources of their estates, particularly in cash terms. One way of achieving this was by creating urban communities and then granting them a degree of autonomy. Consequently, in about 1200 or probably a few years before, a charter was granted to the men of Lymington by William de Redvers, grandson of Richard.[9] Unfortunately, this charter seems no longer to survive, but it is known through the very precise reference made to it by Baldwin de Redvers, William's grandson and the 6th Earl, who, in a later charter, referred back to, and confirmed, that granted by his grandfather.

A later medieval copy of the charter made by Baldwin survives in the *Cartulary of Beaulieu Abbey* and can be dated to 1256-7.[10] Amongst those who bore witness to this valuable grant were Andrew, the abbot of Quarr Abbey on the Isle of Wight, the priors of both Breamore and Christchurch priories and other local notables. The purpose of Baldwin's charter was to legally confirm the terms and conditions set out in the original grant and then to add to that borough by an

extension 'on the north side of the church of Lymington . . . the burgesses shall hold the new burgages of the said extension' on the same terms as those in the existing borough.[11]

The grant of borough status to Lymington almost certainly relates to its importance as the best port to serve the Isle of Wight. In the early 1180s Baldwin had created Yarmouth as a borough.[12] No doubt an important reason for this was that its harbour was where ships from Christchurch docked, even though so short a voyage was fraught with hazards. It is a reasonable hypothesis to suggest that the de Redvers, with their land and great defensive and residential castle at Christchurch and their ownership of the Isle of Wight, came to realise the advantages presented by Lymington. The sheltered harbour here offered a convenient crossing place for the family, its servants and representatives. The direct sea journey from Christchurch to the Island was made dangerous by having to negotiate the Shingles off Hurst Spit and sail through the disturbed and turbulent waters of the narrows. The

15

alternative was an easy land journey to Lymington followed by a sheltered crossing to Yarmouth (see map 2).

The charter is of considerable interest, as through it the burgesses of Lymington were given freedom from paying tolls and custom dues on all the extensive lands belonging to the de Redvers. Such concessions had real commercial value, especially for those engaged in the maritime coastal trade. The benefit to the lord derived from the fact that he compounded his disparate rents and dues, collected by a reeve, for a regular annual payment of £1 10s. in addition to the individual property rents. The ringing tones of the charter's opening sentence are still stirring today.

> Know ye all men present and to come that I, Baldwin de Redvers, Earl of Devon, have granted and by this my present charter have confirmed to my burgesses of Lymington all liberties and free customs . . . throughout all my land in towns and villages, by land and by sea, at bridges, ferries and gates, at fairs and markets, in selling and buying . . . in all places and in all things...

Having laid out the borough one must speculate from where the potential population to occupy the new town was to come. The terms of the charter offered a number of economic advantages intended to encourage people to take up residence on plots within the borough. This was a time of nationally increasing population, but we have no way of knowing exactly where they came from. Some, no doubt, migrated from adjoining villages, but others must have come from further afield. The charter, significantly, mentions burgesses and gives the instruction that each shall pay 6d. a year for his property (messuage) and be free of all other feudal services to the de Redvers, as lords of Lymington, thus permitting them to organise and conduct their own affairs within the terms of the charter. The burgesses are also permitted to elect 'by common assent' their own *prepositus* ('*Concessi similiter predictus burgensibus ut nullus in burgo eorum fiat prepositus . . .* ') or reeve to act as their agent in their dealings with the lord. He needed to be a man of integrity; one who was both respected by the urban community he served and acceptable to the lord. During the thirteenth and fourteenth centuries the reeve (*prepositus*) was chosen by his fellow burgesses to serve a term, usually a year, though he could be re-elected for further terms, presumably at times when there was no other suitable candidate.

In Lymington the office of mayor is first recorded in 1412 when Stephen Holcombe is so described when witnessing a property transaction.[13] The office of reeve continued until at least 1543, which indicates that the mayor was not a replacement for the reeve but a new kind of official who, in effect, was the chief of the borough administration. The term bailiff was also used and this seems, at least on some occasions, to have had the same status as constable. Unfortunately, the surviving records do not enable a clear distinction to be made between the roles of the three offices of reeve, bailiff and constable.

The first Lymington reeve of whom there is a record was Roger de Insula, who was holding office in 1270.[14] He held a property described as 'a cottage' in New Lymington for which he paid 6d. a year rent, the allocation for a single burgage plot. The office of constable at that time was held by Hugh de Maneby.[15]

It is from this charter that we can see the emergence of a very real, self-governing community set within a deliberately planned urban layout, paralleling that of many other places, including Newport on the Isle of Wight[16] and, most spectacularly, New Sarum (Salisbury).[17] It is possible to deduce the position of the burgage plots, the rented messuages of the burgesses, laid out at right angles along a wide, straight street, in blocks, each with a frontage measuring five-and-a-half yards (16½ feet). The noted Lymington historian, Arthur Lloyd, has been able to demonstrate this by measuring the frontage of several present day properties which still conform to these dimensions. However, even at an early stage many of these plots were being amalgamated or divided and subdivided so the uniform pattern that existed initially must soon have been modified. An example of the way properties were divided is clearly revealed in a gift of land by William Burgeys to William Burgess in 1335. Here three portions of land within a curtilage comprised plots measuring 50 ft. by 40 ft., 40 ft. by 30 ft and 20 ft. by 10ft.[18] The first of these plots was abutted to the north by the property of William

The wide High Street as created by William de Redvers. The properties on the right illustrate the width of the burgage plots.

Lytecane, one time reeve and bailiff and an influential burgess.

There are many surviving documents clearly indicating a considerable number of transactions concerning properties in New Lymington, as the borough was called. These refer variously to tenements, messuages and gardens situated in Gosport Street, New Lane, Robyschones Lane[19] and the High Street. Although most property deals are concerned with those living in Lymington a number also give some indication of those residing beyond the town, for example, John Cole of Lyndhurst, Peter Otre of Gorley, Juliana Barstaple of Winchester.

On the death of Baldwin, Earl of Devon, in 1262 we obtain a picture of both the borough, which had become known as 'New Lymington', and the original settlement, 'Old Lymington'. Importantly, both remained within the manor of Lymington and were subject to the authority of the manor courts. By this date, which is only about 70 years after the granting of the first charter, we find that there are thirty-four plots in New Lymington, some described as 'cottages' and some as 'places'. With a solitary exception the rent payable on each was 6d a year. The unexplained exception is for two plots occupied by a man called Eberic rendering 10d, *i.e.* 5d. each.[20] There was, at this time, a total of twenty-one tenants of whom one, Hugh of Buckland, held 5½ 'places' while another, Godfrey Mercator, held five (he also held ½ an acre in Old Lymington): other individuals held single plots or, in the case of Andrew Arni, just half a place and others one-and-a-half or two plots. From this record it can be seen that the borough was already occupied in a complex way and, plainly, those tenants holding more than one property would have sub-tenants in actual occupation.

The layout described here (see Map 3) comprised the present day High Street and was probably planned to utilize the steeply rising area between Lymington River and the agricultural *Lentune* hamlet. Though conjectural, it does seem probable that by the mid- to late twelfth century, a small

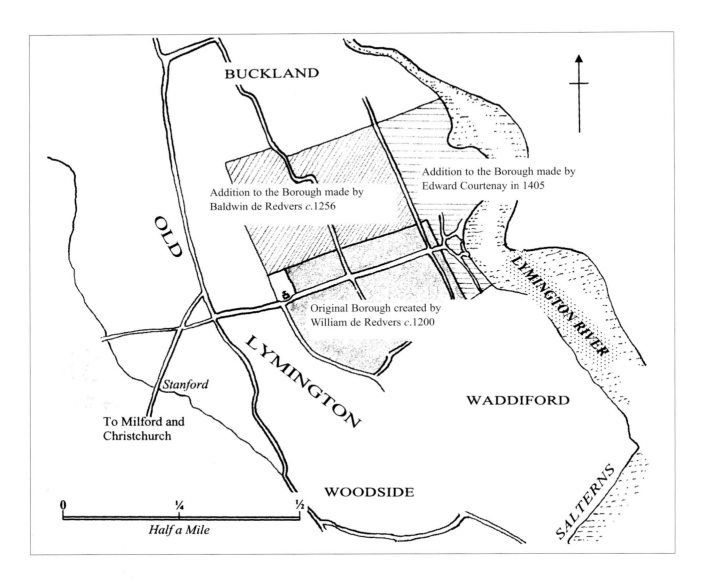

BUCKLAND

Addition to the Borough made by
Edward Courtenay in 1405

Addition to the Borough made by
Baldwin de Redvers *c.*1256

OLD

Original Borough created by
William de Redvers *c.*1200

LYMINGTON RIVER

Stanford

**To Milford and
Christchurch**

WADDIFORD

SALTERNS

0   ¼   ½

Half a Mile

WOODSIDE

Map 3. The three phases of development of the Borough of New Lymington. Isabella de Fortibus confirmed the original ('old') borough and that adjoining it to the north added nearly 60 years later by her brother. The quay area was added in 1405 by Edward Courtenay so completing the whole borough.

fishing or maritime settlement was established at the river's edge (around the quay) and the still irregular layout of streets and alleys does strongly suggest the pattern of a spontaneous and unplanned community. If this hypothesis can be accepted it makes the de Redvers' borough, laid out in a form that was becoming widely established throughout the country in the late twelfth and thirteenth centuries,[21] a practical link between the original agricultural hamlet on the higher ground to the west and the maritime one.

The words of a later charter conclusively show that the latter settlement was absorbed into the borough of New Lymington in 1405. In this document it is stated: 'Moreover we have given and granted to our said burgesses and their heirs the whole of the Quay with all things belonging to it . . . '. This was the final grant and it established the size of the borough until 1835. It is this area, often known as 'the hundred acres', which became New Lymington whilst the surviving settlements surrounding it to the north, south and west became Old Lymington, an administrative division which persisted into the nineteenth century.[22] The holdings in Old Lymington, in contrast to those in the 'New' borough, were defined as land specified in acres to a total of 115½[23], reflecting its agrarian origins.

In the year (1256) Baldwin de Redvers issued his charter, King Henry III granted him the right to hold an annual fair in the manor of Lymington lasting three days, 'to wit, on the eve, on the day and on the morrow of St Matthew the Apostle' (20-22 September).[24] The medieval fair was a commercial institution of great importance and granting the right to hold one was usually in the gift of the king. Traders from far afield came to these fairs offering a range of exotic products not normally available locally or at the weekly markets. Fortuitously, due to the report of an attack by a Frenchman[25] on a ship plying from the Isle of Wight to Lymington we get an insight into the importance of Lymington's fair. The ship, *Passager*, (its name suggests a ferry[26]) was recorded as carrying merchandise valued at £2,000, specifically ear-marked for the Lymington fair of September 1411; on board was £254 'of gold and silver of the king's coin', eight 'pakkes' of woollen cloth valued at £300, ten 'pakkes' of linen cloth 'to the value of £400', and other packs and bales of mercery in addition to a cargo of jewels worth £500.[27]

When a borough, such as New Lymington, was established by charter it required an administrative organisation so that its affairs could be properly regulated. As the lord had granted a range of rights to the burgesses so they, in turn, needed to develop within the terms of their charter necessary regulatory mechanisms. In the first instance they had to ensure that the annual payment of 30s., as required by the charter, was made to the lord. The manor court was modified so that trade and marketing could be properly regulated. The members of the manor court comprised all the tenants of the lord, known collectively as the homage. From the part of the homage comprising the burgesses would be elected the officers, charged with the responsibilities of running the borough.

The carved effigy between the arches at Boldre church may represent Isabella de Fortibus.

Unfortunately, no details of these arrangements survive in the charter of Baldwin de Redvers, but when Isabella de Fortibus, the last of the direct de Redvers line, granted a further charter to Lymington in 1271 a clearer picture emerges, though it also created a confusion which has dogged historians subsequently. Isabella's charter states 'The burgesses . . . shall pay me out of their property either in the old borough aforesaid or from any increase thereof'. Here the term *old borough* means that created by her grandfather, William de Redvers, called originally the borough of New Lymington and she uses the term merely to distinguish that *first* borough from the extension made to the north of the church by her brother, Baldwin. Her reference is not to 'Old Lymington' as has been assumed by earlier historians (see maps 1 and 3).

Isabella de Fortibus (1237-93) inherited great wealth from the de Redvers estates and consolidated this through her marriage to William de Fortibus (or Forz), Count of Aumale (sometimes named Albemarle). His death in 1260, when she was only 23, left her as probably the richest woman of her time, owning properties from Cumberland to the Isle of Wight. She took up residence in the de Redvers' castle at Carisbrooke and, undoubtedly on her many journeys to her mainland properties, travelled frequently from Yarmouth to Lymington. She died in 1293 and was laid to rest in the de

The seal of the Borough of Lymington. The Corporation's seal dates from the time of the Courtenays and shows their arms hanging from a ship's yardarm.

Redvers' mausoleum in Breamore Priory.[28]

Under her charter the borough was still to be held at a gross yearly rent of 30s. and the individual burgage plots continued to be rented at 6d. a year (usually payable in two 3d. instalments, as specified in Baldwin's charter). The meetings of the burgesses and the manor courts ultimately required a hall in which they could regularly gather to conduct their affairs. Possibly, at first, meetings were held in the house of one of the burgesses or even in the nave of the parish or town church, for we have no record of a town hall until 1299 when a building designated

Part of the medieval boundary wall marking the southern extent of the borough revealed when excavated by Avon Valley Archaeological members in 1996 at the author's request.

as such was described as being in need of repair, which suggests it may have been standing for some time.[29]

The last medieval charter granted to Lymington was issued by Edward Courtenay, Earl of Devon, a descendant of the de Redvers, in 1405. After fully reciting and confirming the charter granted by Isabella in 1271 it clearly defines certain other rights and importantly adds to the borough 'the whole of the Quay with all things belonging to it' and also grants to the borough the payments of the tolls known as anchorage and wharfage levied on vessels and boats using the quay. This unequivocal statement demonstrates that Edward Courtenay had definitely enlarged the borough by the inclusion of the already settled quay area which had not been mentioned in any of the previous charters. The resultant total area, to be known as 'the 100 acres', conforms precisely to that depicted on the oldest known authentic map of the borough made in 1795,[30] some three hundred and ninety years after it was defined in Edward Courtenay's charter. Confusion arising from the wording of Isabella's charter was no doubt responsible for the misinterpretation made by Edward King when he reproduced, partly redrew and annotated a map of about 1680 giving the incorrect geographical location of the boroughs and the wrong dating.[31]

ECONOMIC LIFE

Apart from the agricultural activities conducted primarily in Old Lymington and continuing to some extent within the borough, the local population was also engaged in the salt industry, itself well established by the early twelfth century. At high tides the sea water was allowed to flow into specially constructed shallow ponds, called pans, where the action of the sun and wind evaporated the sea water to brine.[32] The brine or liquor so produced was then boiled in pans until evaporated, leaving a deposit of salt crystals. The fuel to heat the furnaces seems to have been wood (and, possibly, charcoal) as there is a reference to timber being taken illicitly from 'the demesne wood of Bolrewood to Lemyngton and to the saltworks'.[33]

Some six miles to the north-east of Lymington,

across a desolate stretch of forest heathland, Beaulieu Abbey had been founded in the beautiful valley of the River Exe by King John in 1204-05.[34] As the community of Cistercian monks established there flourished and grew wealthier they formed commercial links with the urban centres within reach of their abbey. Most of their dealings were with the major port of Southampton but Lymington, being nearer, also played a role in their affairs. An incidental and isolated example of this contact is recorded in about 1230 when Richard of Brockenhurst, who held a messuage in Lymington as a sub-tenant, granted to the convent of Beaulieu his rent of 1*lb* of wax from that property, expressing at the same time his wish to be interred in the abbey.[35] Isabella de Fortibus in her charter singles out the property held by Beaulieu Abbey in Lymington and states that their 'two districts' shall 'hold none of the said liberties' granted to the burgesses. Even 260 years later, at the time of the Dissolution in 1538, we learn that Beaulieu Abbey was still receiving rents of 2s. from properties held

in Lymington. As early as 1262 the abbey tenanted one cottage in New Lymington and owned a saltern.

Another abbey having contacts with Lymington was the Cistercian monastery of Quarr on the Isle of Wight. This connection should be expected as the de Redvers, lords of Lymington, had also founded Quarr Abbey in 1132. The tithe, or tenth part, of the salt produced at Lymington was granted to Quarr Abbey[36] and, in order to store this prior to shipment, it had a storehouse or granary (*garnarium*) built on the quay. So also did Beaulieu Abbey, presumably to store the salt from its own saltern as well as that purchased from others. Sadly the remains of these two medieval stone-built warehouses were destroyed under the impact of redevelopment in the 1960s though some of the stone was incorporated in the modern buildings.

A surviving fragment of a medieval house is preserved in the stone work on the east of the Red House in the High Street.

The Lymington reeve was responsible for seeing that the tithe was collected annually, for which duty he was paid 1s. As Father Hockey states, 'Salt was a valuable and important commodity for the abbey; besides its culinary importance, it was used for curing skins, for preparing leather and even [as a flux] for soldering the joints of pipes and gutters.'[37]

Beaulieu Abbey also held other property in Lymington, known as the 'Abbotes tenure'. This almost certainly was situated in Gosport Street, close to its junction with the High Street, and therefore not far from the quay. As stated this property was expressly excluded from the liberties granted to the burgesses by the confirmation charter of 1271: thus the brethren of the abbey were prevented from holding any hereditary rights or being responsible for any urban duties. No doubt as a consequence to this stricture the Beaulieu monks are recorded as being in dispute with the Lymington

burgesses in 1319 regarding the payment of tolls by the abbey.[38] Following litigation based on the premise that it was the occupier or tenant of a property in the town the abbey was allowed, like any other tenant, to buy and sell in Lymington free of any toll charges. The agreement arising from this action was signed at 'Lementon' on the Feast of the Annunciation of the Blessed Virgin Mary (25 March, Lady Day) in the 12th year of the reign of Edward II (1319), and effectively superseded the limitation imposed by the clause in Isabella's charter. Those witnessing this judgement on behalf of the town were the reeve, William Lytecave, with Hugh Thomas, Robert Le Bryd, Thomas atte Gardyn, Henry le Chaundler and John Robert.

It is interesting to note that in the government's tax of one-twentieth on moveable property, known as the Lay Subsidy and collected in 1327, just eight years after the dispute with Beaulieu, we find the names of William Lytecave (assessed at 1s. 6d.), Hugh Thomas (1s.), Robert le Brid (9d.) and Henry le Chaundelir (3s.). In that record there is also a Matilda Robert rendering a high payment of 4s. It is likely she was the widow of John whose name was appended with those recorded above. All are shown as being residents of *Nova Lemynton*.[39]

The 1327 Lay Subsidy for Lymington is divided into two parts covering, respectively, Old and New Lymington. There are 32 taxpayers in New Lymington (the borough) rendering a total of £3 3s. 3d. and in Old Lymington there are 36 assessed at a total of £3 13s. In both parts there is one individual paying the highest tax of 10s., namely, Roger of Boclonde (Buckland) in New Lymington and John de Cerne in Old. Judging by those who are assessed for tax it would appear that by this date the two parts of Lymington are of approximately equal population and wealth. If the tax is averaged we find about 2s. a head is paid in New Lymington and 2s. 4d. a head in Old. The tax levied in 1334, however, discloses a different result when New Lymington rendered a total of £11 3s. and Old Lymington only £4 0s. 10d. Unfortunately, there is no contemporary evidence to explain this curious anomaly but it is possible that Old Lymington was being taxed as a rural area at a fifteenth while New Lymington, being urban, returned a tenth, even so

this would hardly account for the actual difference after an interval of only seven years.

Henry the Chandler, who rendered a payment of 3s. in the 1327 tax, had been long established in Lymington for he appeared as early as March 1313 when taking possession of a tenement in 'Goseport' street and only a month later, for the price of £2 13s. 4d., he purchased a further messuage in Gosport Street in New Lymington, described as lying between one occupied by the 'Abbot and Convent of Beaulieu' on the south side and Robert Pernele's on the north and, in January 1331, Henry granted his tenement in Gosport Street to Walter of Tisbury which tenement, or house, was then described as lying between one belonging to Beaulieu Abbey and one already in Walter's occupation.[40]

These early decades of the fourteenth century show Lymington emerging as a real urban centre, small certainly, but also functioning effectively. The returns made to the Exchequer in 1300 present a basic yet clear image of the community. From this record we discover Old Lymington contained 40 burgages,[41] 64 messuages and 138 acres of land, this latter referring to farmland. Farming was to some degree carried on in the open common fields of Highfield, Barfield, Fairfield and Waddiford Field. There were also some ring-fenced, or enclosed, farms in the Woodside area and in Buckland. Additionally, the coastal parts of Old

A view of the dilapidated Lymington tithe barn situated on the northern borough boundary but lying in the manor of Buckland. It was demolished in 1926.

Lymington had 12 salterns and 3 granaries for salt. In New Lymington there were 52 burgages owned by forty people and the existence of a hall is also recorded, probably the town's first. The total receipts for the two parts of Lymington came to over £16 and the expenses are shown as being less than £8.[42] Evidently a satisfactory position.

The mention of burgages in Old Lymington poses a problem, for there is no documentary evidence for any part of Old Lymington being constituted a borough. It seems probable that the term is reserved for the properties along St Thomas Street, which represented the urban core of Old Lymington abutting the borough to the west and having a thoroughfare which runs eastward into the High Street.

MARITIME TRADE

The maritime life of Lymington, based on its accessible and well-sheltered, tidal river estuary, was flourishing by the late thirteenth century. The town of Southampton, by a royal decree of King John, granted in return for the payment of £200 to the crown, obtained jurisdiction over all the ports from Portsmouth in the east to Keyhaven in the west, thereby including Lymington. The mayor of Southampton was empowered to act as 'admiral' of all those ports and, in that capacity, was authorised to levy a toll on all produce arriving or leaving, to regulate fishing, obstructions to navigation, control of swans, and he had a right to flotsam and royal fish, which included all the cetaceans and sturgeon. His authority was implemented through the legally constituted 'admiralty courts', in which cases of avoidance of duties or of complaints could be treated.

It seems clear that at the time of this grant Lymington was not regarded as a harbour of any importance, for when King John sent an instruction to Southampton in April 1206 to commandeer merchant ships to back up his navy he neglects to mention Lymington by name, though the ports of Keyhaven, Yarmouth and Christchurch are specifically recorded. This may be explained by the fact that New Lymington, created only a few years before by William de Redvers's charter, was only in its infancy as a town.[43]

Early in the fourteenth century Edward I required all the ports along the south coast to supply fully manned vessels in 'aid of the Scotch war'. For Lymington the demand was beyond the town's means and, like many other ports, it defaulted. As a consequence in August 1302 instructions were issued to punish 'the commonalty of the town of Lymington' for their failure to supply a ship. However, the economic realities which constrained the town from obeying the injunction were evidently recognised by the king, for in November the sheriff of Hampshire was persuaded to 'induce the bailiffs and good men' of Lymington to supply a ship jointly with Yarmouth.[44] As the expense was shared they were now able to fulfil the requirement and the completed ship had to be sailed to Newtown (Isle of Wight) by the feast of the Ascension (*i.e.* 40 days after Easter 1303). In the large build-up of the navy in preparation for a further attack against France in 1345, when most south coast ports sent ships and men, Lymington did rather better by supplying nine ships and 159 mariners.[45] This seems to indicate that the town was now on a sound, not to say flourishing, economic footing.

It is not possible to construct a consecutive story of the life of any community in the middle ages because of the lack of regular and coherent documentation; often that which survives is incomplete or inconclusive. One of those intriguing, yet valued, glimpses into the past is given when, in about 1324, Geoffrey Scurlag, William Culhout and 18 other Lymington men were arraigned in the Admiralty Court for two offences. In the first instance it was claimed they had maltreated Walter Depedene, the official of the admiralty court, and that, secondly, they had taken for their own use customs valued at 11s. on salt, corn, barley and oats landed by the cargo ship *Le Johette* and more customs to the value of £5 on cloth, wax and other merchandise landed from the *Port Joy*. In support of their action the Lymington defendants sought to deny the jurisdiction of Southampton over their port, perhaps basing their case on an agreement made in 1314 whereby Southampton granted Lymington the right to collect customs between Hurst and Calshot for the annual payment of £1 10s.[46] But Southampton, adhering strictly to the letter of the law, stated that £200 was paid annually to the crown for its jurisdiction over Lymington and the other local ports: the jury found in favour of Southampton and Lymington had to pay £200 damages.[47]

A mere four years later, in March 1328, with apparent disregard to the result of the previous adjudication in the Exchequer court, the mayor and commonalty of Southampton were again complaining that certain Lymington men were collecting for their own benefit the customs on shipping entering their harbour to the considerable amount of £600.[48] In view of the fact that William Lytecave, the reeve, was amongst the thirty-six named in the complaint it seems indisputable that they still regarded Southampton's jurisdiction as not applicable to Lymington: after all they had the agreement of 1314 and, in addition, their charters which granted them freedom to trade and collect dues.

A further case implies illegal if not downright criminal behaviour by Lymington officials when William Lytecave with many others was charged with carrying away the goods of a Portuguese ship,

This early twentieth century photograph of the quay captures the character of this vital landing place as it survived from the earliest times.

Jesus Christ, which had been driven ashore at Brighstone on the Isle of Wight, which they took despite the fact the crew were saved.[49] Such events must raise questions about their actions and the genuineness of their complaints. The question of the jurisdiction of Southampton's admiralty courts became a source of continual disputes between the two communities.

As these disagreements rumbled on over the years it was obvious that eventually some kind of solution would have to be found but this did not come about until an agreement was reached on 5 April 1508 following yet another dispute in the previous year. The mayor, bailiff, burgesses and commonalty of Southampton agreed with Robert Mawler, mayor of Lymington, Richard Kent, bailiff and Sir Hugh Conway, lord of the manor of Lymington, that customs on specified merchandise belonged to Southampton but, importantly, that keelage and wharfage dues were payable to Lymington. The penalty for breaking this agreement was set at £20.[50]

In the later years of the fourteenth century, during the second phase of the Hundred Years' War, the south coast was subject to many raids by the French, the worst being against the harbours of Yarmouth, Newtown and Newport on the Isle of Wight in the summer of 1377. No record or other evidence of Lymington being subject to similar raids at this time has been uncovered, despite the persistence of a local tradition that Lymington was sacked and burned.[51] In May 1401, at the time of another threatened invasion, we find a maritime entry in which instructions were given not to allow any ships or vessels 'of the portage of 30 tuns of wine and more' which were lying in the ports of Lymington and Poole to leave for foreign places.[52]

Despite the increasing importance of finished cloth in England's export trade during the fourteenth and fifteenth centuries wool was still a valuable export and a levy was charged on each 'weigh' or bundle shipped abroad. In order to ease the collection of the levy all wool had to be exported through recognised outlets. In 1363 Calais had been set up as the continental *entrepôt*, but many of those exporting wool sought to avoid the levies or tariffs by using other continental ports. As time went on this illegal activity evidently increased and a commission in April 1453 authorized the search of harbours along the Sussex, Hampshire and Dorset coasts (which, of course, included Lymington) to look for 'wool, woolfells and other merchandise brought to these ports for shipping to continental places other than the staple port of Calais'.[53] Various but disparate entries over the years show Lymington to have been a harbour of considerable commercial importance, as highlighted by a mid-fourteenth century record showing the export of 4,000 quarters of salt and 600 sacks of wool, and the import of 1,800 tuns of wine and 3,700 fish.[54]

Ships' cargoes were always a temptation and the account of an isolated incident survives from 1434 when Thomas Freeman of Salisbury captured and robbed the *Marie* of Lymington. He was caught and found guilty of the offence,[55] unfortunately the surviving record does not state the penalty.

An indication of Lymington's trade in the early 16th century can be gained from a few isolated entries regarding ships paying dues in Southampton. A boat belonging to John Haylys, after paying keelage dues of 2d., left for Lymington on 16 November 1509 carrying a cargo of four quarters of bay salt. Stephen Belle arrived in Southampton on 3 February 1510 *en route* for Lymington with a cargo of 1,000 hake on which he paid 1s. 8d. custom dues. The wealthy Southampton merchant, John Garrard, had one of his vessels, captained by John Rogers of Lymington, carry two tuns of ale (*ceric*'), whose loading by crane required a payment of 8d. On the same day, 25 February 1510, William Mayn's boat left carrying 200 flat fish to Lymington.[56] Such evidence helps sustain the view that Lymington played a small but significant role in the coastal trade along the south coast.

SOCIAL LIFE

The lack of continuous documentation can often mean that life was progressing relatively smoothly, for it is mainly when there are problems, disputes and difficulties that we have a record. Thus the everyday details of the lives of Lymington's townsfolk almost always only come into focus when a crime or other offence has been committed. Even Isabella de Fortibus, the lady of Lymington, was obliged to go to court in 1280 to try to establish that her hunting dogs, used in the New Forest, and those of 'her men at Liminton' should not be expeditated, that is, subject to the cutting back of their claws. It was eventually agreed that Isabella and 'her men of Old and New Lymington' could avoid this stricture on their dogs provided they proved it was an established custom.[57]

In 1399, a year of considerable upheaval in which Richard II was deposed, a Lymington man, Robert Swalwe, joined one of the bands of retainers supporting the earls of Kent, Salisbury and Huntingdon in their attempt to reinstate Richard.[58] Henry (Bolingbroke) IV had usurped the throne in September, about four months previously, but the insurrection against him was badly coordinated and consequently failed, all the leaders, on being caught, were put to death. Why so minor a figure as Swalwe was induced to join this rising we do not know. It is known that the earls of Kent had been involved in the New Forest area, for an account records that in 1391 John Bakere, a Lymington butcher, was accused of taking two cows from Latchmoor valued at 20s., both being the property of 'Thomas Holand, Earl of Kent'.[59] So could it be that Robert Swalwe who in 1397 had been granted a burgage plot in Lymington High Street, rented from the Earls of Devon,[60] also with land in 'Couperscroft', had some connections, in his capacity as a yeoman, with the Earl of Kent? Whatever the explanation he was captured and beheaded at Oxford on 7 January 1400, together with 27 other 'persons'.[61] His Lymington properties, comprising a tenement and ½ an acre of land worth 9s. 3d., were taken into the king's hands, as was always the case with the properties of traitors. However, as Robert held his property jointly with his wife, Christina, it was

Quay Hill has been a link between the town and quay since the middle ages.

declared that she should inherit. The escheator of the county of Southampton in making this judgement ordered that the king's hand should be removed and 'meddle no further' in this holding. From the records we discover that Robert had owned goods worth £6 13s. 4d., including a silver cup valued at 8s., a doublet worth 20s., and two horses together valued at 26s. 8d.. To tie matters up legally a royal grant was made to Christina in January 1401 permitting her to enter her late husband's estate to the value of £40.

Interestingly enough, in those last years of Richard II's reign, Lymington made a contribution of 50 marks (£33 6s. 8d.) towards a huge loan of £20,175 for the king.[62]

Debts of the aristocracy, and the more lowly citizens, then as now, were a commonplace problem. In 1409 we find John Baldewyne *alias* Bakere owing Walter, abbot of Milton Abbey (Dorset), and William Lymyngton, a Reading goldsmith, debts of 40 marks (£26 13s. 4d) and £4, respectively.[63] In 1437, the vicar of Lymington, John Tailloure, had failed to appear to answer for a debt of 40s. to John Chook.[64]

Failure to repay debt was then a considerable misdemeanour but crimes of a violent nature were far more serious, so it is unusual to learn of two Lymington men being pardoned for what were very grave felonies. The first concerns Robert Darok (*alias* Botreaux) of New Lymington, a yeoman, who having failed to appear in court became an outlaw. His offence was to enter the close and house of John Fraunceys at New Lymington 'on the Annunciation of 19 Henry VI' (25 March 1449) and there violate Joan, the wife of John, and abduct her together with goods to the value of 20s.[65] The second concerns John Prows (*alias* Prouse, *alias* Prous, *alias* Browes) a Lymington wool tucker, who was described as an outlaw wandering through various parts of the realm 'spoiling, beating and committing other evils'.[66] On the 1 March 1459 the Dorset justices were commanded to deliver him to Dorchester gaol, for he had been active in 'Wymburnmynstre' and Bere Regis. Yet when his pardon was issued six weeks later it forgave him 'all felonies, murders,

27

rapes of women and other trespasses, offences, contempts and forfeitures'. Why these two men were pardoned after committing such serious offences does not appear in the records and compounds the difficulties of being able to provide a clear picture of medieval conditions. However, as early as 1294 a 'decision was taken to offer full pardon, in return for military service, to all men indicted for or convicted of homicide, including felonious homicide . . .'[67] Whether this form of pardon was still operating a century and half later it is difficult to confirm.

Forgery was always regarded as serious and punishments were often harsh. When Thomas Glasier, a Lymington stainer, was sent to Winchester gaol for forgery fear of punishment led to his escaping in January 1440 after first attacking the prison guard, Thomas Parker.[68]

For several Lymingtonians, of all classes, the New Forest must have been seen as a source of fresh meat, mainly in the form of venison, ready for the taking. At one end of the scale we find William Thorner, described as 'a labourer' when arraigned before the Court of Swainmote in February 1486 for taking a young hind at Whitley, near Brockenhurst, and making off with its carcass. At the other end we find William Holcombe, a 'gentleman of Lymington', indulging in poaching on a large scale. The Court of Swainmote learned of offences starting in June 1484 when he killed a buck at Lady Hill, with the aid of greyhounds, continuing through 1485 when a doe was taken at a place called La Estyate. In this he was assisted by Richard Fletcher, a fletcher or arrow maker, of Lymington. Holcombe's offences continued throughout 1487 and 1488 when he is variously accused of taking a 'fawn at Hurst', a doe at 'Butts Lawn' and another from 'Lyndhurst Park'. These were all serious offences yet his penalty seemed remarkably lenient in that he was bound over to be of good behaviour 'under pain of £10' with four other sureties, all London men, who each stood to lose £5 if he failed to obey the court's ruling.[69] In this he was not so fortunate as the Lymington butcher, John Bakere (mentioned earlier) who in 1391 was pardoned for several offences, curiously all carried out on Thursdays, regarding the taking of the king's venison, an ox belonging to William Schepurd of Battramsley and the two cows belonging to the Earl of Kent at Latchmoor.[70] Even the Lymington chaplain, William Johnson, from whom better behaviour might have been expected, was twice accused of poaching does at Rhinefield and Whitley, aided in the latter case by a Lymington baker, John Porchet.[71]

ESTATES, LAND & PROPERTY

The drama of the lives of the ordinary people was played out against a backcloth of frequently changing land ownership by the wealthy and politically influential families. The story is often complicated by the fact that overlords at times granted their lands or parts of them to other individuals or institutions for variously defined periods. Sometimes during the childhood of an heir the lands would be leased until the minor reached 21 and came into his or her inheritance. Overall these dealings had little direct impact on the conduct of the affairs of the ordinary merchants, tradesmen, artisans and farmers: except, of course, that their feudal allegiances, though not commitments, changed with the change of landownership. However, rents in money and kind still had to be met and, where services were due, these had to be fulfilled and the bailiff or reeve was responsible to see that this was done.

During the middle ages Lymington was held by a succession of feudal barons; for a short while the earls of Shrewsbury, later, the de Redvers and finally the Courtenays. But even ownership of their estates, wholly or in part, changed from time to time in accordance with political necessity, family allegiance or religious endowment. It is important to remember that throughout the middle ages all the land ultimately belonged to the monarch and every estate was held 'of the king'. In times of trouble or lack of a suitable heir the land reverted to the crown, either to be re-granted to members of the original landholding family or to a new grantee or tenant.

Freehold land and property is that which is held without owing any feudal dues. The individual to whom it is granted is said to be 'seised' of the land

and seisin applies to him or her alone and is not transferable to any tenant. Tenants therefore owed feudal duties, if demanded, to the person from whom they held their land.

An illustration of this kind of complication is seen when on 8 May 1252 Guy de Rupe Forti granted to Richard Picard, a citizen of London, for the term of four years 'the manor of Lymenton which the said Guy had of the king's bail of the lands of Baldwin, sometime earl of Devon'.[72] In 1262 Baldwin de Redvers granted the manor of Lymington to Breamore Priory.[73] But when Isabella succeeded to her brother's estates she disputed the control of the priory saying that it had been taken by force. During the Barons' War (1264-7) Isabella had remained loyal to Henry III and was alarmed, when taking refuge in Breamore Priory, to find the prior supported the cause of the king's arch opponent, Simon de Montfort. After some threats and disputes, involving also a bribe, the prior acknowledged Isabella's lordship of Lymington.

On Isabella's death in 1293 the manor reverted to the Crown and in 1303 Edward I 'dowered' his second wife, Queen Margaret, with the manor and borough of Lymington. In the following year, apparently in response to legal correctness, he took it back from the queen and granted it instead to Hugh de Courtenay, a descendant of the de Redvers and thus a legitimate successor. A licence was granted in 1385 for the 'king's kinsman, Edward de Courteney', to enfeoff[74] the Archbishop of Canterbury; Robert, bishop of London; Thomas, bishop of Exeter; Walter Clopton; John Hulle; John Wadham; John Isaac and John Barnburgh with 'fourteen messuages, twenty saltpits, two carucates of land, 40s. of rent and a rent of eleven quarters of salt and two cartloads of hay in Old and New Lemyngton, held in chief'. Landholders could enfeoff their land so that at times of dispute, usually following a death or political upheaval, it need not automatically revert to the crown but could pass directly to the enfeoffees. It was a legal mechanism designed to limit the control of the monarch even on estates held 'in chief', that is, held directly of the crown. It applied when the holder of land was seised of the estate, provided the estate was freehold. It was often framed in a way that enabled

the estate to remain with the family without the necessity of seeking a further grant from the crown.

It is not from these records that we get any real understanding of the town's social and economic life but rather from the smaller dealings relating to the occupation of properties. Some of the Lymington tenants held several properties and sub-let these to other townsfolk, and the descriptions often help to build a picture of the times.

Christchurch Priory had been granted land in Lymington by Richard de Redvers, his brother Baldwin and their uncle William.[75] The canons of the priory, not wishing to occupy and exploit the properties directly, leased them to Lymington residents. So we find, for example, round about 1250, the Priory alienating (i.e. giving up direct control) 1 messuage and 9 acres to Christina de Solario for an annual rent of 2s. 4d. The messuage had previously been held by a man called Stephen and was situated next 'to the house of William le Cherchmay'; the 9 acres lay between the land of Geoffrey le Wasyere and Nicholas le Cu. The headlands of this land begin at the New Town'[76]. Undoubtedly, these were part of the agricultural lands that abutted the borough of New Lymington to the north, perhaps the very land on which Baldwin de Redvers was to make an extension to his grandfather's original town, i.e. the High Street, in his charter of about 1256? The Priory, too, was the owner of salt pans in Old Lymington and benefited from income from others.

Another example of how property exchanges can provide tiny glimpses of Lymington occurred in 1335 when 'John, son of Jordan, a Boldre clergyman, granted to William Burgage a tenement in New Lymington opposite the lane called *Alremanne Lane* (i.e. Ashley Lane) at the south end of a way (New Street) leading from the Market Place (High Street) towards Bouclonde (Buckland)'.[77] A further glimpse is provided through a gift made by John le Clerk to Symon Clerk of 'Lymyngstone' of a salt granary 'above the sea gate' (*supra portam mars*)[78], lying between the granaries of Agnes Holewey on the north and another of John le Clerk's on the south.

This John le Clerk, like other Lymington merchants, also had interests in Southampton. It

No 27, High Street. The surviving timber jetty now incorporated within Osborne's menswear shop. Many of the ancient timber-framed houses were given new façades throughout the course of the eighteenth century so that the original structure was wholly concealed. This is a good example of a surviving medieval timber-framed building.

seems certain that merchants with a maritime interest needed bases in more than one town and in the early years of the fifteenth century there are records of Richard Seman, John Sherman and John Bigard, all of Lymington, renting properties in Southampton.[79] Salisbury, by the late thirteenth century an important trading city with a special interest in cloth and wool, also had its merchants holding properties in Lymington. An instance of this occurs when in April 1440 John Stone of the City of Salisbury (*Nove Sarum*) granted to John Hoy of New Lymington 'half a plot of land being built upon with its appurtenances in New Lemyngton, situated between a tenement late of Henry Redyng on the east and a tenement that Geoffrey Borard holds on the west' which ran back from the High Street to land called 'le cartforlong', probably lying in Barfield.

It is evident that the extension made to the borough by Baldwin de Redvers in about 1256 did not lead to any appreciable building of premises, as subsequent records show the land to have remained substantially agricultural in character. For example, on 21 September 1412 a grant by Thomas Stocker of New Lymington to William Pokeswell comprised a close of two acres, hedged and ditched, lying within the borough of New Lymington, 'in the east part of a lane called Newelane' and ½ acre of land in Robeschenes Lane (Cannon Street).[80] Clearly the

built up areas comprised the High Street and Gosport Street but with relatively few buildings in Ashley Lane and New Lane. It is difficult to know why the borough had been extended but not developed in a formal pattern. Probably there were few people available to take up residence, suggesting the borough had reached an optimum point so far as population was concerned.

Within the context of Lymington we know very little about the actual buildings of the medieval period. The tantalising references in an action by Robert de Warham against Geoffrey Bonch in 1321 provide a rare glimpse. In this there is an agreement to build a staircase between their houses in the High Street in order that repairs can be carried out.[81] The surviving rubblestone wall fragments of The Red House, next to the present Post Office, almost certainly indicate the remains of a medieval house of some pretensions but there is little else remaining.

A chance survival, revealed during the rebuilding of a property, has provided a tantalising insight to a Lymington once lined with jettied, timber-framed houses either side of the High Street. Late in 1988 and early 1989, whilst renovating 27, High Street, the builders[82] uncovered some timber beams which, upon examination, proved to be part of a box-framed house. Its street front was 18 feet wide and it stretched back 25 feet. Its plan is characteristic of the type of timber-framed building commonly erected in the Wessex region in the fifteenth century.[83] This at least gives a tangible clue to the appearance of late medieval Lymington.

Of living conditions in the houses nothing directly survives. Archaeological investigations on a variety of urban sites have indicated quite considerable care in the disposal of human waste through cesspits and drains, a practice which appears to have fallen into decline in the fourteenth and fifteenth centuries, leading to a worsening in public health and so allowing an increase in the prevalence of recurrent bubonic plague, most notably the Black Death of 1348-9, and other diseases. Matters must have improved in the Tudor period, as a Dutch physician, Levinus Lemnius, visiting England at that time found that the

'neat cleanlines, the exquisite finenesse, the pleasaunte and delightfull furniture in every poynt for household, wonderfully rejoysed mee; their chambers and parlours strawed over with sweete herbes refreshed mee; their nosegays finely entermingled wyth sundry sortes of fragraunte floures in their bedchambers and privy roomes, with comfortable smell cheered mee up and entirelye delyghted all my sences'.[84]

Lemnius's delight is however diametrically opposed to that written by another perceptive visitor from the Netherlands, the noted theologian and philosopher, Desiderius Erasmus, who visited England on a number of occasions between 1499 and 1517. He considered the houses in which the English lived to be filthy which consequently, in his view, led to the prevalence of plague and the 'deadly sweat'. He described the house floors as being covered with rushes which were occasionally removed, 'but so imperfectly that the bottom layer is left undisturbed, sometimes for twenty years, harbouring expectorations, vomitings, the leakage of dogs and men, ale-droppings, scraps of fish, and other abominations not fit to be mentioned'.[85]

It can now be seen that the story of Lymington in the middle ages is one in which the charters granted by the great landowners created a largely self-governing borough which was intimately associated with and ultimately, integrated within the original manor of Lymington. The borough creations of the de Redvers, William and Baldwin, created the administrative division of Lymington into two parts; Old Lymington comprising the riverside, the coastal marshes to the south and the agricultural land lying to the west and north embracing, as it were, the borough of New Lymington. The holding of the land was also complicated, with many changes of occupation or ownership under the overlordship of the de Redvers. The Cistercian abbeys of Beaulieu and Quarr were involved in both Lymington-based trade and property ownership, as were the Augustinian canons of both Christchurch and Breamore priories.

The maritime life of Lymington was evidently thriving throughout the period, but not without fluctuations, and its custom control was in the hands of the Borough of Southampton administered through the admiralty courts. The lords of Lymington had been granted an annual three-day fair by Henry III and limited evidence we have

suggests that this was a flourishing affair.

It can be seen that this was a community growing to maturity in self-government and commercial life. These were factors that were to stand it in good stead in the ensuing Tudor and Stuart periods when political and religious upheavals were to change the face of England.

THE MANOR OF BUCKLAND

Included within Old Lymington and lying to the north-west of the town was the manor of Buckland. It was a large agricultural estate within the bounds of Lymington parish but with its own ownership and manorial control. Buckland, the word itself means 'Book Land', that is, land held by 'boc' or charter, was not recorded in *Domesday Book*, presumably at that date it was either just waste lying between *Lentune* and Battramsley and Boldre or it failed to be recorded.[86]

The name Buckland is first known through the surnames of witnesses to the charter of Baldwin de Redvers (*c*. 1256) and various deeds where their names appear, for example, Nigel of Buckland and

Map 4, Plan of the manor of Buckland.

31

Buckland Manor House; mostly eighteenth century but built on the site of the medieval manor house.

Roger of Buckland. Its precise origins as a manorial estate are obscure but it must have been in existence as an independent manor by the mid-thirteenth century as Nigel of Buckland and his son, also Nigel, granted a saltern in Oxiheye marsh (now Oxey Lake) and a house to the Cistercian monks of Quarr Abbey for the sum of £5 6s. 8d.[87]

In 1290 the Prior of Christchurch, in exchange for a property in Christchurch, granted to Roger of Buckland a free chantry within his existing chapel at 'Boclond'. The new chapel was dependant on the mother church at Boldre so its ecclesiastical status was much the same as Lymington's chapel or church. The Bucklands had to support fully the chaplains appointed to serve in their chapel. The fact that this privilege was granted to the Bucklands indicates that it was an influential family. In practical terms it enabled the family, their servants and tenants to attend the usual forms of worship in the Buckland chapel saving them the journey to the Lymington chapel (or church) or, indeed, to the mother church at Boldre. Some physical evidence of this chapel survives in the form of fragments of stone window tracery dug up close to the present manor house.[88]

There is no consecutive documentation to reveal the story of this chapel and its chantry until the reign of Henry VIII, when it is recorded as a free chapel 'founded to have a priest there to sing in the same . . . for the ease of the tenants there'.[89] The priest's annual stipend, valued at £3 6s. 8d., was derived from endowed land in the manor and from tithes. The chapel is described as being devoid of 'ornaments, plate juells, goodes and chatells'. In the great survey of chantries undertaken in 1547, in the reign of Edward VI, Buckland is again described, but with the additional information naming the incumbent as Edmund Colne, a scholar in Oxford University, and that the chapel was one and a half miles from the parish church in Lymington.[90]

Of the manor itself we have further details of its size and ownership when in 1300 John of Buckland, probably the son of the younger Nigel, was recorded as holding 28 messuages, a water mill and a saltern in Old Lymington. In 1316 this same John was granted 2 carucates[91] of land, 45 acres of meadow and 57 acres of pasture situated in Buckland, Arnewood and other places. It is likely that this grant extended the manor's holdings to the north of Passford Water to abut the New Forest boundary and along the Lymington River towards Boldre (see map 4).

Ownership of the manor continued to descend through the Buckland family and when Sir John of Buckland died in 1362 it was assessed as one-eighth part of a knight's fee. It was in the hands of Walter Sydelyng in the 1390s and on his death, as he had no surviving sons, his two daughters, Margery and Amflesia, were joint heiresses and the manor was divided equally between them. Though both were married they left no heirs and the manor was subsequently reunited on passing to Agnes, a niece of Walter. It seems that Agnes was married to Henry Popham who inherited the estate on Agnes's death and it was then settled on their younger son, John, in 1417. It remained in the hands of the Pophams until about the 1450s when it was again divided into two. In 1473 one half of the manor is described as being in the hands of John Longe of Wiltshire who died that year. He had come into possession through his marriage to a Margaret Popham.[92] In 1497 another John Longe, probably the son of the previous John, was described as holding 'half the manor of Buckland, 1 messuage, 150 acres of land and 70 acres of wood in Buckland'. In addition he held 'half of 12 messuages, 6 homesteads, 800 acres of land, 40 acres of meadow and 200 acres of heath in Lymington, Oxey, Arnewood, Warborne, Sway' and several other places around the New Forest borders.93 Buckland then, whilst in the parish of Lymington, had a life that was largely independent of the borough. Its own manor courts regulated tenants' holdings and dealt with minor misdemeanours. However, for all administrative purposes, such as the collection of taxes, it fell under the general jurisdiction of Old Lymington.

THE CHURCH & SPIRITUAL LIFE

The first known reference to a church at Lymington appears in the second charter of Christchurch Cartulary, dated to about 1155, when it records, 'The church at Bolra with its chapels of Limnetona and Brokenhurst'.94

It was not the purpose of *Domesday Book* to record churches unless they had some taxable or landholding responsibility, as at Milford where part of the church lands are described as being in the forest. There are occasional exceptions, as when a church is mentioned at Brockenhurst for no obvious reason other than its proximity to a royal hunting lodge. However, no church is mentioned at *Lentune*. It is generally assumed that during the tenth and early eleventh centuries most manors were provided with a chapel or church to meet the spiritual needs of the residents. The lord normally provided the chancel, where the priest celebrated the masses, while the parishioners provided the nave. Whether Lymington was so endowed at an earlier date we now have no means of knowing. However, as a chapel is mentioned in the mid-twelfth century it seems highly probable that a place for worship there was already established. It has to be borne in mind that at this date there was no New Lymington, so if the chapel was on the site of the present church it would have stood at the eastern edge of the agricultural settlement. Indeed, a chapel in such a position may have had some influence on the siting of the western boundary of the borough created by William de Redvers. It would be then in a convenient position for serving the communities of both Old and New Lymington, lying at the boundary of both just within the borough.

The earliest surviving architectural feature of the stone-built church, though only a fragment of a pillar, indicates a date for its construction as about the time of the first charter. It certainly seems likely that in laying out the High Street plots a brand new church would have been built. Indeed the need to import stone for this work would tie in neatly with the possible construction of a stone boundary wall between the borough and Old Lymington. Is it not feasible that the stone foundations to the brick walls along the east side of Church Lane are the remnants of such a boundary? And that the many shiploads of stone needed for this purpose would be brought over at the same time as those for the church?

Whether that was the case or not the church building subsequently underwent a considerable number of changes, many so drastic as to obscure or destroy the original form and materials. It is now impossible to recover the original plan though it was probably either just a nave and chancel or, more likely, a Latin cross plan with north and south transepts and a central crossing (see Church Plan). On the basis of the fragments of attached columns to windows in the chancel it seems likely, as was so often the case in the 13th century elsewhere, that the then existing chancel was extended eastwards at the time of Baldwin's 1256 charter. Of the nave, the only clear piece of architectural evidence is the respond attached to the wall on the north side of the west door, which may date back to the first charter of about 1200. The present chapel on the north side, in effect an eastward extension of the north transept, was used for the interment of members of the Courtenay family and they, of course, would have funded its construction in the fourteenth century. It is not clear from the architectural evidence when the north and south aisles were added, though that on the north possibly dates to the early 13th century.

What is interesting is that Lymington church had only the status of a chapel served originally by itinerant priests from Christchurch Priory, as also were the surrounding churches of Hordle, Milford, Brockenhurst and Boldre. Lymington was also dependent on what later became the 'mother' church at Boldre, and the parishioners were obliged to take 'a fit offering on St John Baptist's day' to

Boldre in return for having their own cemetery at Lymington.[95] Yet it seems to have been served by vicars rather than curates so that the vicars of Boldre had no direct jurisdiction over the Lymington chapel (or church). This is an unusual and anomalous situation yet was evidently the case. John Tailloure, whom we have already met as owing a debt in 1437, was described quite specifically as 'vicar of the church of New Lymington'.

The church was, and remains to this day, dedicated to St Thomas the Apostle, whose feast day falls on 21 December.[96] No parochial records survive to enable a picture of Lymington's spiritual life in the middle ages to be built up so we can only conjecture that the care of souls, the baptisms of infants, the marriage ceremony, the burial of the dead, the celebration of masses on Sundays and

Conjectural sketch plan of Lymington parish church showing possible phases of development during the middle ages. There was a church here before the time of William de Redvers which may have been a structure built partly of stone and partly of timber. It is here suggested that the more substantial stone church and its subsequent modifications relate to the times at which the successive charters were granted to the burgesses of New Lymington. The surviving fragments of architectural detail help to substantiate this supposition.

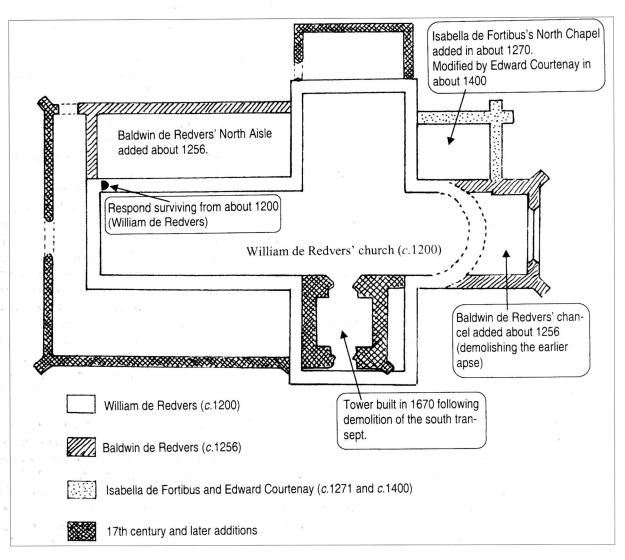

Isabella de Fortibus's North Chapel added in about 1270.
Modified by Edward Courtenay in about 1400

Baldwin de Redvers' North Aisle added about 1256.

Respond surviving from about 1200 (William de Redvers)

William de Redvers' church (c.1200)

Baldwin de Redvers' chancel added about 1256 (demolishing the earlier apse)

Tower built in 1670 following demolition of the south transept.

William de Redvers (c.1200)

Baldwin de Redvers (c.1256)

Isabella de Fortibus and Edward Courtenay (c.1271 and c.1400)

17th century and later additions

feast days and the taking of holy communion were part and parcel of the weekly routine for those living in Old and New Lymington. Sunday markets were commonly held in the churchyard after mass, and in the nave of the church in wet weather until proscribed in the reign of Henry VI.[97] Markets were often sited in the churchyard or close to the church,[98] and so it was in Lymington – with the market lying outside and running eastwards along the broad High Street.

As was usual practice before the Reformation the church had within it a number of chapels dedicated to a particular saint or to particular spiritual needs. By the end of the middle ages in Lymington there were chapels to Our Lady of Deliverance, St George, St Clement and St Katherine. The church interior would have been painted with biblical and religious scenes illuminated by continuously burning lamps and candles, each dedicated to a particular saint or feast day. The oil for these lamps was often paid for from bequests. We find, for example, in the will of Robert Mawler (Maller), drawn up in April 1527, who had been mayor in 1507, not only payments for the lights before the altars of the chapels but also for 'the Epiphany light of the new towne of Lymyngton', 'the Epiphany light of the old towne' and, most intriguingly, to the Epiphany light of 'the towne shippe of woodsyde'. The bequest to each was fourpence.

Another example is provided by a deed issued by Egidia Wolvin (or Walwyn) in 1524. In that year she enfeoffed her property in the counties of Surrey, Sussex and Hampshire to the following trustees: Tristram Fauntleroy, Bartholomew House, John Canterton, John Jutton (or Sutton), John Draper and Henry Ashley of Wimborne St Giles. On her death Henry Ashley, acting for his fellow trustees, was to make an annual payment from her property of 10s. to the churchwardens of Brockenhurst and 10s. to those of Lymington. In the latter case the money was to be allocated to paying three priests the sum of 8d. each to sing three masses for the repose of the souls of Thomas Alwin his wife Joan,

An early nineteenth century engraving of Lymington church from the east.

Reginald Fowlvan, and Thomas Fowlvan (*alias* Wolvin) in addition to Egidia herself. To those assisting in the masses, namely, the orator, the bellringers, the clerk and four serving boys a further sum of 1s. 8d. was allowed. After each mass a penny was to be spent on bread, ale and cheese for the parishioners attending. After the mass on the Sunday following Easter wax candles to the value of 4d. were to be purchased.[99] Although no other connection between Egidia Wolvin and Lymington has been discovered, the fact remains that her deed does further illuminate aspects of the medieval church flourishing in the years immediately prior to the Reformation.

Interestingly elements of the Catholic liturgy often remained in place after the Reformation, as is clearly shown in the will of John Browne of New Lymington made 'the xijth day of Apruell in the yere of o^r lord god anno mccccccxxxviij' (1538) when he bequeathed a shilling towards the maintenance of the rood light. It was not until the provisions promulgated in February 1548, during the reign of the boy king Edward VI, that it was ordered that images, including roods, should be destroyed.[100]

TWO

The Tudor & Stuart Town

RUNNING THE TOWN

It is in the reign of Elizabeth I (1558-1603) that we begin to get a fuller picture of life in Lymington. In 1587 the town's burgesses were required to prove that the borough's rights and privileges derived from its medieval charters granted by Isabella de Fortibus and Edward Courtenay.[1] In this they were successful and it was confirmed that the burgesses were the only ones entitled to a parliamentary vote and that it had been proper for the borough to return two members of parliament in 1584 and at each subsequent election. The first to be elected were probably nominees of the then Speaker, Sir Edward Coke, namely Anthony and Richard Cooke. This was the beginning of Lymington's enduring importance as a provider of members of parliament to meet particular party interests, an aspect more fully described in the next chapter. However, it was only the burgesses who were enfranchised to elect the two MPs; the wider community of Old and New Lymington had no direct involvement in the process.

From a subsidy or tax levied in 1586 we get an indication of the status of the wealthier Lymingtonians.[2] The first name to appear in the list is John Longe (elected mayor in 1588, the year of the Armada) who held half the manor of Buckland and other lands and properties. He is the only one in a list of twenty-four taxpayers who was assessed on land, the remainder were assessed on goods. The valuations in this taxation were on the low side, so Longe's assessment was only a paltry £10, on which he paid one-fifteenth, 13s. 4d. Next on the list is John Clare's widow who paid 12s., equivalent to one-twentieth of the value of her moveable goods (£12) and must be considered as one of the wealthier woman in Lymington. Eleven of those listed were either burgesses or, in the case of two, widows of burgesses. Six had been, or were to become, mayors.

Tax was not levied on those whose goods were valued at less than £3, with the sole exception of a man called William Yenkins, described as an 'alien' who paid, on his person (*i.e.* effectively a poll tax) the sum of 4d. The possessions of the majority of the people of Lymington were worth under £3, including most tradesmen, artisans, and craftsmen, as well as labourers and servants. The clergy, who were taxed separately, were omitted as the subsidy was levied only on lay people.

From 1581 there is a continuous record of the town's affairs in the form of manuscript volumes known as 'Town Books'. The oldest was described by Edward King in 1900 as 'a mouldering fragment'[3] and its condition is now so poor that it cannot be released from its safe keeping in the Hampshire Record Office in Winchester. Fortunately, some early historians of Lymington, notably Charles St Barbe and Edward King, and later the Hampshire archivists, did abstract some occasional items from this record which greatly enhances our understanding of the ways in which the town was administered.

The entries cover the regulation of the market and fairs, upkeep of the market hall, the prison (blind house), stocks, pillory, ducking (or cucking) stool, the market cross and, importantly, the quay (invariably spelled 'Key'). The income for running the borough and Old Lymington came mainly from four sources, namely: (i) the rents on properties, (ii) tolls from the markets and the two annual fairs, (iii) wharfage and other maritime dues and (iv) incidentals such as the sale of surplus materials. The mayor, who was elected by the burgesses annually, was paid an allowance of £2. 10s. a year 'in respect of his travell, dyett, and charge' and this payment was met from the rent received for the corporation's property of Holme Mead, now the site of the Lymington Post Office (built 1960).

The mayor had to be chosen from the burgesses and was elected from three names put forward. The mayor did not have to be a resident of Lymington and those who were non-resident could nominate another burgess to act on their behalf in most matters concerning the borough. It is evident that the matter was taken seriously, for an ordinance of 1622, stated that any burgess elected to office and failing to serve could be fined £5. The mayor could not take on his official duties until approved by the court leet of the manor, which met usually in October. The sitting mayor was obliged to remain in office until the court had taken the oath of the newly elected mayor. The involvement of the court leet in this process further strengthens the principle of the borough being an integral part of the manor.

Though there was a manorial court to deal with offences and to oversee regulation of the market and fairs it was the burgesses who were in sole control of running the town. As Hoskins remarks, 'The incorporated towns [such as Lymington] were governed by medieval charters, and run by small oligarchies which were generally self-perpetuating and closed to all but a carefully chosen few'[4] – a precise picture of Lymington's government which was to continue until the time of the Reform Act of 1832 and the Municipal Corporations Act of 1835.

The election for mayor took place on the first Sunday after the feast of St Matthew the Apostle. Examples include that of 1665 when Henry Bromfield, Thomas Urry and Humfrey Banfeild [sic] were the candidates and the voting was one for Bromfield, four for Banfield and six for Thomas Urry. In the following year Banfield stood again, only to be defeated by the six votes cast in favour of Bartholomew Harmood. There appears to have been a keener contest in 1673 when William Burrard got 5 votes, Samuel Samber 7, and the winner, John Lamport 9.

The first parliamentary election of which we have a voting record took place on 11 February, 1677. The three candidates were Sir Richard Knight (of Chawton), John Button (of Lymington) and George Fulford (of Toller Fratrum, Dorset) and the voting was 13, 11 and 7 respectively, so Knight became the

MP.[5] In 1680, when two members were required, the voting was Henry Dawley 23, John Burrard 21 and the loser, Richard Whitehead, 19.

Control of boroughs such as Lymington was important so the burgesses were 'persuaded', usually by personal reward or some kind of favour, to elect a member who was politically sympathetic to the cause of the landowner, thus ensuring his influence in parliament. Often it was the landowners themselves who stood, as with Sir William Dodington of Breamore House who was elected MP for Lymington in 1620. This practice ensured they had their own voice in the seat of power. At this date there was no specified limit on the number of burgesses and, as we have seen, they could be resident anywhere. Presumably to ensure a greater commitment to the town's interests an ordinance of 1674 sought to restrict membership to people who had lived in Lymington for seven years.[6]

The burgesses themselves were obliged by their oath to be loyal to the monarch but, more importantly from the point of view of local government, they were to use all their 'power, wit and wisdom' to 'maintain and defend' the good name of Lymington, ensuring that their commercial dealings benefited the town.

The burgesses were expected to attend meetings and participate in running the town's administration. Severe penalties were enjoined against those failing to do so. Even as early as 1584 it had been ordered that any burgess failing to attend a meeting called by the mayor, unless he gave good reason, should be fined either 5s. or suffer 'two dais and two nyghtes imprysonement'.[7]

The status of a burgess of Lymington and the influence which could be brought to bear as a voter in parliamentary elections meant that men from far and wide became burgesses. Just a few selected examples of those elected will confirm this characteristic of local government: William Whyte of Moyle's Court (1589), Sir John Oglander of Brooke in the Isle of Wight (1634), Henry Tichborne of Tichborne (1650), Sir John Mill of Mottisfont (1665), John Newburgh of Worth Matravers in Dorset (1667) and Sir Richard Knight of Chawton (1677). Few would have attended

These half bushel and one bushel measures date from the reign of George IV, but accurate measures had been a feature of Lymington's market from its earliest days.

meetings. Many lived some way from Lymington, so were unlikely to be imprisoned, whilst the 5s. fine would have had little impact on men of their wealth. It should be noted however that the majority either resided in Lymington or in the immediate vicinity.

The regulation of the market was the responsibility of the mayor and burgesses acting under the jurisdiction of the manor court. A well-regulated market encouraged trade, and the law laid down strict rules to ensure the proper conduct of all commercial activity. Standard measures were first introduced in Magna Carta in 1215[8] and subsequent governments reiterated this requirement. In Henry VII's reign an act required officially approved and sealed measures[9] to be provided for use in every town. Presumably Lymington obeyed this ruling, but not until 1587 is there a record showing the town spending 7s. 8d. on a replacement bushel measure. Even brass measures would have worn out but the town was sometimes slow to replace them. For example, in 1625 the burgesses were fined £2 for not having available a bushel measure and they then had to pay an additional 4s. 4d. for the 'markett Bushell and sealing it'.[10] In 1652 John Colchester was fined 3s. 4d. for using 'unjust' weights, *i.e.* unsealed weights.

Although no list of these measures survives in the Lymington records we do have an example from Ringwood which must parallel those retained in the borough. There we find eleven brass weights ranging from ½ ounce to 14lbs, a 'pair of brass scales', and a brass bushel measure, wooden measures for half bushel and ½ gallon, copper measures for one pint and ½ pint, pewter measures for a nogin and ½ nogin and also yard and ell measures.[11] Isolated Lymington entries do throw light on this important matter, as in 1633 when a 'paire of gold weightes' were purchased for 7s. indicating either that there were goldsmiths in the town or that some market activity was in gold. A more everyday example comes from 1637 when 4s. 8d. was expended on the purchase of a pair of scales for weighing meal.[12]

All markets depended largely on the sale of live and dead stock and it was imperative for the conduct of business that live animals should not be permitted to root about in the streets, pick produce from vegetable stalls or generally make a nuisance of themselves. To control such matters most markets appointed an official, known as the hayward, whose duty it was to round up stock not properly tethered and place it in the pound. Lymington's pound was situated in New Lane (probably at its junction with Lower Buckland Lane).[13] Those who owned the offending animals were then punished by a fine imposed by the manor court. An entry of 1574[14] orders that,

> no man's or woman's hogge shall go within the New Town unringed and unyoked; and as often as any man appoynted by the maior shal happen to take any suche hogge unlawed, the owner shal paie for evry hogge iiij[d] whereof ij[d] to go to the Towne and ij[d] to the driver of the same hogge.

The dead stock, normally slaughtered in an abattoir in New Lane, was offered for sale on wooden stalls called shambles, whose maintenance was the responsibility of the burgesses. Similarly, fish, offered for sale as 'wet', 'salted', dried or smoked, was displayed on wooden boards in the fish shambles.

Typical entries dealing with repairs to the shambles are recorded in the second town book, where entries include '2 planks for the fish

Shop and premises from the late Stuart period that once stood where nos. 40-2 High Street now stand. Ashley Lane runs down on the right. Drawing by Thomas T. Colborne in about 1840.

Shambles, 2s. 6d' and, prior to market, the 4d spent 'setting uppe of the Fishe Shambles'.[15] An earlier reference to the shambles is recorded in a lease of 1409 when the reeve, Richard Draper, granted a 60 years' lease on a piece of land (measuring 40 x 11 feet) in 'Fleschamelrewe' for the sum of 8s. a year to John Peperwhyt.[16] This record hints at the existence of permanent or semi-permanent shambles in the wide High Street.

Trade and commerce are, of course, the lifeblood of all communities and if their urban function is to be sustained and developed, the corporation must encourage a range of economic activities. Lymington's first town book lists weavers, tailors, drapers, innkeepers and tipplers; the innkeepers providing the ever important victuals, board and lodging for townsfolk and visitors alike.

The production of wool, a cornerstone of life in Tudor and Stuart England, and its export and processing into cloth was crucial to both the national and local economies. The presence of weavers shows that the town sustained a cloth working community, and wool, drawn from the hinterland and the Isle of Wight, was an important export from Lymington throughout the late

sixteenth and the first half of the seventeenth century; in 1615 eighteen loads are exported, 16 loads in 1616, 21 loads in 1617 and so on over the years.

Southampton's probate inventories reveal the close links maintained between its merchants and Lymington's tradesmen. In 1554 we find William Sibill of Lymington owing Thomas Harrison, a girdle maker, the sum of 3s. 7d. In 1573 Lymington's John Pamplyn owed the wealthiest Southampton merchant, Richard Goddard, 48s. 4d. and William Hunte owed him 40s. 2d., whilst William Elliot and Thomas Burad [sic] owed Reynold Howse 49s. 9d. and 47s. 9d. respectively.[17]

Incomplete and partial though the records are the picture emerging is of a vibrant and dynamic commercial community dominated by the annually elected mayor and the (appointed) burgesses, comprising the corporation. As regulators of the town's affairs, they were able to ensure that the greatest influence in both trading and political matters lay always in their own hands. Next to them were those traders and artisans who received permission to conduct their businesses under privileges granted and specified by the burgesses. Other traders were at a greater disadvantage, though not discouraged, and they were generally referred to as 'strangers' or 'foreigners'.

The earliest record we have of the town's income appears in the first Town Book in which it is recorded that in 1587 the receipts equalled £2 9s. 9d. whilst the expenditure, at £2 15s. 6d., showed a deficit of 5s. 9d., which was carried forward so as to be chargeable against the following year's accounts. The income and expenditure accounts vary quite a lot from year to year and sometimes there are surprising contrasts, as in 1619 when income was £9 7s. 9d. while in the following year it soared to £47 4s. 6d. The high receipts for 1620 were timely, as essential repairs at the quay cost no less than £24 17s. 7d.

Typical examples of income are the £6 18s. received in 1616 from the 'Shoppes and Shambles and quarteridges for shoomakers', and wharfage duty on 16 loads of wool earned 13s. 4d., equivalent to 10d. a load. Expenditure in the same year contained items such as 'Repair shops and shambles this yere £1 12s. 8d.', 'It^m for Forest duties 8d.' and repairing 'the Staires to the Key 5s. 10d.'[18]

The wharfage duty is fully listed in 1626 and gives a fascinating insight into the wide range of goods and produce being transported to and from the harbour. Much of it was packed in barrels, the 'containers' of their day. For example, 'For every Barrell of beefe, porke or herringe 1d.' and 'For every barrell of any other comodities not before mençoñed 2d.'. Amongst the produce specifically itemised are 'sea colles', charcoal, wine, vinegar, soap, iron, tar, pitch, earthenware, boards, planks and livestock. Lymington was, of course, an entrepôt for the surrounding hinterland and was particularly important in serving the southern side of the New Forest.

It is not clear from the records of this period the extent of its European trade, but the import of deal boards does suggest a Scandinavian connection and there was certainly trade with the Channel Islands. Undoubtedly the cross-Solent contact with Yarmouth on the Isle of Wight, then as now, was the most important single maritime function for Lymington. The quay was heavily used and it was reported in 1565 that of all the landing places within the jurisdiction of the admiralty court of Southampton only Lymington Quay was 'decayed'.

This was due to the 'lading of the Princesse's timber out of the New Forest', which was then shipped to Portsmouth and to 'all the Fortresses and Castells' within Hampshire, including Hurst, Calshot, Yarmouth and possibly some of the other Isle of Wight forts. Timber was also exported on behalf of the queen to castles on Jersey, Guernsey and Alderney. As the wear and tear on the quay was largely due to the needs of government a sum of £60 was allowed for repairs.[19] This sizeable sum stands in contrast to the much lower costs incurred by the burgesses.

The constant repairs to the quay emphasised its importance, and a list of 1620 provides an insight into the materials used and work required. Surprisingly perhaps from this record are the large quantities of faggots needed; their use is not specified but may have been as fuel for lime kilns or for providing foundations in the mud for the stonework. Thirty tons of stone and large amounts of chalk for making lime were landed. The lime kilns were fired, at least partially, with gorse. The provenance of the stone is not always recorded, but much must have come from the Purbeck quarries as in 1617 there is a reference to Philip the Mason being paid 1s. 6d. for 'Purbicke' stone.[20]

The market hall, as in all towns, was a building of considerable importance. One market hall existed as early as the late thirteenth century, when it is described as having attached to it half an acre of garden and to be worth 7s. per annum, 'saving repairs'.[21] This hall probably belonged to the manor for the corporation, comprising the burgesses of New Lymington, was a member of the manor of Lymington and in that capacity was subject to the rulings and decisions of the manor. In the reign of Edward III it was described as a house with 'a little close used for holding courts and worth

nothing beyond repairs'. By the seventeenth century the hall had come to be regarded as the property of the burgesses, the manorial courts were also held there.[22] So we have this medieval hall in which the business of the burgesses was conducted and the courts of the lord were held. About its structure and form we know nothing, although evidence suggests that it was a building of no particular architectural merit perhaps standing on the site of the later Holme (or Home) Mead.

Its shortcomings were no doubt recognized for in 1465 a widow, whom we only know by her name, Juliana Tevant, granted two messuages and ½ an acre of land to John Quicke, the reeve, and all the burgesses for their use. The property lay on the

Robert Groves's pencil drawing shows clearly the terrace of seventeenth century properties that made up the south side of Quay Hill. They have all been modernised but retain their basic architectural form and character.

south side of the High Street and ran back to land held by Christchurch Priory. In exchange for this gift the burgesses were to give 3s. 4d annually to the poor.[23] On this land, according to Edward King, the town hall was built for upon the back of the document is inscribed: 'the deed of the Town House late in the possession of Giles Samber'.[24] The site of this building is not known but King, tantalisingly states, 'we can pretty closely identify its locality', which he assumes to be 31/33 High Street, near the brow of the hill.[25]

41

The oft repeated tale that this was the town hall burnt in a French raid in 1545 appears to be without substance. On 19 July a large French fleet entered Spithead. The *Mary Rose* in preparing for action was swamped through her gun ports and sank with a loss of all lives. The French then landed on the Isle of Wight but were defeated and withdrew the next day when their fleet sailed eastwards with the prevailing wind and attacked Seaford and burnt Brighthelmstone on the Sussex coast.[26] So the evidence for an attack on Lymington, lying in the direction opposite to that taken by the French, is contrary to the tradition.

It is likely that the 'Town House' and the 'Market Hall' were one and the same building. If a new market hall was built on the land given to the town by Juliana Tevant it probably would have consisted of an open arcaded ground floor, the shambles, and an upper chamber for the conduct of the corporation's business and the manor courts. Although the building was later demolished it probably conformed to the traditional style, of which numerous examples survive.[27]

Some idea of its situation, condition and structure can be obtained from entries for its repair recorded in the Town Books. For glazing and mending the Market House in 1620 the sum of 9s. 8d. was spent. In 1631 Edward Collins supplied twelve loads of gravel to improve the road around the Market House. A sum of 6d. was spent on clay, no doubt for the daub for wattle panels, for we find from the record that Andrew Studly 'and his boy' were paid 1s. 4d. for a day's work when they set up boards and rods for daubing '2 panes of wall'.[28]

Associated with the Market House was the communal town well. From its many mentions in the records it was probably the main permanent source of water for the borough residents supplemented by a number of private wells, often shared, and by rainwater collected in butts attached to individual properties. In 1620, 2s. 6d. was spent on cleaning the town well and three years later boards were bought to make a cover for it. The following year saw the purchase of two loads of gravel to be 'layde about the well'. A new bucket was supplied in 1631 which cost 2s. 6d. In 1656 a kerb costing 5s. was constructed around the well.[29]

The care of the well and its surroundings was a ongoing concern and in May 1707 the court orders that 'the dung about the town well to be carried away' within four days and when that is done 'that gravel be laid round it'.

The market cross also had to be maintained at the expense of the borough and regular charges for its repair and upkeep are found in the records. As the focal point of trade in the town it was essential that the area around it be kept in good condition. The to and fro of livestock, wagons and carts would have quickly turned the street into a quagmire, so it comes as no surprise to find the burgesses in 1640 spending 10s. on ten tons of pebble stones to be set about the market cross.

Manorial courts were empowered to inflict penalties on those who disregarded and disobeyed the laws regulating conduct within the manor. The implements of punishment, also sited close to the Market House, were maintained by the burgesses. This is a further indication of the integral relationship of the manor court, which authorized the various punishments, and the burgesses. It was the latter who financed, from the town income, the stocks, cucking (or ducking) stool, pillory, whipping post and blind house. Indeed if the corporation failed in its responsibility to properly look after any of these it would be arraigned in the manor court and fined. Thus repairs and replacements form a regular expense in the outgoings of the burgesses: in 1629, for example, a carpenter was paid 16s. for making a new pillory and cucking stool and a glazier was paid 1s. 'for coolering the Pillory with Oyle'. The 'blind house' was a name commonly used for tiny local prisons or lock-ups, the term deriving from the absence of any windows.[30]

TRADE, COMMERCE & BUSINESS

Apprenticeship was the standard way whereby a boy learned a trade. No doubt most apprenticeships were within the town but at least three boys were sent to Southampton to be indentured. For example, Edward Knowles, described as a Lymington mercer, sent his son, also Edward, to be apprenticed to Francis Knowles, a merchant, for a period of eight years in 1625. It would seem likely

Lymington trade tokens issued in the reigns of Charles II and James II. The one on the left shows flax, indicating possible linen production.

Woodside Manor House, as drawn by Thomas Colborne in about 1840. This building represents a surviving example of a substantial house belonging to the time at which the Hearth Taxation was in operation.

that this arrangement was within the family as the surnames of apprentice and master are the same. More intriguing perhaps is Thomas Hurst, described as a 'gentleman' of Lymington, sending his son, Edward, to be apprenticed to Thomas Mason a Southampton grocer for a term of nine years in 1630. And another Lymington gentleman, John Scott, sent his son, John, as an apprentice to Edward Tatnell, merchant in 1633.[31] Owning a grocery business could evidently be profitable for Thomas Glevin, who issued more than one Lymington token as 'grocer', was recorded as living in a house with 7 hearths, indicating a substantial residence.

The dearth of small coinage in the years following the execution of Charles I, persisted during much of the Commonwealth period and, by the time of the Restoration, local trading communities were facing real difficulties in small-scale retailing. As a consequence of this shortage of small change, affecting most particularly farthings (¼d), businessmen sought a solution by issuing their own coins, called 'trade tokens'. Local traders were permitted to advertise their businesses by having their names, and sometimes symbols of their trade, struck on the tokens. In Lymington at least seven tradesmen produced and issued these now rare copper/tin alloy coins.[32] Two were of half-penny (½d.) value and the remainder of one farthing. Several carried the grocers' arms and others were decorated with flowers, possibly illustrating flax, indicating involvement in linen production. However, the circulation of this local, private coinage was seen as a threat to the national

standard coinage and left open the possibility of counterfeiting. Ultimately, low value coins were minted nationally and legislation forbidding the use of trade tokens was introduced.[33]

At this period shipbuilding did not figure prominently in the economic life of Lymington. When a government commission was appointed in 1698 to look into the provision of shipyards it reported that Lymington was 'a place more short and scanty in the accommodations [than] to be found in Beauly river'.[34]

Central to the economic welfare of the town remained the manufacture of salt. Salterns ran along the western side of the estuary and thence along the coast to Oxey and continuing on to Keyhaven. Each had it own name, such as Five Rankes, Nineteen Rankes and Twenty-two Rankes, North Croft and South Croft, Lawrence and Oxey. Many of the saltern owners were men of considerable status in the town and lived in substantial houses, as is shown by the Hearth Tax returns. The following served as mayors: John Edwards, Francis Guidott, John More and Thomas Urry (or Urrey) and a number of others were burgesses. The Burrards were deeply involved in the salt industry: in the mid-seventeenth century Thomas Burrard owned a number of salterns and constructed new ones.[35]

The majority of the burgesses of Lymington and, no doubt, many of the townsfolk supported Parliament against the king when the Civil War broke out in 1642. This was typical of many ports and coastal towns, due largely to the festering opposition to the re-imposition of the Ship Money tax by Charles I in 1634. There was also a strong non-conformist element amongst the burgesses, ensuring their sympathy for the strongly puritan parliamentary cause. Typical of these was Thomas Burrard. Two years after the start of the war he was spared paying tax, principally because he had given £40 to the support of Lymington's garrison and had had a barn burnt down in a skirmish with the Royalists.[36]

An anecdote indicating the pro-parliamentary stance of Lymington is revealed when a mercer of Ilchester, George or John Smith, a member of the Royalist garrison of the Somerset town, rode out to accost John Stone of Lymington 'on whom he drew his sword . . . and threatened to kill him, as he was a round-headed rogue, whereupon Stone was forced to leap over a hedge and escape for his life'.[37]

However, when the first phase of the Civil War was over and Charles was imprisoned at Carisbrooke Castle, we find that the mayor, Bernard Knapton, supported the Royalist cause so that when, in 1648, Prince Charles arrived off Yarmouth with a fleet in an attempt to rescue his father, Knapton and some burgesses offered their help.[38] This stance may represent a change of heart which affected many who had started out supporting Parliament but had become disillusioned or, more simply, it may reflect political divisions within Lymington's ruling elite, with the majority supporting Parliament and others siding with the king. There is no record in the town of that other disaffected body, the 'Clubmen', who made a such a mark in Dorset, standing for their rights against both sides.

Only one major skirmish took place at or near Lymington and on that occasion three Royalist troops of horse were attacked by a Roundhead force from Sussex, killing seven and capturing 24.[39] Regardless of actual battles troops and sailors made use of the town and harbour during their movements across the south, and the burgesses soon learnt that billeting troops was an expensive business involving a direct charge on the funds of the town. In 1642 the 'next Mayor' was reimbursed the sum of £4 for the expenses he had paid out of his own pocket for the billeting of seamen. In the following year we find 5s. laid out for quartering for one day and one night 20 soldiers 'going westward for the Parliament's Service'. And in the traumatic year of 1644 there is a list of items concerned with the expenses of war:

for relieving divers companies of souldiers coming from Cornwall £2. 10s.
for straw to lodge soldiers 5s.
For Mr Guidott at Basingstoke, in mony 10s.
to Captain Green for him and his men £1 00s.
paid to James Garrett's wife for a sicke souldier 5s.
for a shrowd for him 3s. 6d.
to Belman for a barrell of beer for the soldiers 4s. 6d.
for relieving 2 sicke women which came out of Cornwall 5s.[40]

Over the war years repeated expenses occur when providing accommodation and victuals for soldiers. Bartholmew Bulkeley is paid 5s. 10d for providing cheese in 1645 and Thomas Bellman 5s. for a barrel of beer.

The town had to be protected and it seems as though at least one earthwork was thrown up near the church to safeguard it from the west; for in 1646 an entry in the Town Book records that 6s. was paid 'For pulling downe the Worke to make way into the churchyard'. The town was also guarded by watchmen every time a threat seemed imminent. Because of these potential dangers the burgesses sent the town records to be stored safely in Hurst Castle, which had been held by Parliament since 1642. In 1647 when the danger had passed 2s. was spent in 'bringing the Towne Chest from Hurst Castle'.

Even after the conclusion of the Civil War Lymington was still subject to considerable expense in hosting military forces, as the following entries show:

To Bennet Pigen for quartering souldiers 4s.4d.
To William English for quartering of souldiers 4s.6d.
And for carriage of his sicke souldiers 1s.

For quartering souldiers at my house 4s.6d.
Paid Andrew Lockyer for grasse for their horses
4s.8d.
Payd to Sir Thomas Firyffas soulders goeing for the
Isle of Wight with their general's passe 12s.6d.
For quartering of Sir Thomas Firffax solders at my
home 6s.6d.

COMMOMWEALTH, RESTORATION & REBELLION

The upheaval of the Civil War had an adverse effect on the economic life of Lymington, and an economic depression characterised the years of the Commonwealth. Nor the did the Restoration of 1660 bring an immediate revival of the town's fortunes.

Two years later the government of Charles II introduced the Hearth Tax, which required the sum of 2s. to be levied on each hearth or stove in every house whose rental value was above £1 per annum. It was occasionally modified, but the details given when it was collected do provide us with an insight into the types of dwellings to be found in late seventeenth century Lymington.

In the returns for 1665[41] the Borough (New Lymington) had 95 households, of which 30 had one hearth, 27 had two and six had 7 or 8 hearths. In Old Lymington out of a total of 53 households 23 had one hearth and 16 had two while one house, Buckland Manor, by far the largest domestic property, had 19 hearths. Twenty-seven residents in the Borough and 23 in Old Lymington were excused payment because of poverty.

The returns of 1673[42] show that in the Borough most houses had two hearths (38) and 26 had one. Of all houses 59% were equipped with one or two hearths. In total there were 106 hearths, representing an increase of 11. In the Borough of New Lymington two properties boasted as many as 7 hearths, one belonging to Thomas Gleven, a grocer, the other shared by John Ensor and John Barwick. Buckland Manor House is still recorded as paying tax on 19 hearths. Through poverty 19 were excused payment in the Borough and 20 in Old Lymington.

Though useful in providing a general view of the quality of houses and the changes which occurred, such a picture is essentially statistical and lifeless. Nevertheless, on the surface the returns do seem to indicate some improvement in economic life, especially as revealed by the reduction of those excused payment through poverty. However, it is only when we look at the probate inventories attached to wills that a more detailed picture of the homes of the people becomes apparent.

On his death in 1676 Edward Smith, who had lived in the property now numbered as 27 High Street, had his goods assessed. From these details we discover that his main bed comprised a feather mattress and a bolster and was topped with a tester. Its value, including the bolster, a pair of pillows and sheets and blankets was given as £5. The bed was heated with a warming pan which appears to have been kept in the kitchen. As was common practice at the time clothes were kept in coffers or chests, but his two chests contained bedding, table cloths and napkins. Candles provided the main source of illumination, for he owned a total of five candlesticks distributed around the house.

The kitchen was equipped with two brass kettles, two skillets, a frying pan, an iron pot, and such things as tongs and hangers in the hearth needed by his wife or maid cooking at the large open fire. When joints were spit roasted the fat was collected in either an iron dripping pan or one of the two latten (brass) pans. There was a grater, a salt cellar and a pepper box. For most meals the family sat on forms or joint stools at a table board and ate their meals off wooden plates (trenchers). Beer was the usual drink and the household had five beer vessels and a flagon.

Edward was evidently literate for he owned five books and had six chairs. He was a shoemaker by trade and his workshop contained 72 lasts, two hammers, a cutting knife and cutting board and an unspecified quantity of leather for uppers and soles. In stock at the time of his death were 21 pairs of shoes for men and women and 13 pairs for children.

Tradesmen, craftsmen and artisans often had interests subsidiary or additional to their main enterprise and in this respect Edward Smith was no exception. He held a quarter part interest in a ship called the *Elizabeth* and a sixteenth part interest in another called the *Nightingale*. This was then a common form of investment, as the value of the cargoes carried by the vessels brought in a proportional profit to the partners. And there was an inbuilt safeguard in that if a vessel was lost only the proportion held by each partner was at risk.

The total assessed value of his worldly goods and interests came to £207 9s. 3d., placing him in the category of a small but successful businessman.

Leather was perhaps even more valuable in the seventeenth century than it is today. Not only shoes and boots, but also clothing, thongs for chairs and beds and covers for books, buckets, saddlery required leather. The office of 'searchers and sealers of leather' was important in trying to ensure and maintain the quality of leather sold at market. Consequently it is not surprising to find Richard King of Lymington arraigned before the manor court in 1650 to pay a fine of 3s. 4d. for sending his leather to Christchurch 'unsearched and unsealed contrary to statute'.[43] Leather was used for fire buckets and examples from this period can still be seen today, as in Puddletown church in Dorset or in the hall of St Cross, Winchester. In 1697 the Lymington churchwardens paid £4 for 24 leather buckets to hang in their church.

The succession of the Catholic James II to the throne in 1685 must have sent shivers through many of those self-sufficient urban dwellers who had supported, even half-heartedly, the parliamentary forces during the Civil War. There had been widespread rejoicing when Charles II was restored after the partly dictatorial authority of Cromwell and the short but wholly ineffective rule of his son Richard. Yet uneasiness at the possibility of absolutist monarchy cannot have been far beneath the surface for Lymington men were suspected of involvement in the doomed Rye House Plot of 1683.[44] The plot involved assassinating Charles II and the Duke of York (the future James II) as a means of preventing all Catholic claims to the throne. John Burrard hired a ship named the *Thomas* of Southampton to go to the western ports of England and Ireland to seek support for the conspiracy. Bad weather prevented them reaching Ireland but on turning back they called at

Plymouth, Dartmouth, Topsham, Weymouth and Poole in order to meet with conspirators to try to prevent the eventual accession of the Duke of York as James II. Burrard was accompanied by other disaffected Lymington men including Thomas Wansey and Thomas Dore. In September 1683 a warrant had been issued to search for Thomas Dore and his daughter Melior, 'to answer to what shall be objected against them on suspicion of being privy to the late conspiracy'.[45] Little wonder that when the Protestant Duke of Monmouth landed at Lyme Regis in June 1685 to claim the throne he found sympathisers in Lymington. A John Tutchin, a stalwart supporter of Monmouth, is reported to have gone to Lymington to get backing for the ill-fated rebellion.[46]

The Dore family was in the forefront of local support. As early as 1661, just a year after the restoration of Charles II, Philip Dore (mayor in 1652-53) refused the oath of allegiance and was debarred from office.[47] It is no surprise to find Thomas Dore, mayor of Lymington 1684-85, amongst the most ardent supporters of Monmouth's Protestant and dynastic cause. James II was aware of his sympathies and a warrant was issued on 9 June for Dore's arrest and also to make a search for arms.[48] Dore eluded his pursuers and declared his support for Monmouth. Ten days later he was described as 'hovering about the New Forest' with a band of some 80 horse and foot soldiers.[49] A week after that the Earl of Sunderland, James II's Secretary of State, was informed that:

> those rebellious and disorderly persons who were gotten together about the New Forest are willing to come in upon assurance of pardon, and [the king] being inclinable to extend his mercy to such as may have been misled, commands me to tell you that he would have you promise a pardon to all such as upon publication of his intentions come in and claim the benefit thereof except Dore, the Mayor of Lymington . . .

By 6 July it all was over. Monmouth's luckless followers were either wounded, on the run, or lying dead in the dykes of Sedgmoor. The defeated Duke was heading towards Lymington and sanctuary in anticipation of making his escape by sea when he was captured at Horton Heath, just a few miles north of Wimborne and taken to Ringwood. In the face of imminent arrest Thomas Dore made his escape, probably through Poole, and lived abroad for three years, only returning in 1688 (though a pardon had been granted to him in August 1686).[50] In 1690 he was returned as one of the MPs for Lymington. How fortunes can change in the world of politics.

Understandably, James II must have viewed Lymington as an antagonistic borough and sought to diminish its role by calling into question its political authority. It was George Burrard, who had received training as a lawyer at the Inner Temple, who presented Lymington's case for the legitimacy of its liberties and privileges. The outcome was successful for the town.[51]

THE POOR & CHARITY

In Elizabeth's reign legislation was passed making provision for the poor on the basis of parochial responsibility. Of the poor of Lymington prior to the Tudor period we have no detailed knowledge. It is known that various kinds of charitable provisions were made by the church to aid the poor and the sick but records are few. There is the isolated reference to Juliana Tevant, mentioned earlier, requiring a payment of 3s. 4d. to be made annually to the poor. But it is with the adoption of the Elizabethan Poor Law that some documentary evidence does survive; little at first but abundantly later.

In August 1608 Alice Ingram, wife of John Ingram of Lymington, was found wandering around Salisbury, running into people's houses and declaring she had the plague. For this behaviour she was punished and then sent back to her husband at Lymington. We later discover that John Ingram was an itinerant pedlar and by 1617 had made his home in Harbridge.[52]

Private charity seems to have played a small but significant role in the seventeenth century and a number of individuals made provision for the poor. Nearly every will proved in the ecclesiastical courts allocated a small sum to aid the poor at the time of the funeral. More permanent provision was made by men such as Thomas Brown who in February 1668 (1667 O.S.) bequeathed £2 per annum to the poor of Lymington and, additionally, 10s. for a sermon to be delivered on the 1 January each year for ever. Brown desired that any poor persons who wished to benefit from his largesse should come to church to hear this sermon.[53]

A curious insight into the operation of legislation and the way it could aid the poor is given in the case of Widow Penny of Sway who was buried at Lymington on 15 December 1685 in a linen shroud. In order to encourage the woollen cloth industry the law required that everyone should be buried in wool[54] and affidavits had to be sworn at the time of the funeral (or immediately afterwards) to the effect that this had been done. In Mrs Penny's case a fine of £2 10s. was levied against her estate for her failure to abide by the law, and the money was then given to the poor of the parish.[55]

RELIGION & THE CHURCH

The Civil War had given further encouragement to freedom of worship, especially for those sects essentially puritan in character. The Anglican Church remained legally the established religion and as such dominated the spiritual life of the community. The ecclesiastical courts were under the jurisdiction of the Church of England. All sacraments were to be administered in the parish church, including baptism, marriage and burial. Attendance at church was required and those who failed to attend were fined 1s., and even those leaving services early suffered the same penalty. Sunday was to be kept sacred so far as possible and in Lymington those who travelled for business on the Lord's Day were liable to a fine of £1. Boatmen, perhaps because of the unpredictability of the weather, were treated rather more leniently and were subject to a fine of only 5s.

The irony inherent in Sunday being a day of rest was that it gave the working population an opportunity to gather for leisure pursuits in a way not possible during the working week, and absenteeism from church, either wholly or partially, was often due to men playing games. Those baiting bulls or bears or engaging in plays or sports in Lymington were subject to a 3s. 4d. fine or, if they

The initials RC and the date the tower was built commemorated on this stone in the buttress. It is not clear who RC is as the builder was Mr Mitchell, the churchwardens were John Burrard and Richard Eden and the Rev. Samuel Torksey was the minister.

could not pay, punished by being locked in the stocks.

The parish church played a central role in local administration. Money was raised by levying a church rate and this was collected and disbursed as appropriate by two elected churchwardens. The basic rate was 1d. per property but could be collected more than once a year although, in general, the sums were relatively small. For example, early in the seventeenth century two 1d. rates raised £4 3s. 8d. but by the end of the century two identical rates raised £14 10s. This confirms the fact of an increasing population, also indicated by the Hearth Tax returns.

One major structural change to Lymington's parish church came with the addition of the great, stone south tower in 1670, probably erected on the site of the south transept. For this fine limestone structure Mr Mitchell, the builder, was paid £389 5s. 4d., and £1 10s. when he laid the first stone. This tower, constructed in the traditional late gothic style, continues to dominate Lymington and the date 1670 can still be seen carved on a buttress near the south door. Among the donations received towards this enterprise were gifts from several Lymington burgesses, including John and William Burrard, Bartholomew Bulkeley and, perhaps surprisingly in view of the political predilections of his family, £10 from Philip Dore.

One donation particularly worth noting is £8 from Sir Thomas Badd. Badd had his home at Cam House in Fareham but for some reason held the lease of Lymington parsonage in 1647. As a Royalist he was examined by the Committee for Compounding with the view to his forfeiting his estate for supporting the Crown. At that time the inhabitants of Lymington sought permission for the lease, which had five years to run, to be given to their own minister. Badd agreed to settle £30 per annum on the minister and as a consequence the Committee reduced Badd's forfeit of £530 by £60. There was some procrastination, but by 1650 the 'Lymington Rectory' (as it was then designated) was settled for 80 years, or three lives, on Lymington.[56]

Amongst other expenditure incurred by the churchwardens was the purchase of fire fighting equipment to be kept in the church. In 1697 £4 was spent on two dozen leather buckets and £4 16s. on fire hooks with chains. These latter were designed to pull blazing thatch from house roofs. Probably most fires started in the thatch or, most certainly, were spread by sparks catching in the roofs of adjoining thatched properties. A hand-pump engine was bought for Lymington in about 1720.[57]

A portion of the church rates was also expended on the maintenance of the parish roads and two parishioners were elected annually to fill the post of surveyors of the highways.[58] The first two of which there is a record are Henry Wale and John Blake, who were elected in 1685; from thence onwards there is an annual record through to 1708. These officers were empowered to provide labour and materials for the general care of the roads, drains and smaller bridges within the parish. Detailed accounts were maintained which describe the work carried out. This system remained in place until 1835, though from 1708 the post was separated from the church administration and transferred to the Poor Law.

From time to time briefs (notices of fire, flood and other disasters) were read out after the church service and the money contributed was then sent to relieve the victims, or to help rebuild or maintain a parish church in some other part of the kingdom. In Lymington sums ranging from under 5s. to over £2 were collected on each brief in the year 1682-83. Briefs were not a satisfactory solution to raising aid and they are adversely commented on by Pepys and by Lady Mary Coke who in 1768, when living in Notting Hill, stated, 'We had a br[ief] for the rebuilding a Church in your County [Yorkshire]; to which I own I did not contribute a single shilling. To tell you the truth, I think you ought to keep Your Churches in such good repair as to make it unnecessary to send to Us in the South to furnish money for the rebuilding'.[59]

Anabaptism, later to be known as Baptism, probably had its roots in Lymington in Civil War times, for in 1646 Thomas Collier 'by incessant labours and extended usefulness is represented by his adversaries as having done much hurt in Lymington'. He is further described as the person who first sowed the seeds of 'Anabaptism, Anti-Sabbatarianism and some Arminianism in these parts'.[60] As was usual with dissenters, because of the legal disabilities they suffered, they first worshipped in private houses and at Lymington the

first such meeting place was believed to have been in a property in Captain's Row. By 1688 their first proper chapel had been founded in New Lane (now New Street) and its first pastor, the Rev. John Rumsey, was appointed in 1693. With the passing of the Toleration and Licensing Acts in 1689 and 1695 the Lymington Baptists, with their new freedom, became active proselytizers and soon carried the tenets of their beliefs into the surrounding countryside.

The Presbyterian, later and interchangeably called Independent, was another important sect in the seventeenth century religious life of Lymington. In 1672 Robert Tutchin took out a licence to 'teach' as a Presbyterian and licensed his home for that purpose. As was often the case with dissenting ministers, he had been ejected as Anglican curate of Brockenhurst for his non-conformist views and is recorded as preaching in Fordingbridge in 1669. Early days for the Presbyterians were a struggle, and a survey made by the Common Fund in 1690 reported that Lymington (together with other nearby towns) 'have noe Settled Ministers for the present. Att Limington the maintenance is small . . . There might be a greater meeting if there were a Settled Minister and Competent Maintenance'.

Presumably some slight easing of the situation encouraged an outstanding individual to become for just a few years, 1692-8, effective minister of the Independent congregation. John Farrell was born in 1619 and became vicar of Selborne but, like Tutchin, was ejected for his non-conformity. His commitment to his faith led to imprisonment but even after his release he continued to preach, his enemies then declaring they would not send him to 'Prison again because he liv'd there better than at home'. His friends took a more affectionate view:

'At last he remov'd to Limington in Hampshire, where he did not continue idle, but preached frequently as Opportunity offered and Providence favour'd him; Till by a gentle Decay (for he would still say he did not find himself either sick or in pain) the Candle of Life burning down to the socket, he expir'd, not with a Stink, but a sweet Savour . . . in the 80th year of his Age. He was of an active disposition, and being a noted Florist and Herbalist, made his Garden his Domestick Diversion.'

THREE

The Age of Elegance

POLITICAL LIFE

The seventeenth century was marked by a succession of national upheavals and conflicts. It was also a century of immense change, particularly in the development of religious non-conformity and in political awareness, the two going hand-in-hand. These events had a direct impact on Lymington although the surviving records inadequately tell the full story.

One legacy was a growing desire for involvement in civic and political affairs. There were undoubtedly a number of Lymingtonians who believed they should have a greater say in the running of their town and, more widely, in the nation's affairs. Evidence to support this is borne out by the two parliamentary elections of 1690 and 1695[1] in which the commonalty, that is the substantial citizens of the borough, elected their own representatives in direct opposition to those elected by the burgesses.

In 1690 Thomas Dore and John Burrard were returned by the mayor whilst the townsfolk elected Thomas Jervoise and Oliver Cromwell (grandson of Oliver Cromwell, the Protector). In 1695 the mayor returned the same candidates as before whilst the commonalty of the town elected John Pitt and William Clarke. This curious situation was referred to the House of Commons Committee of Privileges for resolution. Its findings were that the franchise was legally vested in the burgesses alone and that the commonalty had no right to vote.

This decision placed Lymington in the same category as many other boroughs who had small privileged electorates, and which in due course became known as pocket or rotten boroughs. Initially this arrangement favoured the Court or Tory party, indicating that the ordinance of 1674 restricting burgess membership to residents in the

This view from the bottom of the High Street shows the street much as it must have looked in the eighteenth century. Most of the foreground buildings on both right and left are of that time. Note the deep gutters on each side. The one thing missing from this view is the Town Hall, which then stood in the centre of the street.

town, who tended to be Whiggish in character, was abandoned as being politically restrictive. But this was to change once the Burrard family began to flex its political muscle: they, like so many of the landed classes at that time, were Whig supporters.

Although obliged to accept the judgement of the Committee of Privileges there is little doubt that a new sense of political awareness was abroad in Lymington. Though seemingly dormant throughout much of the eighteenth century (there were no contested elections from 1713 to 1832), it was finally to surface with renewed vigour and enthusiasm at the time of the debates leading to the Reform Act of 1832 and the election that followed.

The parliamentary election of January 1700 saw the return of two Whig candidates, Thomas Dore and Paul Burrard, who won comfortably receiving 33 and 32 votes respectively. The Tory party candidates, James Worsley and Thomas Fullerton received 11 and 10 votes. One elector, rejoicing in the improbable name of Wilderness Watson, hedged his bets by casting one each of his two votes for candidates from both parties.[2]

As the franchise in parliamentary elections was now firmly in the hands of the mayor and burgesses it meant that Lymington was one of the boroughs favoured by any prospective candidate eager to become an MP and wealthy enough to 'buy' votes

Grove House once one of Lymington's fine town mansions. Built by George Burrard between 1710 and 1720 but subsequently much enlarged and redesigned. It had many owners and occupiers, the last being the novelist, Dennis Wheatley. It was then bought by developers and demolished in 1970.

of a restrictive electorate (*i.e.* a small number of voters who were relatively cheap and manageable). This was effectively bribery, and was borne out by the much later example of Robert Colt, who in the six years from 1784 spent over £1,500 for the privilege of serving as one of Lymington's MPs.[3]

Although not directly connected with a particular election there can be little doubt that the 19s. spent by the 2nd Duke of Bolton in 1708 on a 'fat buck' plus a present of 5 guineas for the corporation was a 'sweetener' for future support. The Hampshire Powletts were influential in national politics at the highest level, and the dukedom of Bolton had been conferred on Charles Powlett by William III in 1689. The 2nd Duke was made Warden of the New Forest in 1702 and shortly afterwards was appointed Lord Lieutenant for both Hampshire and Dorset.[4]

This Whig family had a strong interest in Lymington and forged a political alliance with the Burrards in an attempt to ensure that the parliamentary representation was always in their pockets. Lord William Powlett had been a burgess, voting in 1700 for Dore and Burrard, and was himself elected MP for Lymington in 1715, together with Sir Joseph Jekyll, a protégé of the Powletts. This provides a good example of how Lymington was used for political convenience as he had sat first for Eye in Suffolk from 1697-1713, then for Lymington 1715-22, and for the last sixteen years of his life for Reigate, always in the Whig interest.

Powletts and Burrards often sat together for Lymington, as in 1722 when Lord Harry Powlett sat with Paul Burrard, Lord Nassau Powlett with Harry Burrard in 1741 and Charles Powlett with Harry Burrard in 1747.

The Burrards and their supporters were prepared to add burgesses in their interest whenever necessary and in 1722 Paul Burrard could remark, 'all the old burgesses now alive (except one) from the year 1686 to 1701 were made by us'.

The politically influential branch of the Burrard family lived at Walhampton. In 1668 Elizabeth Burrard, widow of Thomas, had bought Walhampton House and estate from Thomas Gookey for £1,060[5] and the family's direct involvement with the town continued into the mid-nineteenth century. A cousin called John Burrard[6], whose brother, George, had built Grove House in Church Lane, sought to exercise his own control on the town. He was made burgess in 1726 and was High Sheriff of Hampshire in 1738, but he never succeeded in breaking the hold of the Walhampton Burrards.[7]

Inevitably, disillusion developed on the part of the Burrards, who feared they were being used politically by the more influential Powletts without proper regard for their own interests.

In 1745 a further attempt by the 3rd Duke of Bolton to obtain sole control of the borough was defeated by an alliance between the sitting Members, his nephew Colonel Charles Powlett and Harry Burrard, who secured a majority on the corporation by calling a surprise meeting and creating new freemen.[8]

The succession of offices held by Harry Burrard (1707-91), eldest son of Paul, clearly indicates how the family extended its political influence and how, in return for supporting the government, it could

Serampore Place on the west side of Church Lane, a row of late eighteenth century cottages, named after the Indian town in West Bengal Province.

expect to be rewarded. Harry was created baronet in 1769, but was already in receipt of a government pension of £500 a year as a reward for offices he held, including that of Page of Honour to Princess Amelia, gentleman usher to the Prince of Wales (1728-36), Collector of Customs for London (1731-91), Bow-bearer of the New Forest (1754-91) and Governor of Calshot Castle (1761-87). He was MP for Lymington from 1741 to 1778[9] and mayor on ten occasions between 1734 and 1781.

Other influential landowning families of the eighteenth century included the Buttons (owners of Buckland Manor), the Knaptons and the Harsnetts; all were involved in the political intrigues of their day. Often the families' alliances were reinforced by marriage, as when Mary Burrard married Robert Knapton, himself a nephew of Elizabeth Button.[10]

Fascinating though it is, the detailed political history of Lymington's parliamentary significance is not our direct concern in tracing the overall development of the borough. Lymington's MPs were often no more than placemen serving their political masters who used the town as a manageable base from which to secure their interests. Figures such as George Rose and Edward Gibbon, famed as the author of *The Decline and Fall of the Roman Empire*, represented Lymington on behalf of their political patrons.[11]

THE MANOR COURT IN THE BOROUGH OF LYMINGTON

The manorial court continued to play its administrative and regulatory role throughout the seventeenth and eighteenth centuries. Mundane matters were dealt with, such as ensuring that chimneys were in good repair and traders were using correct weights. The evidence, however, suggests that the court's influence was beginning to decline, here as elsewhere. No fewer than 54 absented themselves from the 1650 court, amongst them members of the most influential residents, including William and John Dore, Christopher Knapton, Thomas Burrard, Phineas Wright and Bartholomew Bulkeley. As attendance at the manor court was a legal requirement; each was fined 3d. for his failure to appear. Even more dilatory was the non-appearance at that court of three of its elected officials, namely, the two constables and the aletaster.

The close interconnection of manor and borough is clearly revealed in entries in 1653 when William Burrard was fined 45s. for 'not taking upon him the office of a Mayor as he was enjoyned att the last lawday' and a further 41s. for failing to take the mayoral oath.

The town's traditional forms of punishment were still in regular use. In 1697 the pillory and the stocks were repaired and a few years later the pound in New Lane mended; while in the early 1720s orders were issued for repairs to the ducking stool and the pillory post.

It is from these records that we get an occasional insight into the commercial life of the town; some of which is of considerable interest. In the early 1720s those appointed to measure the sea coal arriving in Lymington (known as coal meters) were ordered to shovel the coal into the bushel measures and 'not pour it in with baskets', failure to abide by this instruction would lead to a fine of £1. It is evident that coal spilled by tipping became, no doubt, a perquisite for the men doing the measuring!

In 1726 butchers were forbidden to throw the guts of the slaughtered beasts into the street on pain of a 3s. 4d. fine and Thomas Coombes, who was tenant of the markets and fairs, was ordered to cleanse the streets.[12]

THE WORKHOUSE & THE POOR LAW[13]

In 1722-3 an act of parliament, called Gilbert's Act[14], enabled parishes to build workhouses if they thought it necessary. Lymington, like many other provincial towns, did not immediately adopt the provisions of this act and waited until 1738 to erect its first workhouse. The promoters, included John Burrard, John Northover and five others who raised £248 10s. to meet the cost of the building. This was situated just outside the northern boundary of the borough in what is now called East Hill. Most of the records for the first forty years (1738-75) are missing so the full history of its early days cannot be recorded.

Workhouses were intended to provide decent but basic accommodation for those too poor to maintain themselves, such as the infirm, the crippled, the insane and those who had fallen into extreme poverty. Those capable of employment were given work. A master was appointed to oversee the general management of the house and the funding was supplied from the Poor Rate. The rate was levied on properties throughout the parish of Lymington and was collected by elected officials called overseers of the poor; they were also responsible for disbursing moneys to the needy and meeting the administrative expenses of operating the Poor Law. Lymington's first workhouse master was Richard Budden, appointed in May 1739 at an annual salary of £10. As the workhouse had the responsibility of housing the sick and infirm medical care was provided by local doctors appointed by the overseers. The workhouse also had its own resident dispenser in the person of Henry Hackman, who was 'to provide the necessary medicines and proper assistance in surgery' for the same annual salary as the master.[15]

It seems likely that Henry Hackman was the Dr Hackman mentioned as early as 1708 where there is a reference to a James Pitt being sent from Beaulieu to Lymington to be cared for by 'Doctor Hackman, att the Charge of the said Parish . . .'[16] A second mention followed in 1713 when the churchwardens and overseers of Beaulieu decided to 'imploy Doctor Hackman to cure John Drover's Legg'.[17]

An insight into the furnishings of the workhouse is provided by an inventory drawn up in 1741 which lists such details as a long table, undoubtedly for communal eating, which was supplied with two table cloths and four benches. There were also chairs, stools, bedsteads and bedding and a variety of domestic and gardening implements.[18]

The need to isolate those with infectious diseases

Lymington's Georgian legacy.
Top left A good example of a pair of late Georgian town houses in Quay Street.
Left Wistaria House, probably a late seventeenth or early eighteenth century house in St Thomas Street, that was re-fronted in yellow mathematical tiles in the late eighteenth century.
Above The pedimented surround with semi-circular fanlight is a good example of a classical Georgian door case at Southend House, Church Lane.

dates back to the middle ages when accommodation outside towns was provided for lepers.[19] In the eighteenth century a number of diseases were prevalent, amongst them smallpox. In 1741 Lymington's overseers and churchwardens sought to purchase from William Samber 'a house or cottage (with the appurtinces in this parish) called "The Doggs Kennell".

This, from its description and the relatively small cost of £15, can have been little more than a cottage but orders were given for it to be made 'fit, proper and Convenient for the Reception and Entertainment of such Person or Persons as shall happen to be visited with the smallpox or other infectious deseases . . . '.[20] No evidence survives of its location, but it has been plausibly suggested that it lay at the northern end of Gosport Street, just outside the borough.[21] It became known by the generic term adopted for such places, 'Pest House'. Certainly it provided lodging for those with smallpox as in 1775, during an epidemic, we find Elizabeth Badcock being paid 5s. for 'attending at the Pest House'. It remained in use for a long time as 31 years later, straw for thatching cost £1 7s. 6d. and, after a lapse of only five years, we again find it being repaired at a cost of 6s. 3d.[22]

The scourge of recurrent smallpox outbreaks led to the adoption of inoculation for the poorer parishioners, paid for from the rates, but prior to inoculation the parish burial registers reveal the devastating impact of the disease. In the 15 months, May 1768 to August 1769, 59 persons are recorded as dying from smallpox. A further outbreak in 1778-9 claimed at least 26 victims, ranging from infants and young children to the elderly; but interestingly enough none in the age range 20 to 55.

The parish register for 1791 has a note stating that as a consequence of an outbreak of smallpox 'the Parish came to a Resolution of having a general inoculation'. The doctors appointed to carry out this operation were Mr Beckley, Mr Nike and Mr Dollan of Bramshaw. It is recorded that of the 300 inoculated by Mr Beckley two died as a consequence, of the 300 treated by Mr Nike eighteen died and of the fortunate 500 inoculated by Mr Dollan none died. In that year seven died of smallpox 'in the natural way' and 20 as a result of inoculation. What cannot be calculated from a total of 1,100 inoculated is how many were saved from contracting the disease but, based on previous evidence of mortality, it is likely to have been the vast majority. Inoculation against smallpox, first introduced into this country by Lady Mary Wortley Montagu in about 1720, was further refined by Benjamin Jesty and Edward Jenner, quite independently of each other, by using cowpox serum. This treatment became the first major application of preventative medicine and by the 1780s every parish in the kingdom was paying to have its poor residents treated.[23]

Entries from the Lymington Poor Rate books provide an insight into the prevalence of the disease:

> To Mrs Woolfrey for her child in the smallpox   5s.
> Expenses going round to the Inoculators   1s.
> To Ann Bishop her children in the smallpox   £1 1s.
> To Dolly Buckett for attending Mrs Miles in the smallpox three weeks at 7s.

> per week   £1 1s.
> To different people for relief in the Smallpox   £2 2s. 3d.

An entry for 31 May 1756 throws light not only on smallpox but also on parochial responsibility when the churchwardens and overseers of Lymington ordered that they should be 'indemnified of and from all costs and charges that shall or may happen on account of Edward Bradeing of West Cows, bringing to this place Jane Kent with the smallpox then fresh out upon her'.[24]

Other diseases noted as killers in the parish registers are 'putrid fever', 'consumption', and 'measles' – the latter caused an especially severe outbreak in 1790.

Much help given to the poor in the eighteenth century was termed outdoor relief, a reference to the aid given those outside the workhouse. In 1774 there are 31 persons in receipt of outdoor relief: some of this was disbursed as food, especially bread, clothing or shoes and some directly as cash. During the exceptionally severe winter of January 1740 the mayor and burgesses agreed to give £10 as a supplement to the poor rates for the purchase of bread and meat for the poor.[25] Medical help at times of sickness and in cases of midwifery was paid for from the Poor Rate. A local barber, Thomas Thirle, provided a bleeding service, as is revealed in 1775 when he is paid 6d. 'for bleeding Elizabeth Haines', and also dentistry as in 1783 when he received 6d 'for drawing a tooth for Mary Sheppard'.[26] The records show a considerable expenditure on health care, which rose considerably during epidemics.

REMOVAL OF PAUPERS

The business of the removal of paupers to their parish of origin occupied much effort, time and expense on the part of the Lymington overseers of the poor, as it did in all other parishes. From 1662 there had been a legal requirement for all paupers needing assistance to receive it only from their parish of birth or of 'legal settlement'. Those who required help in Lymington but who belonged to some other parish had to be examined under oath so that their parish of origin could be determined and, once this was confirmed, they were then returned to it. The examinations were carried out by the local magistrates, who issued the orders for the removal of the paupers to their own parish.

The earliest removal order to survive for Lymington, dated 25 March 1728, involves the case of William Young, labourer, and his wife Ann who were being returned to Ringwood. Another example from 1767 involved a whole family, namely Thomas Light, Mary his wife, and their three children, all of whom were under seven, and who were sent from Lymington to Portsmouth.

Conversely, of course, the system also meant that Lymington residents who sought relief in parishes elsewhere would be examined and returned. A case in point relates to George Franks, his wife Hannah and their infant son, William, who, out of necessity, sought relief in Beaulieu and, after examination, were returned to Lymington under a removal order dated 4 March 1780. On occasion the distances involved were considerable, as when two overseers from Melbury Osmund in west Dorset travelled to the Isle of Wight in September 1765 to collect their parishioner, Richard Peach. Their journey took them through Lymington where they spent 5s. 10d. in the town and a further 2s. for their passage to Yarmouth.[27] Similarly James McIlwain and William Noake of Lymington had to convey the Hewings family to 'Colliton Rawleigh' (Colaton Raleigh) in Devon, part of the journey being by boat from Weymouth, at a total cost of £11 2s. 9d.[28] Colaton Raleigh parish authorized Lymington to give Robert Hewings £5 for the journey, which they reimbursed.[29] These examples are selected from dozens of surviving removal orders,[30] clearly reflecting the complexity and the expense of the system.

There is no doubt that initially the Poor Law Settlement Acts tended to immobilise the working population. This was a problem recognised at an early stage and, in order to encourage men and their families to seek work in more favourable places, orders of indemnity were issued by their parishes of origin. An early example of this comes from Somerset, where on 26 April 1708 Thomas Symes and his wife Elizabeth were given a certificate acknowledging they belonged to and were the responsibility of Evercreech, but 'for theire better Livelyhood and maintenance is willing and desirous to Inhabite and dwell in Your Said parrish of Lymington'.[31] Arriving in Lymington they deposited this certificate with the overseers of the poor. This meant that should the Symes family need relief at any time, the town's overseers would be fully reimbursed by Evercreech. There are tantalising baptism records of the children of a Thomas Symes (or Simms) from 1709 to 1720 and the burial record of Elizabeth Simms on 19 November 1733 and of Thomas Sims on 24 November 1738. It seems very probable these records do refer to the Symes from Evercreech and indicate that they lived successfully in Lymington for thirty years.[32]

Occasionally a parish would disagree about a particular pauper legally belonging to it, leading to a dispute. This happened in the case of Catherine Harvey, a single woman residing in Lymington, who was adjudged, after examination, to belong to Blandford Forum. She was sent from Lymington to Blandford but then returned pending a court case to determine the matter. At the foot of the order was written, 'the above Order was Appeall[ed] to By the Parish officers of Blandford at Winchester the 12 day of Jany 1813 when the Order was confirmed By the Court'.[33] In other words Lymington's decision was confirmed and Catherine Harvey had to return to Blandford to be cared for by that parish.

There were occasions when, due to illness or injury, the pauper could not be moved and had to be looked after by the parish in which they were then living. We have an example of this from Leigh in Dorset when in 1767 the vestry there decided not to remove 'Peter Masters of Lemington who hast unfortuneingly brokin his they [thigh] and we order the Overseers to take care of him till he can posebly be removed'.[34] Even over relatively short distances the removal could be delayed, as happened to Thomas Renyard of Hordle who could not be removed from Lymington 'by reason of Bodily Infirmity'. In fact he remained in Lymington from 18 August 1810 to 25 May 1811 and Hordle parish was obliged to reimburse the £13 6s. it had cost the town to care for him.

BASTARDY

Bastardy was another problem confronting the overseers of the poor and churchwardens. There was always a small number of unmarried women who became pregnant and were therefore likely to become chargeable to the parish during their lying-in and the delivery of the child. The problem of illegitimacy became worse in the late eighteenth and early nineteenth centuries. Wherever possible the overseers would try to discover the identity of the father by examining the pregnant woman under oath. The man would then be persuaded to marry the woman if he was free to do so and, if not, then obliged to contribute to the child's maintenance.

In February 1770 Sarah White was examined by Lymington magistrate, William Hawkins, regarding the putative father of her child. Under oath she declared that:

> John Dunn, late of the Parish of Northwood in the Isle of Wight in the County of South'ton, Servantman, had Several Times Carnal Knowledge of her Body in the months of July, August and September last, and did beget the said Child, or Children – and that John Dunn and no other Person is the true Father thereof.
> the mark X of Sarah White.

The impact of maritime communication and contact on this aspect of social and moral life is made clear when Thomas Wills, a Cornish sailor, was declared (in a voluntary examination taken before Charles St Barbe, the Lymington Mayor, on 19 September 1809) to be the father of 'a Female Bastard Child' born of Mary [Woodford] of Lymington in the house of Sarah Woodford.[35]

An insight into the operation of both the bastardy and removal legislation is provided by the case of Fanny Lacey, whose parish was Sturminster Marshall. Fanny became pregnant in Lymington and in August 1831 William Noakes, the Lymington Guardian of the Poor, sent the following letter to the overseers of the Dorset village:

> Sir,
> We shall send you a bargain but not of the most profitable sort. It is Fanny Lacey who is confined in childbed at present. The order of removal is suspended until she can bear the journey.
> Wm Noakes,   Guardian.[36]

APPRENTICESHIPS

Parish apprenticeships were another mechanism for trying to alleviate poverty. Young boys and girls were indentured as apprentices by the parish officers and in Lymington the taking of apprentices was deemed a duty of the local employers and gentry. This can be seen when the Countess of Delaware was fined £10 to be excused taking an apprentice.[37] Apprenticeships had the immediate effect of removing the child from the list of paupers requiring relief whilst simultaneously providing a training. The number of children so indentured in Lymington between 1700 and 1773 was 141, about two in each year[38] (probably there were more as the complete records do not survive). In March 1807, 12-year old Elizabeth Fugate was apprenticed to John Ryall, surgeon, whilst a year later Sarah Haskell started her apprenticeship at the age of 13 with Joseph Skeats the butcher. Even as early as the tender age of 10 a child could be apprenticed, as with William Youngs, who went as a servant to Major-General Popham at Heathy Dilton in the New Forest.

The length of apprenticeships varied but were usually until the age of 21 or, in the case of females, until married if under twenty-one. Children were mainly, but not exclusively, apprenticed in their own parishes. Those who went to another parish and served out their apprenticeship became legal residents of the parish of adoption.

Some boys were particularly suited to a life at sea, as in 1780 when Lymington ordered that if James Alexander did not contribute towards the maintenance of his son, also James, 'the parish will endeavour to get him on board a Man-of-War'. In fact James must have gone into the Newfoundland trade for his marriage in 1836 is recorded at St John's, Newfoundland where he is described as 'of Lymington'.[39] Moses Kittier in 1787, on leaving the Lymington workhouse, was sent to Poole to enter into the Newfoundland trade.

By the late 1780s the workhouse was too small to meet its needs. In 1788 it was proposed that a larger replacement workhouse be built with provision for and help from the surrounding parishes of Boldre, Brockenhurst and Beaulieu.[40] When this issue was put to the vote Lymington unanimously rejected the idea, but went ahead with a proposal to enlarge the existing workhouse. This work was completed in 1789 and on 28 May William Tarver was appointed master at an annual salary of £25 and accommodation was to be provided in the building for his wife and two youngest children.[41]

MILITIA

From time to time parishes had been called upon to supply men to serve in the militia, a home-based force to protect our shores against enemy incursions. During the wars with Revolutionary and later Napoleonic France, when the threat became significant, men were enlisted for three years. This requirement led to a rather curious arrangement whereby each parish had a given allocation of men who were then selected by lot. In most cases those with the money and who did not wish to serve were permitted to pay £10 for a substitute to serve in their place. It was not a requirement that the substitute should be of the same parish, for example James Macilwain's substitute was James Smart of Christchurch and Joseph Sharp of Alverstoke stood in for William Wickenden of Lymington. The substitutes were mainly labourers and unskilled workers. As they were invariably the breadwinners their families had to be properly maintained during their absence on militia duty. The cost initially fell on the poor rates but the overseers could apply for reimbursement from the government. Because of the paperwork involved a number of records survive. In 1798 William Newsam served as a substitute for James Rawlins which meant that Newsam's wife, Susannah, and their daughter Mary had to be maintained by the parish.

From the poor rate funds the parish was required to subscribe to the county rate, used mainly for the maintenance of bridges, prisons, asylums and the expenses of legal administration. For example, Lymington's assessment for 1805 was £8 15s. 6d. which had to be taken to Winchester by the constable who was enjoined, 'NB You will bring the Money ready counted, not to require Change'.[42]

The Poor Law from its inception in 1601 through to the Amendment Act of 1834 was a key factor in the development of local government. The poor rate was raised by levying a sum on each property owner or occupier based on the assessed annual rental value for that property. The rate was agreed by the elected overseers of the poor and churchwardens. The rates varied but typically could range from 3d. to 1s. in £1, but the money could be levied on a number of occasions throughout the year, as needs required. In the early eighteenth century there were about 96 'housekeepers who paid church and poor' rates.[43] In the year Easter 1774 to Easter 1775 (the first year for which accounts survive) ten rates of 3d. each were collected bringing in a total income of £490 16s. 9d. To this must be added the surplus of £13 16s. 10d. from the previous year and other sundry credits amounting to £14 14s. 7d. This gave the parish officers a total of £519 8s. 2d. During that year the overseers disbursed £503 0s. 10¼d. in relieving the poor and so remained in credit. From about 1795 economic conditions worsened so the call on the rate became more demanding and the amounts collected soared, as the following table demonstrates:

Year	Expenditure	Balance
1800-01	£1,571	(£13)
1801-02	£1,899	£22
1802-03	£1,267	£39
1803-04	£1,177	£16
1804-05	£1,311	(£13)
1805-06	£1,615	£34
1806-07	£1,568	£16

(Figures in brackets are annual deficits).

In 1817 the rate was collected on seven occasions, each time netting around £336 and bringing the annual total to £2,353 6s. 9d.

Lymington's high expenditure on poor relief was matched both in the county of Hampshire and nationally.

Such a high level of expenditure was not sustainable and there were increasing protests demanding that something must be done to relieve the burden. We shall see later how this was accomplished.

Charity, as distinct from the official poor relief, was still a small but significant element in providing support for the disadvantaged.

George Burrard in 1721 made a bequest of £100 for the purchase of land on which was to be erected houses for 'lodging, maintaining and employing the poor of Lymington'. As the bequest was too small the overseers of the poor and the churchwardens were empowered to raise an additional rate 'not exceeding 4s.' to make up the deficiency. The sum then raised enabled four small houses to be built and administered as part of the workhouse, regrettably their location was not recorded.[44]

In 1790 the Rev. William Gilpin, vicar of Boldre, gave an account of what must be one of the earliest women's friendly societies.[45] It was designed to 'be of great benefit to distressed females' of Lymington, 'which being a little sea-port, and frequented by the seamen of small coasting vessels, and boatmen, their wives are often put to inconveniences by the misfortunes . . . by the absence of their husbands'. Mrs Pierce, the promoter of the scheme, first ascertained that there would be sufficient support to enable the society to function and found 'Between thirty and forty inhabitants of Lymington, and its neighbourhood, were ready to subscribe each 14s. a year, or 3d. a week'. The charity endorsed the friendly society requirement of a contribution from members; in this case 6d. on joining and 1½d. every week. Membership was available to those who were aged between 15 and 50 years and of each 'It was required that she should be a parishioner, of good character, and in good health at the time of her entrance'. Initially the prime aim was to provide for women during their lying-in, but this was extended to care for 'the sick of every denomination'. The conditions set down are of some interest:

> Before she receives relief, her name must have been a year on the books; she is then entitled to 3s, a week during any illness with which she may be visited; but she receives it only during the term of thirteen weeks; if she is not then recovered, she receives 1s. a week only, while it is thought necessary.

Additional financial support was raised by an annual charity sermon, preached on the second Sunday in August, which Gilpin suggests raised between £10 and £16.

> All poor members who are able to go to church, walk in procession to the town-hall, with their patronesses at their head, who treat them with cake and wine. This is a pleasant day for them, and makes some return to the healthy, for not having had occasion to draw upon the fund for sickness.

Apparently most of the 65 members at some time received assistance and Gilpin says 'of these thirty-five were women in child-bed', two others with 'lame hands received 1s. a week' and a third who was 'in deep decline' had long-term aid.

The hard times of the late eighteenth century are reflected in Gilpin's concluding sentence.

> In the late scarcity of bread-corn, each poor member received a half-gallon loaf every Wednesday, for six weeks; and during the last two winters, each had three bushels of coals.[46]

As well as scarcity, costs were also rising, causing the magistrates and 'principal Inhabitants of the Borough and Town of *Lymington*' to meet in the Angel Inn on 28 October 1795 to enquire into the 'Practice of the BUTCHERS in selling out their Meat, and the Cause of the present high Price thereof'. The meeting resolved unanimously,

> That the Butchers of this Town demand a higher Price that those of Ringwood, Christchurch, Poole, or any of the Neighbouring Towns; and that the manner of obliging their Customers to take a considerable Quantity of what is called *Rough Meat*, to be weighed in with the *Prime*, is peculiar only to the Butchers of Lymington.[47]

The outcome of this episode does not appear in the records but judging from the authority of the magistrates it must be assumed that the Lymington butchers were obliged to conform. This action clearly demonstrates how, even in an age of *laissez-faire* economics, the authority of local government could be wielded on behalf of what was seen to be the general good.

THE BRIDGE & TRANSPORT

Access to the eastern side of Lymington River had been by ferry from the Town Quay to Walhampton, the alternatives to this being a journey of about a mile-and-a-half upstream to cross by a ford known as the Shallows or, if that was not passable, a little further on to cross by Boldre Bridge.

A watercolour of the bridge and dam looking upstream. The trees on the left are growing around The Common.

The building of a dam across the river in 1731 on the site of the present bridge produced not only ultimate benefits but also immediate problems. This dam, which was in fact a causeway, measuring 20 feet high, 30 feet broad and 500 feet long was built on the instructions of Captain William Cross of Boldre. It was well constructed with pilings and interlocking boards and, although not specifically recorded, it must have included a bridge beneath which sluices were fitted to allow the flow of the river. However, the net result was that the natural scouring effect of the free flowing river was interrupted by the dam, leading to the build-up of mud immediately downstream. As it was generally believed Cross had no legal authority for building it in the first place the Lymington burgesses protested that it would injure the navigation of the river and, additionally, that it had intruded on Lymington's common to the detriment of its users (see map). So in January 1732 the Corporation started an action against Cross. This threat of legal proceedings made Cross dig his heels in still further:

'It being then apprehended that the dam would in time destroy the navigation of the river, a design was formed by some of the Town to cut down the piles and timber work, and put a stop to the building thereof, which Mr Cross prevented by threatening to shoot the first man he met, and for that purpose armed himself.'

The death of Captain Cross in October 1732 did not end the problem, for his widow Rachel[48] proved just as obstinate. In 1737 she leased the dam to William Lyne, one of her Boldre tenants, and he erected an access gate in Croydon Lane, and proceeded to charge a toll to those passing through it to cross the dam.

Incensed by this disregard for its authority, the Corporation determined to pursue the legal action and 17 subscribers raised £200 to fight the case. Viscount Lymington made a handsome donation of 50 guineas in support of this cause. The case was presented at Winchester Assizes in July 1738 but adjourned for eight months to allow the jurors to inspect the site. Charles Colborne, counsel for Lymington Corporation and also a burgess, claimed that between two and four feet of mud had settled on the river bottom to the detriment of the town's maritime trade. Interestingly enough, four Lymington men, Daniel Reeks, John Newman, both aged 75, Jeremiah Wilkins (60) and William Blake (56) stated that the river had been navigable from 'Jack in the Basket, three miles below the town, to Boldre Bridge two miles above until obstructed by the dam'.[49]

It was stated that there had been a lucrative trade in timber for the Royal Navy, destined for the Portsmouth shipyards, which was loaded near the place where the dam was built. Other vessels of 50 or 60 tons burden used to carry bricks from the Walhampton brickyard and lighters travelled as far as the Shallows. It was further stated that vessels of,

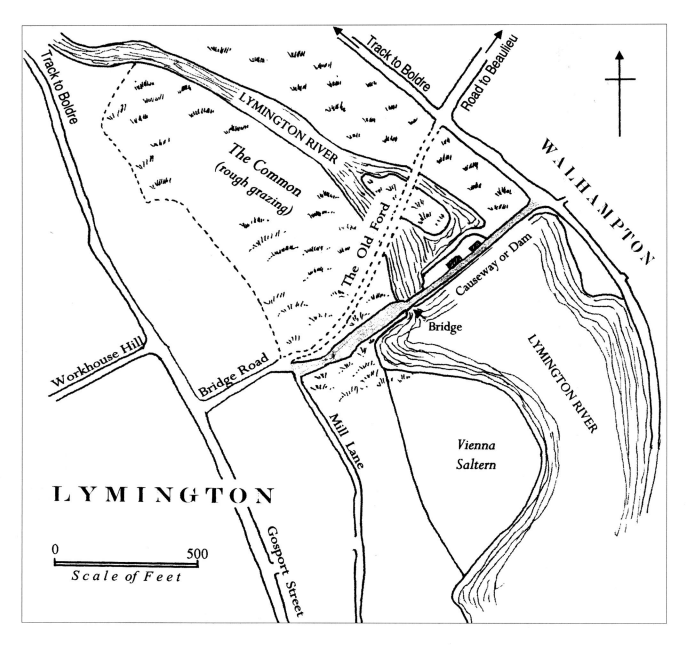

A sketch map showing the position of the dam or causeway (shaded) that was constructed across the river by Captain Cross (see main text).
It is a composite plan based on the lost map of 1680, the map of Mr Richman's estate appearing in the Morant Estate Book, 1793 and later maps.
Prior to the construction of the causeway the only way to cross at that point was by the old ford, and this could only be done when the river was low and the tide out.

'considerable burthen sailed from the town to near two miles above the dam'.[50]

The defendants, for their part, presented four clauses stating: (i) that there had anciently been a dam across the river; (ii) that it had belonged to Dr Cademan, Rachel Cross's grandfather; (iii) that the cause of the build up of silt was due to Mr Bevis's saltworks and (iv) that the river had not been navigable above the dam before its erection.

In due course the judge directed the jury to find

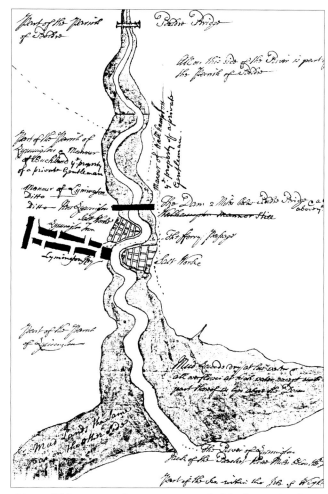

the dam no nuisance, and this they obediently did. One can only assume that the judge, if he was being genuinely impartial, failed to understand the evidence, wrongly assuming that the construction of a dam above the navigable river would not affect conditions below it. The townsfolk and Corporation were convinced that the jury had made up their minds in advance of delivering their decision and 'on the whole they behaved with great dishonour . . . all unprejudiced and disinterested persons declared they never heard a verdict given more fully against the evidence'.[51]

The dam, eventually to become known as the Tollbridge, did offer a more convenient route to the eastern side of the river and improved links with Walhampton and the road to Beaulieu. The earliest surviving entry from 1774 confirmed its use when 4s. was paid for turnpike costs and toll for the carriage of tiles to Lymington.[52]

Lymington was linked to the turnpike system under the provisions contained in a private parliamentary act passed in 1765.[53] This act enabled the creation of a road running northward from the town through the New Forest to Rumbridge in the parish of Eling,[54] where it would join the Southampton to Salisbury turnpike. The only surviving tollhouse on this road is at Buckland, immediately to the north of and almost adjoining the Tollhouse Inn. For a short period in the late twentieth century it became the museum of the Buckland Trust[55] but is now used as a storehouse. In the manor court (about 1785) the commissioners of the turnpike were ordered 'to pay 1s. a year to the tenants of the said manor for building a House on the Lady's Land at Buckland Hill'.[56]

Full details of the tolls charged by the trust do not

Above This manuscript map was probably drawn in about 1738 at the time of the court case over the building of the dam across the river. The proposed dam is the thick black line crossing the river.

Below An early twentieth century photograph from the Walhampton shore, showing the causeway, bridge (far left) and the toll house with, between the two upstairs windows on the left, a white board listing the tolls.

Above A postcard view of the closed tollgate. Looking east towards Walhampton and the Undershore.

Right A horse drawn wagon passes through the toll gate on its way to Lymington.

Below & Opposite page The yard of the *Angel Inn*, as drawn by Thomas Rowlandson, probably in the autumn of 1784 (see page 66 for a plan of the yard).

The tollhouse at Buckland in about 1905 from a watercolour painting by Wilfred Ball. Although by this date it had long ceased to function the atmosphere of earlier times is captured.

survive, but the accounts for 1830-31 show that Buckland Gate took £218 in tolls.[57]

The route westwards from Lymington was not turnpiked and it is most salutary to read the comments made in 1810 by Charles Vancouver about this road:

'Nothing can possibly exceed the goodness of the roads through the New Forest, and the southern parts of the county. It is no less true than strange, to say that the traveller may pass from Lymington to Christchurch, and thence to Salisbury, without a turnpike, and all the way on parochial roads, which may vie for goodness with the best turnpikes in the kingdom.'[58]

Before the eighteenth century nearly all land transport was by foot or horse. A few wagons did travel the roads, but most goods were moved by pack animals. The mid- to late eighteenth century saw considerable improvements in road

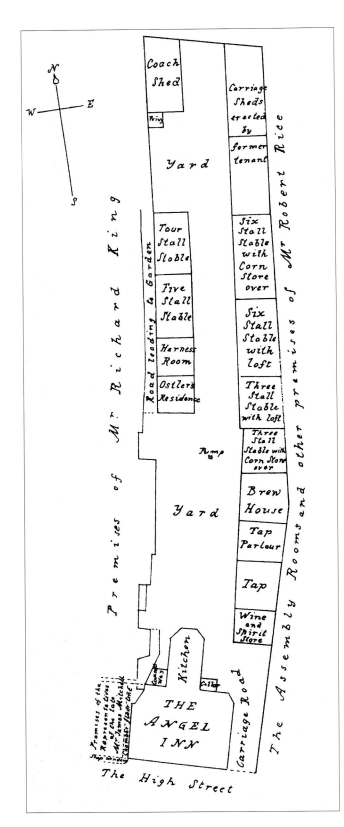

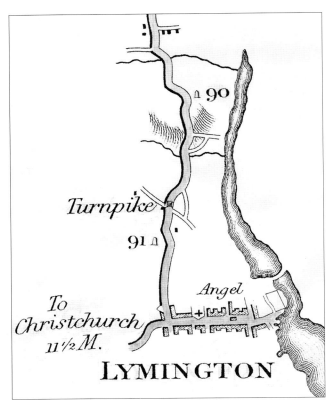

Above Map of the turnpike road by Mogg, 1817. The tollhouse is sited where the word Turnpike appears.

Left Plan of the *Angel Inn* yard from an early nineteenth century deed.

construction, which was particularly encouraged under the turnpike system and led to marked advances in vehicle design.[59]

It is difficult to know when the first regular coach services were introduced to Lymington but certainly by 1765 we have the record of a coach called the *Rose* leaving Holborn for the *Angel Inn* at Lymington on Sundays, Tuesdays and Thursdays, making the return journeys on the following days.[60]

By the 1780s Lymington had a coach, the *Diligence*, making return journeys three days a week to Southampton on Tuesdays, Thursdays and Saturdays. And commercial wagons travelled to Ringwood on Mondays and Saturdays and to and from Christchurch on Saturdays.

At this time all letters were processed by the Royal Mail Service and post could be sent to London on Monday, Thursday and Saturday nights at 11

The *Angel Inn* with its first floor balcony from which so many of the town's proclamations were announced flanked by the Assembly Rooms to the right. These rooms were the centre of much of the social life of Lymington and provided the accommodation for the borough council from 1858 to 1914.

o'clock and on Wednesday at 3 in the afternoon. The mail arrived on Monday, Wednesday, Thursday and Saturday mornings at 7 o'clock.[61] The time taken from Lymington to London was between 13 and 14 hours. A unique bill survives giving exact details of the mail between Southampton and Lymington on 25 March, 1797. The mail was dispatched from Southampton post office by A. Beare, the postmistress, at 7.05 a.m. and it was received by A. Shepard, the Lymington postmaster, at 10.35 a.m. The returning mail left Lymington the next day at 5 p.m. and arrived in Southampton at 7.30 p.m. In this bill the road distance is given as 18 miles each way.[62]

By the early nineteenth century communications had much improved, with several coaches journeying to Southampton which connected with those to London. Roger's coach, *The Lymington Mail*, left the *Angel*, a coaching inn in the High Street, at 4.45 p.m. and reached the *Coach and Horses* at Southampton 3½ hours later, returning to Lymington the following morning: *The Telegraph* left the *Anchor and Hope* at 5 a.m. daily and reached Southampton at 7.30, while *The Independent* started from the *Nag's Head* (later renamed *The Londesborough*) at the same time and arrived at the *Star* Southampton between 7 and 8 a.m., both coaches returning the same evening. There was also *The Weymouth Commercial Coach* which left the *Golden Lion*, Weymouth at 8 a.m. on Tuesdays, Thursdays and Saturdays and arrived at the *Anchor and Hope*, at about 4 p.m., before continuing its journey on to Southampton.[63] All these coaching inns were in the High Street with only the *Angel* now remaining as a hotel.

An example of these developments is clearly revealed in the following advertisement:

In addition to the passenger traffic here were also
a number of goods-carrying commercial wagons
that regularly rumbled to and fro between
Southampton, Salisbury, Blandford, Wimborne and
other places.

INDUSTRY, COMMERCE & RETAILING

When the observant and seemingly indefatigable
Celia Fiennes visited Lymington in about 1698 she
noted that it was a seaport town having a few small
ships belonging to it but 'the greatest trade is by
their Salterns'. She must have closely examined the
operation and spoken to those engaged in it. Her
description of how the sea water was drawn into
ponds, which were always kept in good repair, and
there allowed to partially evaporate until a briny
liquor remained is carefully observed. This, in turn,
was pumped into iron or copper pans situated in
brick buildings where it was boiled dry. Five of the
wind driven pumps which carried the brine from the
ponds into the boiling houses are clearly depicted
on a map of 1698.[65] She described the metal pans
as being shallow but measuring 'a yard or two if not

Drawing (after Edward King) of one of the salt boiling
houses, showing the sails of two of the windpumps in the
distance.

more square', arranged in rows with a fierce furnace
blazing beneath to keep them boiling. As the liquor
boiled away so a deposit of salt was left on the sides
and base of the pans. She described this as 'very
good Salt', which was scraped off and collected in
great baskets. As soon as all the salt had been
removed from the pans they were refilled and the
operation repeated. She went on to say,

'They told me when the season was drye and so the Salt
water in its prime they could make 60 quarters of Salt in
one of those panns which they constantly attend night
and day all the while the fire is in furnace . . . their
season for makeing Salt is not above 4 or 5 months in
the year and that only in a dry Summer.'[66] [a quarter of
salt weighed about 4 cwt.]

In 1645 there is a record of 39 salterns owned by
well-known Lymington men, many of them
burgesses: George Burrard owned four, Thomas
Burrard three, Bartholomew Bulkeley two and
Francis Guidott, who then owned one, extended his
interest by purchasing a further five in 1653 for
£110.[67]

In 1694 an act passed through parliament
imposing a tax on all salt produced. Home
produced salt was initially rated at 1s. 8d. a bushel
(about 56 lbs.) bringing the price to 4s. 4d.;
however, salt destined for fisheries was exempted.
Only three years after its imposition the tax was
doubled to 3s. 4d. a bushel.

Government collectors were appointed to gather
the tax. Amongst these was Joseph Slater who in
1715 collected £25,110 from the Lymington saltern

owners. In 1745 the collector, John How, took the huge sum of £48,994 19s. 2d. but the peak was reached ten years later when the astonishing amount of £57,891 was collected on the General Account.

Such figures give a clear indication of the size and importance of the industry throughout the first half of the eighteenth century. This rate of increase is confirmed by the fact that by mid century there were at least 178 pans operating. These pans were owned by 21 owners who in 1743 formed themselves into a legal co-partnership. Of these the largest single owner was James Perkins with 28 pans. Two women were partners, namely, Susanna Hicks with eight pans and Mary Blake with two. This body of saltern owners had formed what was effectively a cartel whereby prices and trading arrangements were controlled. It was reckoned that this group produced about 178 tons of salt in a season.[68]

For the 19 years between 1724 and 1766, for which records survive, we find that 4,612 tons of salt was exported from Lymington in 64 ships, an

The steamy interior of a salt boiling house showing the men at work with the boiling pans of brine.

average of 72 tons per ship. Twelve cargoes were destined for Newfoundland and 33 for America, others went to Norway, Ireland and the Channel Islands. The quantity of salt used in the Newfoundland fishing industry must have been vast, for though it could obtain foreign salt cheaper than that produced in England[69] it was evidently insufficient as large quantities of home produced salt were also required.

Local supplies were obtained by coastal vessels from Lymington, and by 1740 'English white salt' was a regular importation into Poole. By the 1750s, vessels were making regular trips to Lymington carrying wheat, barley, and assorted cargoes of timber, pitch, and Purbeck stone, and returning with salt in bulk. From Jan., 1758 to July 1759, 322 weys of English salt were imported from Cowes and Lymington . . .[70]

Incidental references throw some light on ships and their cargoes of salt, as when Saltash

This little engraving by G.W. Bonner about 1840, shows the boiling house on the left with the cistern for the brine in front. The windpump in the centre was for drawing the brine into the cistern from the ponds.

Corporation in 1760 collected dues from James Rossiter master of the sloop *Briewell* of Lymington, carrying a cargo of 25 tons of salt.[71] This ship was one of 10 such vessels from Lymington visiting the Tamar in 1760-1, but is the only one for which a cargo is specified.

However, signs of the impact of competition were clearly discernable when in 1789 Glauber wrote a letter to the inhabitants of Lymington expressing dismay at the decline of the industry.[72] He refers to its 'present unprofitable condition' and points out that men who 'from earliest youth have been maintained by their labour in the salt works' are now in distress. He blamed the expense of running the salt works in competition to those of Liverpool, where the brine was mined and there was ample coal for the furnaces. Lymington owners had to pay carriage for their coal and were much more subject to the vagaries of the weather, pointing out their 'salt works are exposed to the fury of wind and sea' and constantly need repair.[73] The position was so dire that Glauber refers to one proprietor having given up 'works which paid a rent of £500 per annum' but had a prospect of being retenanted again.

The notebook, compiled in 1805, by one of the largest saltern owners, Charles St Barbe, throws much light on the Lymington salt industry. As Celia Fiennes stated the salterns only operated for a few weeks in the summer but the period could be drastically shortened by bad weather, as in 1802 when operations lasted for only two weeks, or it could be exceptional and last for 22 weeks. The average seems to have been around 16 weeks. The boiling was done on a continuous weekly basis starting at midnight on Sunday and running through to 8 o'clock the following Saturday. Huge quantities of Newcastle or Sunderland coal were consumed in the furnaces, amounting to as much as 1,030 chaldrons (1 chaldron = 36 bushels) in 1805. St Barbe's calculations for quantities and costs, though approximate, are of some interest:

100 tons of salt at £1 18s a ton brings in £190.
50 chaldrons of coal required at £2 a chaldron costs £100.
Rent and taxes £18.
The process of manufacture at 5s. a ton is £25.
Wear and tear (general depreciation) is £20.
Net profit on 100 tons of salt is therefore £27.

A saltern consisting of two pans could make about 6 tons of salt in a week so if the operation was conducted for 16 weeks 96 tons were produced. Generally wages paid are not recorded but a solitary reference indicates that a boy at the works was 5s. a week.

There were two main by-products of Lymington's sea salt. One was Epsom salts (epsomite or hydrated magnesium sulphate), and was produced by the residual 'bitters', as they were called, which remained after the white salt had been produced, and were treated by separate boiling and crystallizing processes. The other was Glauber salts (mirabilite or hydrated sodium sulphate). Both, which were used medicinally, fetched a greater price than white salt but were subject to the same rate of tax as ordinary salt and because of the more complicated manufacturing process were probably no more profitable.

The salt making process was apparently assisted by a small shrimp (*Artemisus salinus*, Lamarck) which was first noticed in 1740. King states,[74] 'that it lived in the brine tanks only, where no other creature could have existed . . . It was supposed by the salt makers, to cause a clearing of the brine; and was carefully transported to those vats which seemed to be deficient'.

In around 1800, and a little after, Lymington was producing approximately 5,200 tons[75] of salt a year and though this represented a falling off from

Pencil sketch of the salt works by Thomas Colborne in about 1840. He has named the owners, Dimmick, Tizard's and King's.

that produced in the mid- to late eighteenth century it shows the long decline had already started. Despite this it remained the second largest producer in the kingdom. By 1825 there were only three salterns operating and Lymington was importing salt from Liverpool![76]

The repeal of the salt tax in 1825 had no appreciable effect in arresting the decline of the salt industry and by 1865[77] it was reduced to a single saltern, Rowe's, and reputedly closing by 1868.[78]

Daniel Defoe in his travels in about 1720 described Lymington as chiefly noted for 'making fine salt, which is indeed excellent good'. More critically he goes on to comment that though the town was well situated for shipping it did not seem

to have any foreign commerce 'except it be by what we call smugling, and roguing; which I may say, is the reigning commerce of all this part of the English coast'.[79]

Smuggling was indeed an important part of Lymington's economic life. It became profitable following the 1671 Customs Act, when tariffs were placed on certain imported goods, particularly wines and spirits. Over the years the duties were generally raised, making smuggling increasingly beneficial to those engaged in this 'free trade'. It was an industry receiving wide support from the local community, much of it of a tacit kind.

Thomas Baskerville writing in the 1670s noted that Lymington 'since the Act of forbidding French wines to be brought over lies very commodious for stealing wines ashore, and that perhaps of late has contributed to their wealth, for here are now built some handsome houses'.[80] Regrettably only two houses of this period now survive, namely, Monmouth House, opposite the parish church, and Woodside Manor House.

Owling, which involved the illegal export of wool was actively engaged in, as is revealed when a Customs Officer at Lymington called Hugh Harsnet, with a sailor named Daniel Gates, sought recompense and a reward of £40 for prosecuting Thomas Tanner, mariner, for the offence in 1714. Tanner had loaded 17 bags of wool on a vessel called the *Endeavor*.[81] In the same year a man

A surviving salt boiling house which once operated in the Oxey salt works, near Creek Cottage.

A curious newspaper account (*Morning Post*, 11 May 1789) about a gang of smugglers, supposed to occupy a cave at Ampress. It has not been possible to verify any part of this account through historical legal sources though it appeared in two national newspapers and was the subject of a published eight-page broadsheet.

called Vaughan 'of the Salt Duty' gave an account to the Customs Commissioners of 'great quantities of wine and brandy being run between Christchurch and Lymington'.[82]

Lymington, lying as it did in the centre of an area of coastal marsh and creeks, provided an ideal base from which Preventive Officers could patrol the marshes and adjoining coast to search for smugglers and contraband goods. The customs establishment in 1799 comprised a Principal Coast Officer, William Trattle, assisted by two clerks, J. Brown and Mr Edwards; the Acting Comptroller of Customs and Comptroller of Coals, Slate and Stone called William How; the Supervisor of Customs and Coast waiter[83] named John How and five riding officers, as well as the Sitter of the Boat, William Rutter, and four boatmen.[84]

The harbour was too public for smuggling, and most contraband was landed in the creeks to the east and west of Lymington River estuary. But the customs boats were based at Lymington and included a cutter called the *Rose*, which is often recorded as being involved in anti-smuggling activities. And, as might be expected, some Lymington merchant vessels were involved in smuggling: The master of the *Mary Ann*, John Bath, was caught carrying contraband goods from France to Keyhaven in 1699.[85]

The late eighteenth and early nineteenth centuries, including the period of the wars with France, were when the trade was most fully developed and when the quantities smuggled were immense. This was when most of the violent affrays between customs officers and smugglers took place. John How, was assaulted and so severely injured by smugglers in May 1786 that the surgeon's bill for his treatment came to £11 14s. 6d. and he received £30 compensation.[86] Five years earlier, Thomas Hanson[87] had died of wounds incurred when the smuggling lugger on which he was a crewman was engaged by the customs cutter, the *Rose*. The death of a customs officer is mentioned in an obituary in the *Hampshire Repository*, of 10 July 1799, which records, 'At Lymington, Mr C. Colborne, officer of the customs; his death was occasioned by a shot from a smuggling cutter'.[88]

The problem when trying to assess the economics of smuggling is that only the contraband taken or reported can be calculated, the quantity landed safely is unrecorded. This is, of course, the nature of illicit activities. However, there can be no doubt that the quantities of contraband goods were huge, and most arrived safely without detection. Some indication of the scale is revealed when in 1816, after the Royal Navy had taken responsibility for the Revenue cutters, 370,000 gallons of gin and brandy, 42,000 yards of silk, 36,000 packs of playing cards, numerous other items and no fewer than 875 smuggling vessels were seized.[89]

There are tales of underground passages in Lymington being used to secrete smuggled goods.[90] Of course, there are no verifiable records to substantiate these legends but as Lymington men were engaged in the trade it is probable they would have used whatever hiding places were at hand. It is interesting to note that 'in 1720 the mayor and burgesses of Poole petitioned the House of Commons to clamp down on smuggling because it was seriously undermining the legitimate trade and impoverishing the town'.[91] There seems to be no equivalent complaint from the Lymington Corporation yet its concerns were probably similar to those of Poole. Sympathy swung towards the smuggling gangs later in the century. Many a shopkeeper benefited from being able to offer customers a little illicit something from below the counter. The duties on wines, spirits, tea, tobacco and dozens of other commodities had gradually become exorbitant, and few people lost sleep when uncorking a bottle of wine on which duty had not been paid.

Despite its size, shipping was economically important to Lymington throughout the eighteenth century. Defoe had stated 'that though the town was well situated for shipping it did not seem to have any foreign commerce'. Records are relatively scarce but the Southampton Petty Customs Book for 1723 gives a remarkable insight into the cargoes shipped and landed at what, in reality was no more than a small but busy port specialising in the coastal trade. On 28 March 1724 John Edwards, a Lymington merchant, loaded 20 hundred of cordage, 15 hundred of ironmonger's ware, 150 cwt. of biscuit, 500 bushels of salt and 17½ quarters of wheat on board the *Blessing* bound for Newfoundland. The same ship returned to Lymington arriving on 9 July 1724 carrying 385 casks of oil (almost certainly cod oil), 500 seal skins, 10 beaver skins valued at £2, two fox skins valued at 5s. and three otter skins valued at 3s. 4d. In March 1725 the *Blessing* weighed anchor again for Newfoundland, with a cargo of 10 lbs of

cordage, 10 lbs. of iron ware, 8,000 biscuits, 50 quarters of salt, 20 quarters of peas, 21 quarters of wheat, 14 quarters of barley and 5 bushels of salt (presumably this second consignment of salt was listed separately as it was destined for a different receiver). By December the ship was again crossing the wintry north Atlantic, laden with over £82 worth of fox and martin skins destined for Moses Kittier of Ringwood.[92] An entry in the burial register for 17 March 1789 highlights the continuing link with Newfoundland, as we find a certain Robert Thumb, aged 52 years, buried in Lymington churchyard after he 'had been in Newfoundland 31 years'. Between 1836 and 1842 eight Lymington men were married in Newfoundland.[93]

Lymington ships were also plying to the West Indies, the American colonies and to Ireland. Occasionally journeys were made to France with bricks, tiles, wheat and salt. The import trade saw Scandinavian ships bringing in large quantities of timber, much of it destined for the shipbuilding yards at Bucklers Hard.[94]

By the end of the eighteenth century we find the following ships engaged in trade from Lymington to Portsmouth and many also sailed on to London:[95]

The Phoenix: William Footner, master
Polly: Thomas Dukes
London: John Johnson
Dove: John White
Bewley: James White
Weston: John Oake
Friends Goodwill: Robert Badcock
Providence: William Hibbard
Neptune: John Revans
Speedwell: William White
Nancy: William Footner
Owners Goodwill: Capt. Tarver
Good Intent: John Bevis

Of the vessels plying westwards on the coastal trade was one named the *Pilewell* with master James Roseter.[96]

During the periods of conflict with France ships plying coastwise along the English Channel were in danger of attack from French privateers, as happened to the Lymington sloop, *Industry*, in May 1780 while carrying a cargo of salt to Plymouth.

Above & Opposite page Loading cattle for the Isle of Wight from the quay. The warehouses form a backdrop to the activity in this drawing by Thomas Rowlandson.

Opposite page bottom This engraving of a lively maritime scene shows the Jack in the Basket marker at the mouth of Lymington River.

The French vessel, the 22-gun *Princess de Robecq*, captured her about six miles south of Topsham Bar and successfully demanded a ransom of £200 before she was released.[97]

Such risks were, of course, additional to the natural hazards faced at sea, as when a Lymington sloop of about 25 tons skippered by Joseph Nutman, ran ashore in a howling gale at White Nothe on the Dorset coast on the night of 5-6 January 1786 and became a total loss. The cargo contained spirits which were taken off by the revenue officers. But whether the ship was engaged in illegitimate trade or not is unknown.[98]

The navigable channel of the river was defined by markers, the most important, perhaps, was the one near the entrance of the river known as 'Jack in the Basket', which remains to this day as an important guide to those using the river. These markers were maintained by the Corporation. Edward King explains the name with the following anecdote, 'the fishermen from Lymington used to go out in the Solent and to save them time their wives rowed down the river in punts and tied their food and drink in a basket on the last stake in the river. The drink was carried in 'black jacks' (a tarred leather flask), hence the name Jack-in-the-Basket'.[99] The pilots who guided the vessels in Lymington River and around the Shingles were essential to the town's maritime reputation. They brought further advantages when ships in distress or derelict where guided in, 'from which business occurs [for] Attorneys, Shipwrights, rope and sail makers and others'.[100]

The first two decades of the nineteenth century saw Lymington's maritime trade flourishing. In the week 26 January to 1 February 1819 the following ships tied up alongside the wharfs: *Anvil* from Sunderland, the *Albion* and *Rambler* from Southampton; the *Nancy* from Portsmouth and, intriguingly, the *Plutis* from Hamburg which together with two ships from London, the *Duncombe* and *Frances Eliza*, were carrying 600 British and German troops 'all for the Spanish Main'.[101] These troops were volunteers and mercenaries sent to support Simon Bolivar in his liberation struggle against the Spanish in the region of South America which later became the republics of Colombia and Venezuela. Oddly enough, despite such support, the British Government was reluctant to recognise these republics after Bolivar's victory and did not do so for about another five years.[102]

The bulk of the trading vessels were mainly from southern coastal ports, as can be seen from the records for January 1823 when the *Amity* arrived from Cork, the *Dispatch* from Southampton, the *Ceres* from Rye, the *Happy Return* from Newhaven, the *Wittering* from Chichester, *Chance* from Weymouth, *Friends* from Shoreham and *Malta* from Portsmouth. The vessels leaving were the *Hearts of Oak* bound for Sunderland, *Sincerity* and *Amity* for Southampton, the *Fancy* for Teignmouth and the *Duke of Wellington* for Newhaven.[103] Despite the dominance of the coastal trade there were occasional visits by foreign vessels, shown by a cargo of foreign beans being landed at Mr West's wharf 'and selling at a low price for ready money'.[104]

One of the social repercussions of this trade is revealed in a letter addressed to Mr Wm Noake, Guardian of the Parish of Lymington, dated 20 March, 1833 from Andrew Watt, overseer of the poor at Dalton-le-Dale near Sunderland.

> Sir,
> We are much surprised of you not remitting us the Money as Usual, as we are in amediate want of it, for our own Parishoners; Last Market day I visited the Family and found them in great want; the Widow has commenced a Small School for Children at two pence per week; which at present she as got seven. "And she beg'd of me", as I meant to write to you this week for

> you to name in my letter whether you meant to send her money down Once in Six Weeks: or not (if not) She will be Compeld to come up to her Parish the next voyage with the Brig Vine they have not rec'd any relief form any Parish Since they got our last on 21st February, which cause them to [be] in great want and you know their six weeks will be due on the (5th April) If you think proper to remit the money down every six weeks . . . [105]

The polite courtesies of the correspondence mask one of the ways in which the sometimes draconian poor laws could create problems beyond any single individual's control. A Sunderland girl had married a Lymington sailor and raised a family in Sunderland prior to her husband's death. Under the Settlement Laws the marriage made her a Lymington parishioner. When, as a widow, she needed support for herself and her family she attempted a little self-help by running a dame's school to supplement any relief money due to her from Lymington's overseers. They defaulted on the relief payment and unless it was paid she would 'be compeld' to return in the brig *Vine* to Lymington. In reality this would have been a cruel blow for she would have been a complete stranger in the town, but it is from the chance survival of such fragments that we can build a picture of daily life in Hanoverian England.

Lymington remained an important shopping town throughout the eighteenth century. Indeed, as the century wore on so shopping became increasingly sophisticated and the range of goods available widened considerably. The town served the whole of the south New Forest area and, of course, the Saturday markets drew in large numbers from the adjoining villages and hamlets. Lymington's shopkeepers also played a role in supplying bulk provisions for the poor law workhouses in the town and the surrounding area – including such minor items as the paper supplied by Galpine to John Kearly, master of the Hordle workhouse, for him to make up into account books.[106]

When Thomas Rowlandson visited the town in 1784 amongst a number of sketches he made was one of a fruit shop where the fruit is displayed in boxes on tables. In the 1784 directory William House is recorded as the only fruiterer and we may

assume it was his shop Rowlandson portrayed.[107]

We know from the seventeenth century trade tokens that several grocers were plying a profitable business in the town. A little over a century later we have records of seven grocers, some of whom were also operating other enterprises. John Woodford was also a chandler and John Bevis master of the trading vessel, *Good Intent*. Ann Beeston had a shop selling books and stationery which was run in conjunction with selling salt – seemingly a curious combination but not so odd perhaps as that of Edward Elgar junior who is both a stone mason and pastry cook! Three traders are recorded only as 'shopkeeper' but references to drapers, mercers, milliners, hosiers and breeches makers indicate a considerable trade in clothing. Two watch makers set up shop by the late eighteenth century, reflecting the growing use of timepieces.[108]

During the second half of the eighteenth century bow windows became increasingly popular as a means of displaying goods. The architectural evidence and some of the early illustrations show their arrival in Lymington and we can easily visualise Lymingtonians wandering along the High Street and window-shopping, in much the same way as they do today.

Charles King, from Yeovil, established himself as

The drawing made by Rowlandson on his tour illustrates a fruit and vegetable shop in Lymington High Street. The only fruiterer recorded as operating at about that time was William House.

a bookseller in Lymington in 1805 and soon had a thriving business. After his nephew, Richard, completed his apprenticeship as a printer and book-binder in Yeovil, he decided to join him. Richard set off from Yeovil at day break on 4 April 1817 and walked 35 miles to Wimborne, where he rested overnight, completing the remaining 24 miles of his journey the following day. Richard's energy was matched by his ambition. He soon established himself as a capable bookbinder. His hours were long, from 7 in the morning till 8 at night with only Sundays and Christmas Day off, and in the winter he had to use an open fire to warm his tools.

Following his marriage in July 1818,[109] he decided to set up on his own with a capital of £100 and, for the first time in his life, boarded a coach for London in order to buy stock. By chance, it seems he fell in with a bookseller named Thomas Tegg who gave him valuable advice on selling books remaindered by publishers. Showing good business acumen, Richard bought some remaindered books in addition to printing materials and a small

Richard King (1796-1877), the bookseller, stationer and printer.

wooden press. From these humble beginnings a successful retailing enterprise was established which continuously traded as Kings of Lymington until 1988. Although Richard King never met Tegg again their business contacts were maintained until Tegg's death in 1869. By the 1820s King was printing and publishing on his own account and in 1828 produced a guide to Lymington which ran into several editions.[110]

Another old established business was that of the musical instrument retailers, Klitz, founded in 1789 by George Philip Glitz (later to take the name Klitz), a refugee from war-torn Europe. In 1821 he sold to the parish church band a double bass for £13 13s. 6d. which, at that price, must have been a fine instrument. The Lymington directory of 1824 records him as a 'music seller'.[111] The accomplished sportsman, Colonel Peter Hawker, who was also a gifted musician, had a high opinion of Klitz's musical skills and referred to 'old Klitz the Clementi of the place'.[112] This

was considerable praise as Muzio Clementi was a renowned virtuoso concert pianist who was then still living. Today a blue plaque is on the front of Klitz's former shop commemorates this early retailing establishment.

SCHOOLS & EDUCATION

It is a little curious that Lymington's first school was not founded by a local citizen but by a man from Toller Fratrum in Dorset who had been elected burgess in 1667 to bolster the Royalist (or Court) party in the town. George Fulford's family had its origins in Devon but was settled in west Dorset by the early seventeenth century. He was born in 1619, the fifth son of Sir Francis Fulford and his wife Elizabeth.

Presumably the lack of an educational establishment in Lymington must have concerned him for in 1668 Fulford, in cohorts with two other Dorset men, William Coker of Mappowder and John Newburgh, made a gift of land in Buckland Newton to Francis Guidott, a Lymington burgess, and five others. For legal reasons this transaction required Guidott and his colleagues to pay £326, but this was reimbursed to them by way of a gift by Fulford, Coker and Newburgh, and the money was to be used towards the cost of building a grammar school. The gift of land was intended to provide a secure endowment and so ensure a continuing income for the maintenance of the school.

The provision of the establishment was for boys, aged between 7 and 14 years, who were to be 'taught and trained up in learning and the true Protestant religion, and more especially the knowledge of Latin, Greek, writing, arithmetic and 'good life' – what we would now call 'citizenship'. Trustees were to oversee the running of the school and the first governors and visitors were to be Fulford, Newburgh, Guidott and his Lymington colleagues. In the case of a governor dying or otherwise being removed a replacement was to be elected within 30 days. George Fulford, as promoter and founder, was to choose the schoolmaster during his lifetime and thereafter such choice was to be in the hands of the governors. The schoolmaster

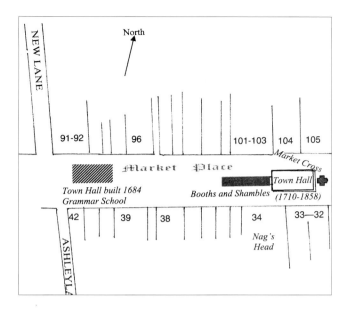

received the income from the lands but, curiously, had to pay out of his own pocket for the replacement of broken glass in any school windows; evidently an incentive to discourage boys playing games like fives around the building.

The governors were to meet only once a year, on the Thursday in Whitsun week, when they would make full enquiries into the conduct and management of the school and, of course, they had powers to 'regulate all matters relating thereto, and to remove the master, usher, or any scholar at their discretion'.

Sadly, the exact location of this school is unknown but it was probably somewhere in the High Street. The accommodation cannot have been satisfactory, for only 20 years after its foundation

Above Sketch map of part of Lymington High Street to show the principal market place and the two Town Halls that were built in the thoroughfare.

Right The pillars that supported the upper room (later the grammar school) of the Town Hall that stood outside Nos. 92-3 High Street from 1684 to 1782. These now form an attractive pergola in Woodside Gardens.

Below This pencil sketch by T. Colborne shows the Town Hall, built in 1710, standing in the High Street. It was demolished in 1858.

the Corporation of Lymington issued a deed enabling the school to move into the upper room of the Town Hall, built 1684, which stood on 18 stone pillars in the High Street, close to the present nos. 93-4.[113] A replacement Town Hall was built in about 1710 a little further to the east but still in the High Street.

A curious, but regrettably undated document[114] has recently come to light which is in the form of a memorial from the governors of the school to the Corporation accusing 'one or more Burgesses' of turning the master and pupils out of the building so that it could be reclaimed as a Town Hall. The governors strongly objected to this treatment and threatened to seek a resolution in law. But as the expense of such a response would be beyond the means of the school charity it was decided to seek a compromise. Unfortunately, the records of subsequent negotiations have not survived but the outcome was that the school was dispossessed and had to find alterative accommodation.

By 1764 the Dorset lands endowing the school produced a rent of only £7 7s. By 1804 the rents from the land still only amounted to £14 and in 1819 to £22 10s with additional income from an investment of £50 made in 1767 in the Lymington Turnpike Trust at an interest rate of 5%. Even these monies were insufficient to properly maintain the school which was now held in the master's private house, where ten boys 'the sons of tradesmen and others in the parish, not in good circumstances' were taught the rudiments of reading, writing and arithmetic. Quite a comedown from the high grammar school ideals envisaged by the founder George Fulford a hundred years earlier. By 1806, and thereafter, all the income was paid directly to the schoolmaster with a deduction being made for stamps, postage and occasional expenses.

Despite a generous legacy of £300 bequeathed by Mrs Ann Burrard in 1777 for the benefit of the school there was insufficient income to enable the trustees to maintain the building given by the Corporation, which almost certainly explains why they wanted to reclaim it. Even so by 1782, the Town Hall building used by the school, was then in such a dilapidated state and 'obstructive to the street' that it was demolished.

Fulford's grammar school was not the only school in the town, for the visitation returns made to Bishop Richard Willis in 1725 record that Lymington had six schools, 'One of them a free school endowed with lands in Dorsetshire of the value of £10 p.a. by Mr. Fulford deceased. Master Mr. John Rigg. Trustees remaining Sir Robert Smyth and William Tulse Esq. The other five private schools are kept by Mr Samuel Belbin, an Anabaptist Preacher, Mrs Coleman, Mrs Mussen, Mrs Cove, Mrs Brent'.[115]

It is worth recording that the trade directories of the late eighteenth century do not mention any educational establishments in Lymington. It is not until the appearance of Pigot's *Directory* in 1824 that the town's five 'Academies' were listed, two of which were day schools and three were for boarding pupils.

WAR & THE MILITARY

Because Lymington was conveniently placed for servicing shipping in times of war the town played a role as a port of embarkation. It lay between two important coastal defences, Calshot Castle to the east and Hurst Castle to the west, while the forts on the Isle of Wight were a bulwark against foreign attack.

Military personnel, particularly sailors, either on their way home or to join their ships, received relief whilst passing through Lymington. Britain had been embroiled in a succession of wars with France since 1744 and had brutally crushed the Jacobites at Culloden in 1746, the same year as the Lymington records state, 'gave to soldiers and sailors several times, 18s. 6d.' and 'Paid by Mr Northover, to four soldiers, per order of Mr Burrard, 12s.'[116] It cannot now be ascertained in which conflict these travelling soldiers had served or, indeed, where their destination lay.

A corps of Hessian soldiers was billeted in Lymington between 1756-9,[117] a period when the Princedom of Hesse was a British ally during the complex machinations of the Seven Years' War.

A memorial in the church of St Thomas captures the character of late eighteenth century warfare, starkly revealing the devastating impact of disease, which then took more lives than military action.

> As a tribute of grateful affection, This Monument is sacred to the Memory of CAPTAIN JOSIAS ROGERS, of his Majesty's Ship QUEBEC.
> Who during the American war, braved every danger, And suffered all the Severities of Wounds and Imprisonment. In the Campaign of 1794, he commanded the Naval Battalions. At the reduction of the French islands in the West Indies, While his services were great to his Country and honorable to his own Character.
>
> In his exertions to save Grenada, he died of the Yellow Fever on the 24th of April, 1795. Aged 40. The COUNCIL OF GRENADA decreed a Monument in Honor of his PUBLIC SERVICES, and in remembrance of his PRIVATE VIRTUES, his widow soothed her sorrows, By inscribing this Tablet to his Memory.
>
> By the same dreadful disorder, on 13th of May, 1794 (after having distinguished himself In the dangers and fatigues of the Campaign) fell at Guadeloupe in his 26th year, JAMES ROGERS, his Brother, and First LIEUTENANT of the same ship; whose generous and manly Principles were admired by All who knew him.
>
> On the 9th of the same month, at the age of 19, the promise of Virtue and Talents, in JOSIAS ROGERS, his Nephew and also LIEUTENANT of the QUEBEC. Died at Martinique, by the same Fatality.[118]

Another important element in national military organisation was the creation of the militia in the reign of Elizabeth I. After the Civil War it became moribund but was revived in 1778 to meet the possible threat of a French invasion.[119] It became the central plank of home defence during the wars with Revolutionary and Napoleonic France, and men were called to serve from every parish.

Three companies of the South Hants Militia were established at Lymington in their own barracks in August 1793. Percival Lewis, a Lymington magistrate, was appointed captain of the North Hants Regiment in 1803 and ensign in the South Hants Regiment in 1809.[120] As captain of the Volunteers he received 9s. 5d each day he was on duty. A number of other Lymington men served as part-timers in the Volunteers, including John King

Rear Admiral Thomas Rogers (1764-1814), younger brother of Josias Rogers who is commemorated on the monument in the church. By his will he founded the charity known as 'Rogers's Gift' (see page 133).

and James Brown, who were lieutenants at 4s. 4d. a day. There were also non-commissioned officers, four drummers and 78 privates who were paid 1s. a day.[121] George Burrard also served as an officer in the South Hants Regiment.

The North Hants Militia embarked from Newport, Isle of Wight, for Lymington, 22 May 1779, six companies remained based in the town and two companies marched to Christchurch on 4 June 1779 where their principal role was to support the Revenue Officers in their operations against the smugglers.

In terms of military affairs, however, it was the arrival of the French troops loyal to Louis XVI that provided one of the most dramatic episodes in Lymington's history. With the declaration of the French Republic in 1792, following the imprisonment of the French royal family, families of noble birth and others supporting the royalist cause came to accept the *fait accompli* and sensed that escape from their homeland was a wiser course than offering resistance. Large numbers crossed the Channel to land along the south coast. As a rule these refugees were hospitably received but gradually the British government realised that some kind of control would have to be exercised if bands of disaffected foreigners were not to be left wandering around the countryside. Instructions were issued to gather the military emigrants together to form corps, which were placed under the overall control of the Duke of York. They could then be organised into regiments to fight alongside the British in the war against Revolutionary France.

After one such regiment had fought unsuccessfully in Flanders the remnant force, comprising about 400 men, came to Lymington to set up quarters. King describes these men as 'tried, trusty, and brave: lives too valuable to be wasted; but preserved for important occasions'.[122] Once established in barracks in the town, with the officers lodged with the tradesmen, they became known as The Loyal Emigrants.

A second band of about 600 officers and men of the French (Royal) Naval Service were billeted in barns and farm buildings in Buckland. Meanwhile, a third corps, the French Artillery, commanded by Col. Rothalier, and numbering about 400, occupied the Malt House in New Street (now the Lymington Community Centre) and some stables opposite. Other units included: Meuron's, Willot's and those bearing their commanders' names: Col. Dresnay, Count d'Hector, Count d'Hervilly, Col. de Mortemar and Count de Puisaye.

Both the Lymington and Boldre parish registers throw some intermittent light on the lives of these Frenchmen. A number of the officers and serving men had brought with them their wives and families. Those children born to them in Lymington were baptised by their Catholic chaplain, who then had the entry recorded in the Lymington parish register:

1794: Aglae-Angélique, dau. of Count Hervé Louis Marie Du Plessis-Pascau (of Landerneau in Brittany, formerly a Lieutenant in the French Royal Navy, and now in the regiment of General Count d'Hector,

quartered in this place) and Anne Buisson de la Vigne, his wife (of L'Orient) born May 6 and Baptised the 7th, inserted at the request of the Priest, the Chaplain of the Regiment.[123]

Some Dutch and German refugee soldiers united with the loyalist French or were formed into regiments of their own nationality. The Dutch certainly had their own regiment at Lymington as is confirmed in the following tragic event:

'Amarante Emilie de Soulange, the wife of Captain Charles de Menard of the Dutch Artillery, died at the age of 27 while giving birth to their son, Charles-Augustus, on 19 June, 1798.

There was even an Italian, Joseph Siciliati, who, at his burial on 28 August 1814, is recorded as a 'soldier'.

The many detachments of foreign military personnel must have brought a colourful life to the town as they walked through the streets in their distinctive uniforms. Men from Dutch regiments, the King's German Legion and the various French regiments integrated into the lives of the local people.

Relationships with local women were inevitable as is revealed by the marriage at Boldre of Sarah Datchens of Mount Pleasant, lying between Buckland and Sway, to John Baptiste Louis van Overloop, Baron de Meudonck, of the 2nd Independent Company of the 60th Regiment, in February 1813. By 1817 she had joined her husband in Brussels.[124]

There were also irregular liaisons. The baptismal register records the baptism of Jane Dibden's son, Robert, on 25 November 1795 and her declaring the father to be Capt. Honnor of the 19th Regiment.

A number of soldiers who returned to Lymington died of diseases and wounds incurred whilst fighting abroad and were buried in either Boldre or Lymington churchyards. Some, had their names recorded as belonging to the regiment of General Count d'Hector, while many others were nameless and entered anonymously in the burial register as, 'A French emigrant soldier', 'A French emigrant officer' or 'Five emigrant soldiers buried'.

It is evident that the British government wished to

make the best possible use of these emigrant regiments and saw the potential for using them to establish a foothold on French territory. As a consequence the loyalist French regiments (the 3rd, 19th and 42nd) were engaged to mount an expedition to Quiberon for the purpose of supporting the royalist supporters already established in Brittany and La Vendée. The invasion force was to be escorted by a British naval squadron. George III, writing to his Secretary of War, Henry Dundas, in June 1795 notes that the French emigrant forces 'under the mixed command of the [Royalist] de Puisaye and d'Hervilly' were under way.[125] They were placed under the overall command of the Earl of Moira[126] and had been based in Lymington about a year and a half[127] before the expedition was launched.

The expedition proved to be a fiasco. Inadequate preparation, divided leadership, treachery and timidity ensured defeat. Of the 3,600 emigrés and released French prisoners (most of the latter seem to have been republican in sympathy but had professed support for the royalist cause to escape imprisonment) who made up the force no fewer than 1,102 officers and men were killed and about 1,000 were captured, of whom 690 were shot. King observes:

> The most fortunate died sword in hand, after exhibiting the greatest bravery; others despairing turned their weapons against themselves; a few were saved through the waves, by the English boats, and conveyed to the ships.[128]

Those who re-embarked on the British ships returned to this country. How ironic that George III should have recorded on 5 July, only a fortnight before their disastrous rout, 'The happy landing of the French corps in Quiberon Bay is a pleasing prelude of a change of events in France'.[129]

A sense of the personal tragedy brought about by this military blunder is summed up in a solitary pathetic entry in the burial register: 'Baptist Grôss, a French Emigrant soldier, one of the few who returned from the unfortunate Expedition to Quiberon, 28 Oct. 1795'.

A further invasion was planned later in the summer. This time the Île de Noirmoutier, lying about 55 miles south-east of Quiberon, was the destination. In a letter to Henry Dundas, Secretary of War, dated from Southampton 19 August 1795, the Earl of Moira states:

> I have the honour to enclose the embarkation return of the four regiments. Everything of the British will be at Spithead tomorrow. As the French corps cannot be brought from Lymington & Rumsey on the chance of our receiving powers to allot vessels to them, their embarkation cannot take place till Friday . . .[130]

The wording smacks of lack of organisation. This too proved a disaster and the troops and ships had to be withdrawn in December.

The Royal Artillery (Foreign) returned to Lymington and is recorded as being there in 1804-07. The marriage at Boldre in December 1805 of Francis Beretze of the 1st Battalion of the 60th Regiment of Lymington strongly suggests that this was an emigrant regiment or, if British, comprised perhaps a foreign contingent. This is reinforced by the record of Sergeant John Manvia (or Manera) of the 4th Battalion of the 60th Regiment who married Sarah Collings of Lymington in the following April.[131]

The Chasseurs Britannique Regiment established a major base in Lymington in the early nineteenth century. This comprised soldiers drawn from a variety of other regiments and earned the name of 'Wellington's Mongrel Regiment'.[132] They served on a number of campaigns, especially in the Peninsula, but, eventually, were disbanded at Lymington in 1814 with many remaining as civilians in the town.

Lymington became also the temporary base for British soldiers, who were billeted not only in the town but on the surrounding commons. Amongst the 27 regiments recorded as being present in the area were the 19th and 42nd regiments (1794), the 29th Regiment (1796), again the 42nd Regiment (1794), the King's German Legion (1809-13), Queen's German Legion (1796-7), 4th Dutch Regiment, Dutch Rifle Regiment, the North Hants Militia (1799), North Devon Regiment of Militia (1799), Berkshire Militia (quartered at Buckland 1800), the Monmouthshire Militia (1796), the Flintshire Regiment (1801).[133]

King describes the Lymington of these troubled times where the 'miscellaneous body of soldiers, the débris of various armies and troops that had fought on the Continent . . . a turbulent and unruly set of men' often carried out criminal activities. He continues, 'Several murders were committed: one was just opposite the parade ground: suicides were frequent. The sailors from gunboats and cutters in the Solent, were the cause of frequent tumult and riots'.[134]

It is difficult to find proof of all this as the burial register records two murders only, the first is of Daniel Baumbeck, aged 34, of the 60th Regiment who was killed 'by his comrade' in September 1808 and the second was Pierre Lafruy, aged 24, who was murdered at Woodside in January 1814 and buried on 2 February.[135] Amongst the naval war vessels lying off Lymington at various times were the HMS *Cyclops* in 1804 (six of her sailors married in Lymington church), and HMS *Sisiphone* from 1806 to 1813.

The bulk of the foreign troops were housed in barracks but a number of others lodged with residents in the town. These men were issued with small paper dockets or certificates giving their names and the name of the person with whom they were lodging. For example, we find Augustin Minguet, a surgeon with the Loyal Emigrant Regiment, lodging with Elizabeth Mitchell in Nelson Place. In 1802 he married her daughter, Catherine. Another was Charles Warin, corporal in the Company of Gentlemen Veterans (part of the Loyal Emigrant Regiment) lodging in a house opposite the *Angel Inn* in the High Street and Antoine Grange, an ensign in the same regiment, lodging with William Rutter in the Old Town. In 1801 he married the daughter, Jane.

These foreign troops and their families had a considerable impact on Lymington. During the period 1794-1815 there were 192 marriages of foreign military personnel and 50 marriages of British sailors and soldiers. Several individuals were to remain and establish themselves as residents in the area.

A curious glimpse into the convoluted effects of the foreign influence can be seen in the sworn deposition, made on 19 August 1818, of a young woman calling herself Mary Vinnard, a widow. In her statement before the magistrate she declared that in about 1815 she had married 'Elias Vinnard who was a Foreigner and a Pensioner of the Board of Ordnance at 3d. per Day, by whom she had one Child named George about 24 weeks old that about three weeks since her said Husband dying she returned to Ringwood'. In the Boldre Marriage Register is the following brief record: 'Els Werward and Mary Anne Kendel both of Lymington. 1 April, 1815'. It seems certain that the marriage referred to is that of Mary Vinnard. Following her husband's death she had no financial resources and became chargeable to Ringwood parish. It is evident that her husband had been unable to make any kind of provision for her.[136] It is quite obvious that the former foreign troops and refugees remaining in Lymington represented an unacceptable burden of expense to those paying the poor rate. In 1816 the overseers of the poor wrote a complaining letter to the government stating that over a quarter of those in the poorhouse were foreigners.[137]

The country was not reliant on foreign soldiers for defence, although where they could be effectively organised they were a welcome addition. During the period of invasion threats from France, mainly from around 1796 to 1802, the Lymington Fusilier Volunteers, which formed a part-time force to protect the coast, was 'disembodied' in May 1802.[138]

FOUR

The Nineteenth Century

IT IS NOT always wise to segregate one century from another in telling the story of any community. So many threads are intertwined and the events of one century pass imperceptibly into the following. But it might be said, with justice, that the nineteenth century represents a major turning point in the history of Lymington. The town and parish of 1800 still had much in common with those of the preceding two or three centuries but by the time Victoria died the changes both in the physical nature of the town and its administration had altered dramatically.

The population of England and Wales during the nineteenth century rose from close to 9 millions in 1801 to nearly 18 millions in 1851 and up to 32½ millions by 1901, in other words more than tripling in a century. One consequence of this was the growth of government involvement at both a national and local level. Events in Lymington cannot be separated from national influences, although their impact was modified in response to local circumstances.

From the point of view of local communities the nineteenth century was a period of immense, and at times rapid, change. These effects were largely generated by legislation resulting from the deliberations of various parliamentary committees. The legislature was driven by an increasing desire to more effectively organise society at a time when the population was inexorably increasing, technology was beginning to have a real impact on everyday life and when new political philosophies were developing.[1]

An engraving by Benjamin Ferrey of Lymington High Street in 1832, looking west from the Town Hall.

The turn of the century saw the first census, which at once placed individual statistical information on a national scale in the hands of government.[2] The desire to rectify the inequalities of parliamentary representation was first addressed by the Reform Act of 1832, soon to be followed by the Municipal Corporations Act of 1835 which sought to democratise local government. By these acts Lymington saw some statutory changes. Although two members of parliament were retained this was only achieved by an enlargement of the borough to incorporate a great swathe of Boldre parish lying to the east of the Lymington River. The administration and control of the borough changed three years later when councillors were to be elected on a wider franchise, abandoning the former system whereby votes were vested only in burgesses. From the body of councillors the aldermen and a mayor were to be elected.

In 1829 the Catholic Emancipation Act effectively and legally enabled Roman Catholic citizens to engage in administrative and military life without any legal disadvantage. It also enabled them to structure their church organisation in the way that suited them.

The year of Victoria's accession saw the introduction of civil registration for births, marriages and deaths and just four years later the census sought unprecedented details about every person in the kingdom. It would not be wrong to see this as one of the first steps in the gradual secularisation of society, reinforced later in the reign by the two Education Acts of 1870 and 1880. From 1858 wills were no longer proved in ecclesiastical courts but by a secular probate registry.[3]

The Public Health Act of 1848 provided the option for local communities to establish local boards of health and for those who failed to fully respond, like Lymington, compulsion was enacted in 1866.

The Local Government Act of 1888[4] replaced the administrative role of magistrates under the old Quarter Sessions system with that of county councils. Under further provisions in that act Lymington Borough was enlarged to become coextensive with the ecclesiastical parish. The enlargement was not without regret, for a mourning

Sacred to the Memory
OF THE
OLD BOROUGH OF LYMINGTON,
WHO DEPARTED THIS LIFE
31st OCTOBER, 1889.
AGED OVER 700 YEARS.

"THE WAIL OF THE 29."
Brief Life is here our portion,
Brief sorrow, short lived care;
We all do live in loving hope,
To sit beside the Mayor.

A mock mourning card issued to commemorate the demise of the 'Old Borough'. The expansion of the borough in 1889 was fairly modest, merely enough to embrace the whole of the ecclesiastical parish.

card with a black border was issued declaring, 'Sacred to the Memory of the Old Borough of Lymington who departed this life 31st October, 1889 aged over 700 years'.

Policing too moved away from the parish or borough constable to that of the county constabulary and Lymington, despite protests about expense, was to be served by county constables.

Apart from these major administrative upheavals by which many centuries' old practices were overthrown the world of technology moved on. The steam engine generated faster and more efficient and reliable transport both on land and sea. Domestic gas, which had become available in the 1820s gradually penetrated most establishments and became the universal form of reliable street lighting. It was introduced into Lymington in 1832 largely through the beneficence of the Burrards, almost their last contribution to the borough they had ruled so long. As with most towns Lymington generated its own gas in premises established in Gosport Street.

The electric telegraph, which arrived in October 1852, speeded up communications and the wires were sealed in gutta-percha within clay pipes which ran alongside the railway to Lymington and then westwards through Pennington, down Lymore Lane, from thence along Hurst Beach to the castle.

Mass production of domestic wares and proprietory foodstuffs gradually displaced local manufacture.

These are just a few of the many major events that helped create Victorian Lymington. Not all had an equal impact and not all old ways and traditions were abandoned. Yet, despite a good deal of public reaction to the impending changes, they did come and the town and its surroundings at the time of Victoria's death in 1901 was markedly different from that existing at the time of her accession sixty-three years earlier.

PARLIAMENTARY REFORM IN LYMINGTON

During the last decade or so of the eighteenth century there was increasing clamour amongst some of the populace for a greater say in the governance of the country. There was no agreed programme as to how this should be implemented and at the same time there was fierce and concerted opposition to any change. However by the 1820s some of the Whig party had become committed to implementing wider representation. Probably, the key factors were that many large urban, industrial centres had no members of parliament while a considerable number of small boroughs returned two members each. The growth and support of radicalism underpinned the desire for reform and despite many setbacks in parliament an act for changing the representation was passed.[5]

A consequence of the 1832 Reform Act was that many boroughs which formerly had returned two members to parliament were either disfranchised or reduced to a single member. But in Lymington, by the ingenious extension of the borough to include a significant area of Boldre parish within its parliamentary boundary, the right was retained to send two members to parliament. The number of voters was increased from the handful of burgesses to 264, including 32 from the Boldre part.

The citizens of Lymington, like those in most other parliamentary boroughs, divided into two camps over the issue of reform. On the one hand there were those who supported the changes leading to wider representation and on the other those who sought to retain the *status quo*. When the details of the Reform Bill were being widely debated a group rejoicing in the name 'Friends of Reform' began distributing pro-Reform literature. Its leaders were two brothers, Captain John Blakiston and the Rev. Peyton Blakiston, curate of Lymington. Those opposed to reform were quick to respond with counterblasts. C.P. Jones neatly describes this situation as leading to

'a flood of broadsheets containing political lampoons, which lasted two or three years, and the like of which Lymington has never seen before or since. Half the residents in the town turned political writers, and the printers were kept busy with the publication of squibs of all kinds which heaped vituperation, not only upon the candidates and the sitting members, but on everyone who was at all in the public (*i.e.* in the Lymingtonian) eye'.[6]

These political satires, often a combination of astute comment, humour and virulent attacks throw light on the strong views held at a time when the public voice was beginning to be heard and heeded.[7] The Reform candidate, a Whig, was viciously pilloried:

THE HYPOCRITE UNMASKED!!!
Independent but insulted Electors of Lymington!
Thomas Hyde Villiers the raving abuser of West Indian Proprietors, and virulent declaimer against Colonial slavery is deriving a considerable income from slave Labour!
Yes Villiers the Tory apostate, Villiers the Placeman, Villiers the supporter of Gross Jobs is the agent for the slave colony of Berbice, and a hired supporter of that system which he so hypocritically denounced!!![8]
Independent electors!
Let Mawworm, Midstream, Puff-puff Fumigant and others of the Nine[9] continue to spout by the hour against local slavery; but I defy them
to prove . . .
One of the Insulted.

Thomas Hyde Villiers (1801-32) was a remarkable young man who had first been elected the Tory MP for a seat in Yorkshire at the age of 25, and who later changed sides to support Earl Grey's Whig administration. In the end he did not contest Lymington, but became a candidate for a Cornish constituency, where he died suddenly before the election.[10] He was succeeded as candidate in Lymington by John Blakiston, a captain in the army and son of Sir Matthew Blakiston Bart. (1761-1806), who had lived in Milford and Lymington and who has a large memorial tablet in the chancel of the parish church where his other son, Peyton, was curate from 1830 to 1833. Captain Blakiston seemed initially reluctant to take on such a responsibility but he at least possessed credentials by virtue of having served as chairman of the Reform Committee.

Another fine example of the political squib is worth quoting as it expresses unequivocally the reformers' view:

NOTICE
Public Exhibition of the Humguffin Raree Show!

The Inhabitants of Lymington are respectfully informed that the two principal Humguffins, Baron Munchausen[11] of Stoneham and the Great Runaway come to Town (both of whom are recently drawn from the side pocket of the Duke of Wellington and sent here to exhibit their great and marvellous powers in the science of Humbug!!! and Gull catching!!!) will enter the town to-morrow morning at half-past ten o'clock on their way to Hungry Hall[12] to the Hole and Corner Meeting at the Angel Inn by the man "entirely unconnected with either party!!"[13]

They will be attended by a numerous body of the Aristocratic Excrescences of this Neighbourhood in their different characters of Intimidators, Wheedlers, Diddlers, Feeders, etc., besides a regular Mob of the Minors consisting of Slaves, Touts, Swillers, Spongers, Rats, and Dogs for dirty work. They will likewise be attended by a Band of Music. The principal part of this *public* exhibition will be held in *private* . . .

By Order of the Mayor no dogs will be allowed in the streets during this imposing exhibition.

The attack on the local gentry and the ordinary townsfolk who could be persuaded to support them is clearly expressed in this handbill. However, despite a strong campaign the reformers did not succeed in Lymington. Even the throwing of a great open air dinner on 7 August 1831, supported by the mayor, James Monro, for all men of the labouring classes (most of who would not be franchised) ultimately did not persuade voters to support the

This political cartoon depicting the nine, who comprised the Reform Committee, in a wrecked ship by Jack in the Basket in which the Rev. Peyton Blakiston perches, preaching to his brother Captain John Blakiston and the other supporters. Many squibs were issued attacking 'The Nine'. And, of course, they responded in kind.

reform candidate.

Sir Harry Burrard Neale, seven times MP for Lymington and for long the sponsor of Lymington MPs, decided to contest the election himself and seems also to have supported, albeit surreptitiously, John Stewart, an independent candidate, who spoke in favour of reform but opposed the more radical reformers gathered around John Blakiston. The ballot at this time was still public and votes were cast in accordance with the list of names in a poll book which was afterwards published.[14] Each elector could cast two votes and, after two days of polling on 10 and 11 December, the final result was 158 votes for Sir Harry Burrard Neale, 128 for John Stewart, while the reformer, Blakiston, received only 77 votes. Thus, despite the changes made by reform, the long-established Burrard political interest was retained.

The fact that Lymington continued to return two members meant the borough retained an influence disproportionate to its size. A letter from John Templer, a Lymington grocer, to the Earl of Radnor, a supporter of the Reform Bill, took issue over the reformers attempt to limit Lymington's representation to a single member: 'Sir H. Neale was listened to; as, I suppose, because, he made a promise, that, if the two Members were continued, he would get them if he could, to support the Gov[ernment]...'[15] The enlarged parliamentary boundary, according to Templer, was designed to incorporate Burrard Neale's property and that of his 'personal and political friends' this 'will give him much greater influence at any election under the bill, than he would have professed, if the right of voting were to be confined to persons residing in the Parish of Lymington only'.

This aspect is well revealed when the Pylewell estate, at South Baddesley, lying within the parliamentary borough of Lymington, was put up for sale by the Welds in 1850 and the sale catalogue announced:

> Nearly the whole of the HOUSES & LANDS being within the BOROUGH OF LYMINGTON, Thereby possessing such commanding influence that it may be said it RETURNS TWO MEMBERS TO PARLIAMENT . . . [16]

Perhaps a reinforcement of this influence is revealed in a letter written by the Town Clerk, James Brown, a Catholic convert, dated from Lymington 28 April 1859 – just two days before the election – to Joseph Weld, junior, at Lulworth Castle. In it he states that he wishes Joseph 'to accompany your good kind Father and "*in case of positive need*" only to oppose the two anti-Maynooth Candidates[17] – I expect a very close run and if my heart's desire could be accomplished, I should indeed rejoice that the majority should be 5 only and that Majority should be the precise number of Catholic Votes . . . '[18] Of the three candidates in that election, namely, W.A. Mackinnon (Liberal)[19], Sir John Rivett-Carnac (Conservative) and John Bramley-Moore of Liverpool the first two were elected, receiving 157 and 140 votes respectively.

The comment of James Weld, who had proposed Arthur Atherley for Southampton at the Reform elections, is of some interest when he contrasted Southampton, which he described as 'a free borough', with Christchurch, Lymington and Andover, 'the people of which . . . had no more

Sir Harry Burrard Neale (1765-1840), one of the three candidates in the 1832 election. Shown here in the uniform of admiral, the rank he attained in 1830. He was a scion of the long-established and politically important Burrard family.

interest in the return of their members than the lamp posts in their streets'.[20] Nevertheless he later offered himself as a pro-reform candidate for Lymington in the 1835 general election but for some reason withdrew and consequently there was no contest.

A by-election writ was moved on 18 May 1860 when the sitting member, Sir John R. Carnac, took the Chiltern Hundreds. A contest was assured when the bookseller and printer, Richard King, a forthright Conservative, proposed Lord George Charles Gordon Lennox while his opponent for the seat, Henry Riversdale Grenfell, was proposed by Nicholas Adams, a Lymington doctor and supporter of reform, and seconded by Rear-Admiral Thomas Edward Symonds of Yeatton in Hordle. Polling on Thursday 24 May lasted from 8 am to 4 pm and saw Lennox returned with 147 votes against Grenfell's 123. When Lennox, a Liberal-Conservative, took his seat he represented the borough with the sitting member, W.A. Mackinnon, a Liberal.[21]

Lymington's parliamentary representation was

reduced to a single member with the passage of the second Reform Bill in 1867. Eighteen years later, in 1885,[22] the town ceased to be a constituency in its own right and was incorporated in the New Forest Division.

STRUGGLES FOR NEW MUNICIPAL GOVERNMENT

As with most market towns Lymington was gradually drawn into the range of responsibilities that ushered in modern urban local government, but old traditions die hard and there were many attempts to avoid the growing civic duties the law saw fit to place on the councillors.

The Municipal Corporation Act of 1835[23] entailed major changes for Lymington's self-government. Teams of commissioners were appointed to examine the municipalities throughout the kingdom but only one commissioner came to Lymington who, in collecting his evidence, was faced with a few puzzles which could not be satisfactorily resolved.

In the first place he could not accurately identify the boundaries of the borough 'as it contains several extra-borough tenements within the very heart of it, and several borough tenements at the extremities, entirely separated from it'. Historically this has always presented a difficulty, for whilst a general view of the borough could be presented it was often flawed in specific detail. As well as mistakenly concluding that the 'Borough has no Charter', he decided that the borough 'is comprehended within what is called "The Hundred Acres" and there being some doubt as to the exact boundaries of this tract, a deed was executed in the year 1795, by Mrs Elizabeth Guitton, the lady of the manor, and the corporation, on which was drawn a plan, which it was agreed by both parties *should be considered* as within the manor of New Lymington'.[24]

The commissioner reported both on the state of local government in the town and gave prognostications about its future. Much of what he said had little lasting importance but he did discover that the mayor was assisted by a recorder, who had to be a burgess, but 'has no duties whatever to perform'! There was also a town clerk, whose duties included keeping minutes of the corporation's meetings and sending notices of meetings. He received a salary of £3 a year plus certain fees on the election of burgesses and the members of parliament, which netted him, on average, another £7 or £8 annually. The Sergeant-at-Mace had the ceremonial function of bearing the corporation mace but he also collected the quit rents from the borough properties. His salary in 1833 was £8 a year.

The new burgesses were each elected by the mayor and burgesses only. The commissioner reported, 'The number of burgesses has varied considerably. At present there are 32, of whom 9 are resident in or near the town . . . they are all persons in the higher classes of life'. He went on to describe how the numbers elected were manipulated from time to time by the unnamed ruling family, plainly referring to the Burrards. The burgesses alone had had the right to elect the two members of parliament until the Reform Act of 1832 widened the franchise.

The commissioner found that 'there are no borough courts whatever'. The anciently established manorial courts carried out the functions which otherwise would have been exercised by borough courts. He pointed out that there was no jail but there was a lock-up which he described as 'a small cell for placing disorderly persons in during the night, and which is never used but for very temporary purposes'.

The income of the borough was derived mainly from rents and from tolls on markets and fairs. For administrative convenience the corporation leased these at £42 a year. The tolls levied on the fairs and markets were either on 'almost all wares offered for sale' or on the stalls themselves. Saturday was market day and the two fairs were held in May and October. The commissioner noticed that a table giving the rate of tolls was exhibited on a painted board hung in the market house. Dues were taken on all goods imported or exported from the corporation-owned town quay. This included 'wheelidge', a charge of 2d. on every load drawn by waggon across the quay and 1d. on loads drawn from neighbouring quays. As with the market the collection of these dues was leased at £7 a year on a 7-years' lease.

Further income was derived from river dues payable by all vessels using the river from Jack in the Basket inwards. The amount charged depended on the size of the vessel, ranging from 4d. to 2s. 6d. The leasing arrangement for the collection of these dues was on exactly the same terms as those for the quay.

The quit rents were 'small acknowledgements paid by such as have made encroachments, by building on wastes of the corporation or making any projection into the streets'. The commissioner reported that the corporations' average income was £80 10s. but observed 'the rents are seldom collected'.

In the year ending October 1832 the annual expenditure of the corporation was £79 12s. 4d., a sum which came close to the average, and is here reproduced in full:

	£	s	d
Salary and bill of town clerk	6	16	9
Ditto of town serjeant	10	14	7
Quit rent to the lord of the manor for the market-place	7	12	0
Rates paid in respect of the market	3	19	6
Church ringers	2	2	0
Wine for the court leet jury	3	4	6
(It has been customary from time out of memory to give 1 doz. of wine to the leet jury.)			
Some small incidental expenses	2	16	8
Various tradesmen's bills for repairs to the market, town hall, wharf, etc.	42	6	4
	79	12	4
The income collected in this year was	68	19	5
Leaving a balance due to the mayor	10	12	11

Expenditure exceeded income by over £10. The mayor was obliged to meet the cost of any overpayment but was reimbursed the following year.

When the new Act came into force in 1835 Lymington found the old familiar system of burgess control had been replaced by an elected council of 12 members. There was to be a much wider base of voters, similar to that established in the 1832 Reform Act. The mayor and aldermen were to be elected from the councillors. Of the 42 candidates who stood for the first election the following 12 were successful. (The number of votes cast for each is in brackets after their names.) Charles St Barbe (100), Edward Hicks (100), James Monro (96), Robert Lillington Rice (94), William Colborne (84), James Corbin (82), Richard Galpine (82), Isaac Withers (78), Charles Fluder (71), Thomas Gatrell (70), Joseph Keats (70) and Henry Figg (60). The first aldermen were Edward Hicks, James Monro, Richard Galpine and Isaac Withers. Charles St Barbe recorded in his personal memorandum book, 26 December 1835, 'Elected councillor of the Boro' and, a few days later on 1 January, 'Elected mayor (the 1st under the new Municipal Law.'[25]

The Town Hall, sited in the centre of the High Street, in which the corporation had met for so long, was found now to be an obstruction to traffic so in 1858 the council decided to have it demolished.[26] However, there were at that time no funds available to build a replacement so for its future meetings the council leased the Assembly Rooms of the *Angel Hotel* for 21 years at an annual rental of £25.[27] In fact, the council's deliberations continued to be held there for almost another 60 years.

The first Town Clerk following the Municipal Act was James Brown, junior,[28] who had succeeded his father on his death in that year. His annual salary in the mid-nineteenth century was £25.

Edward King (1821-85), author of *Old Times Revisited*, in his private notebook provides a rare personal glimpse of James Brown, junior, a solicitor. He observes of him:

in the good old days, when there was nothing to do and plenty to get, if you were a burgess, and on the right side. The elder Brown had an office just before you came to the Quay, where (with 3 assistants) he had nothing to do except draw his salary'. His son was a "loose fish".' He continued by noting that there was 'always a sort of suspicion about his honesty' and that he had always been 'a free living man and mixed up with women. He left only a daughter; but one or two illegitimate sons (as I have heard) whom he had to bring up. He passed as their guardian . . .He had turned Roman Catholic a year or two before his death but if he confessed his sins, I never heard that he made any restitution as enjoined by religion and morality.[29]

James Brown (1787-1868) relinquished the office of Town Clerk in 1860 and was succeeded by

The restored commemorative gas light column which stood outside the Town Hall in the High Street from 1832 to 1858. After the hall was demolished it was moved to a position outside the church and, finally, when it became defunct, to its present location outside the Royal Lymington Yacht Club.

Edward Horatio Moore, senior partner in the legal firm of Moore and St Barbe.

PUBLIC GAS LIGHTING

In December 1831 an act for providing a lighting and watching system for the town was adopted. And in the following year it was decided to provide gas lighting in the borough under the aegis of the curate, the Rev. Peyton Blakiston, and a progressive townsman, Richard Andrew Grove. The 72 subscribers supporting this scheme raised £3,000 to start the project while two local doctors, John Beckley and William Towsey, proposed the formation of a joint stock company to be called the Lymington Gas and Coke Company to manufacture the gas and maintain the lighting. The iron columns for the gas lights were presented by Sir Harry Burrard Neale (known from the time of his marriage in 1795 as Sir Harry Neale) while his brother, George (later Sir George) Burrard, supplied the lamps. An event commemorated by the construction of a large ornate cast-iron gas standard comprising a tall fluted Doric column bearing two lamps. This standard was first sited opposite the Town Hall and, following the building's demolition in 1858, was transferred to a position outside the parish church. It is now re-erected on the south side of, and close to, the Royal Lymington Yacht Clubhouse and painted silver[30]. The inscriptions cast on the pedestal tell the story:

ERECTED BY SUBSCRIPTION
AS A TRIBUTE
OF RESPECT AND GRATITUDE
TO
ADMIRAL SIR HARRY NEALE BT GCB
FOR HIS MUNIFICENT GIFT
OF
THE IRON COLUMNS
FOR
THE PUBLIC LAMPS
IN THIS TOWN
1832
and on the other side:
THE WHOLE OF THE PUBLIC LAMPS
WERE PRESENTED TO THIS TOWN
BY
GEORGE BURRARD ESQUIRE

POLICE

Elected councillors, though aware no doubt of the changing world around them, were often reluctant to change. There appears to be an innate conservatism running through the habits and behaviour of those responsible citizens who became the local governors. The old system of constables elected by the manorial courts was not adequate for an increasingly complex society. Lymington, considered the problem in 1836 and decided to delay making any changes and retain the services of George Banks and Thomas Bridle as constables 'until further arrangements can be made for a more extensive police'. In the report required by the Home Secretary they stated that as the borough was only small, two officers were sufficient for its care and the council had appointed 'a respectable officer as Chief and [a] night constable' to replace the two constables formerly elected by the court leet. On 12 October 1836 the Sergeant-at-Mace was appointed as the chief constable at a salary of £12 per annum and a constable, George Jerome, at £10 annually.

Though pressed by Captain William Harris of the newly formed county police force to adopt a proper system, in keeping with national directives, the corporation refused to do so because it would require raising a rate to finance the police. This resistance to embarking on a change of policing arrangements was shaken when in 1852 the Chief Constable for Hampshire wrote to the town clerk setting out the terms for replacing the parish constable system with officers from the professional county force. His ultimatum was reinforced in the following months when a number of citizens petitioned the council asking for the county constabulary to take responsibility for the town. This system was implemented from 29 November 1852 and a rate to cover the cost was authorised the following day. By 1853 Lymington had two resident constables and an arrangement to supplement these if it should prove necessary.[31] The first police station was established in an already existing house, formerly belonging to Dr William Towsey, in Gosport Street (now a restaurant).

THE POOR LAW

The Old Poor Law had recognised community responsibility for the care of the sick, maimed, lunatic and the lying-in of women. Much expenditure from the poor rate was devoted to health care. The Poor Law Amendment Act (1834)[32] had the effect of limiting public health care to those in receipt of benefit, initially only to those in the newly erected workhouses. Lymington became the centre for a union of six parishes – Lymington, Boldre, Brockenhurst, Milford, Milton and Hordle – with a combined population in 1831 of 9,501. Twelve guardians were appointed to oversee the administration of the union, four from Lymington and the remainder from the surrounding parishes.[33] The new brick-built workhouse (the 'Union') was constructed near the old parish workhouse on the top of the hill facing New Lane (see plan). In shape it conformed to the 'cross plan'. The building cost £4,500 and was completed in

The south façade of the Lymington Union Workhouse as it appeared about the time of its completion in 1838.

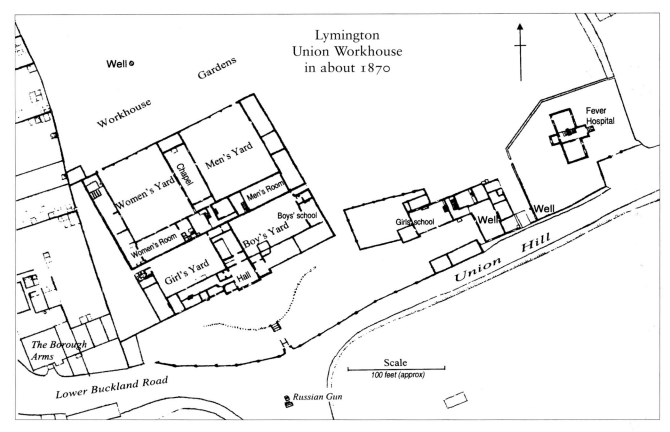

Plan of the Union Workhouse designed by Samuel Kempthorne.

1838. The original plan was to provide accommodation for 270 inmates under the standard principle of 'less eligibility', in other words, that the working conditions within the house should be more rigorous and unpleasant, in other words less eligible, than those outside.

A master and matron were appointed to run the workhouse under a clearly defined set of regulations. Amongst the duties imposed were those of reading prayers and saying grace before each meal. The master was to inspect the dormitories each morning at nine to ensure they were clean and tidy. Inmates had to be in bed by 9 p.m. with lights out. The matron's tasks were similar but dealt especially with the women and children, including responsibility for their moral behaviour.

Under the regime of the New Poor Law the dignity of the individual was effectively abandoned and those arriving at the workhouse had to be examined by the medical officer after being bathed and deloused. They were then allocated a dormitory ward in which to sleep. As males and females slept in separate dormitories married couples were separated. The master was instructed to encourage employment, punctuality, cleanliness and obedience to the workhouse rules[34]. Three acres of vegetable gardens were provided around the house, which it was intended would supply fresh produce for the inmates.

During the first decade of operation under the New Poor Law, workhouses often earned the epithet 'Bastilles' because of the rigour of a regime that at times seemed openly cruel. In due course a Poor Law Board responsible to parliament was created ushering in a gradual improvement of conditions.

In 1851 Alexander and Mary Thompson were master and matron when there were 123 inmates resident in the workhouse. Of these 40 came from Lymington, 33 from Boldre, 18 from Milford, 11 from Milton, 4 from Brockenhurst and one from

Hordle, the remainder came from further afield. By 1857 the number was reduced to 114. This downward trend was to continue throughout the nineteenth century so that by 1895 there were only 44 in the workhouse (including staff). The Workhouse also had its own school and in 1851 the master was James George and a Lymington woman, Amelia Earley, was the mistress.[35]

LOCAL BOARD OF HEALTH

There were significant advances in the health care of the nation's population from the eighteenth century onwards. Unfortunately, these advances were neither uniform in application nor always based on a scientific understanding of diseases or their causes. The government intervened with reports and legislation that sought to make health care more widely available. An important step along this road was the formation of Local Boards of Health. It is interesting to note that W.A. Mackinnon, MP for Lymington, was among those members who strongly supported the Health of Towns Bill which led to the Public Health Act of 1848.[36] The impetus underlying this legislation came largely from the great and frightening cholera outbreak of 1830.

In December 1851 the Lymington council received a letter from the Board of Health stating that 'the prevalence of fever and diarrhoea at Lymington gives strong grounds for supposing that the population are suffering from a neglect of sanitary precautions'.[37] This was undoubtedly true for even the much later report of 1867 described Broad Lane as 'filthy and unwholesome', Station Street as 'becoming offensive from the want of sewerage' and 'the state of the Quays where the principal sewers of the Town now empty themselves' as disgusting.[38] Even the *Lymington Chronicle* had reported that the streets 'in some places have the appearance of an open bog'.[39]

Once again the town's blinkered conservatism was partly to blame. During an earlier national cholera outbreak one person at a public meeting in the town declared that, 'cholera is in the hand of the Most High and if the meeting would but keep His commandments there would be no need of any Health Board'.[40]

The Fever Hospital in the grounds of the Union Workhouse. Later designated 'The Master's House'. This building was preserved from demolition by the actions of the Lymington Society in 2005.

The Local Board of Health was established in Lymington in September 1858 but it was nine years before the first meeting was held when a clerk was appointed at a salary of £65 a year plus £10 for the use of his house as an office. The first rate was confirmed on 9 April 1867 and was intended to raise £533. The responsibilities of the board, taking over some of those previously the preserve of the parish and the poor law officers, covered repairs to highways and paving, cleaning and watering streets, public lighting, and the fire service. Dr Airy, the first medical officer, in returning his annual reports, was at pains to inform the board of the inadequacies of fresh water supply and deficiencies in sewage disposal.

Despite such misgivings William Allingham, both a poet and Lymington's customs house officer, saw Lymington as a safe haven from disease, as he noted in his diary on 1 August 1866, 'Newspaper says cholera is increasing. I ask Ned to come down [from London] to Lymington, with wife and babes'[41].

Some provision for the disposal of sewage, by gravitation, through brick built conduits discharging into the river had been attempted early in Lymington's history. However, as fresh water was pumped from wells situated on nearly every property (Jones states that 'there were over 600 in

Press advertisement for dental services provided by Aaron Samuel Jones at Mrs Rogers's Berlin Repository at 29 High Street on 'the second Monday of every month'.

the district'[42]), supplies could be easily contaminated by seepage from foul water drains, creating potentially serious risks to health. Lymingtonian dislike of change was again revealed when 'two-thirds of the people said that if either a water-supply or a sewerage system were laid down they would refuse to be connected'.[43] The deterrent was largely, though not solely, the concern about the anticipated costs.

A consequence of all this legislation and its promise of greater interference in public life, together with its potential for raising rates, led to opposition. In Lymington this was given substance by the formation of its first Ratepayers' Association. 'An Old Inhabitant' wrote to the *Lymington Chronicle* on 17 August 1883 complaining that 'People who don't like smells must hold their noses . . . If Health suffers send for a doctor, and take physic. If all nuisances were abolished there would be no doctors and people would live too long. It is absurd to be too particular in these matters. Local Boards are no good'. As Jonathan Raban was to remark more than a century later, 'Their conservatism, in every sense of the word, was ardent'.[44]

Typhoid, though never of epidemic proportions, regularly claimed victims. Good supplies of fresh, clean water were essential if outbreaks were to be avoided but years of wrangling and debate failed to achieve anything. It was not until 1880 that positive moves were made and then the first well, costing £1,400, collapsed and became choked with sand. The first reliable supply, calculated as producing 28½ million gallons a year,[45] came from St John's Well at Ampress which supplied water to a tower erected behind the *Hearts of Oak* pub near the playing fields. It was not until 1898 that the geologist and expert on the Hampshire Basin, Clement Reid, then living at Milford-on-Sea, gave his professional opinion that an unlimited supply of pure water could be found at Ampress at a depth of 350 feet. However, it was 1908 before this supply was successfully tapped with an artesian bore pipe giving a sufficient and reliable supply. A new water tower was constructed at Buckland as an additional reservoir in 1931-2.

An increasing population, and a greater understanding of the way in which diseases were transmitted, made continued use of the parish churchyard, though enlarged, increasingly unsatisfactory for burying the dead. The Local Board authorised the purchase of land at Pennington for the construction of a cemetery, which was opened by the Bishop of Guildford in October 1890.

The physical well-being of the population had been catered for by individual doctors. The poorer members of the community received their care during sickness through local doctors and surgeons appointed by the Poor Law officers who were engaged by renewable annual contracts. In the first decades of the nineteenth century amongst the most notable were William Towsey, MD, of Lymington who served, not only the town but the surrounding parishes, and Robert Smith, described as a surgeon. It seems that John Nike had earned a special place of affection in the community for his care and concern for the sick, as his memorial tablet in the church states:

To the memory of John Nike Esqre
who for two and twenty years exercised the profession
of surgeon in this town and neighbourhood, with skill
and exemplary humanity.
To the rich and poor he was alike unremitting in his

attention;while to the latter he was a most liberal
benefactor in humble imitation of his Divine Master
"He went about doing good".
His strength could not keep pace with his exertions
amd he fell a victim to the cause of humanity in the
prime of life on the seventh day of Febry MDCCCXXVII,
aged XLII years.
This tablet was erected by the voluntary subscriptions
of the greater part of the inhabitants of Lymington and
its vicinity,
As a token of their personal esteem, and their
admiration of his virtues.

Dental care in the mid to late nineteenth century appears to have been provided by visiting dental surgeons. From 1850 until at least 1877 Samuel Aaron Jones of Portland Terrace, Southampton visited the town on the second Monday of every month and, when his son Edward Newton Jones joined the practice, an additional visit was made on the fourth Monday also. 'Patients requiring the Nitrous Oxide Gas ensuring all immunity from Pain, will kindly make a written appointment a few days previously', so stated their advertisement in 1877. Another Southampton dentist from Anglesea Place, James McLachlan, held his Lymington surgery on the first and third Tuesdays of every month at 72 High Street and could offer 'A complete set of Teeth from Five Guineas, constructed upon the most approved principles'.[46]

COMMUNICATIONS & COMMERCE

Lymington entered the nineteenth century as a town served by an adequate coaching service. In the 1850s carriers regularly operated to and from Christchurch, Ringwood, Romsey and Salisbury and, with the opening of the Southampton and Dorchester Railway station at Brockenhurst in 1847, omnibuses ran from the *Angel* and *Nag's Head* inns to meet all trains. Prior to the opening of the railway there was even a regular goods service from London operated by M. Lipscomb of the *White Horse Inn*, Cheapside, who had fly-wagons bringing goods to Lymington and the surrounding towns on a regular basis.

The arrival of the railway was to dramatically change the nature of road communication and it was not long before Lymington was clamouring for its own railway connection. A public meeting held in August 1853 pressed for the building of a branch line from Brockenhurst to Lymington. But as is so often the case in the affairs of the town there were delays (on this occasion, it must be said, not of its own making). To maintain the initiative the promoters advertised in the local press inviting individuals to subscribe to the share issue for the proposed railway. The following appeared in the *Dorset County Chronicle* for 30 August 1855:

LYMINGTON RAILWAY, to CONNECT the
Town and Port of LYMINGTON, YARMOUTH,
FRESHWATER, and the WESTERN PORTION of the ISLE OF
WIGHT, with the *Southampton* and *Dorchester Railway*
at
Brockenhurst.
Length of Line 4¼ Miles
Capital £30,000, in Shares of £10 each.
Deposit £1 per Share.
ENGINEER:
Hamilton H. Fulton, M. Inst. C.E.,
8 Great Queen Streeet, Westminster.
JOINT SOLICITORS:
JAMES BROWN, Esq., Town Clerk, Lymington
WM. THOS. MANNING, Esq., 5 Whitehall, Westminster.
A detailed Prospectus will shortly appear, in the mean-
time Landowners and others interested in the under-
taking are respectfully invited to communicate with the
Solicitors.

Subscribers backed the scheme. The private act of parliament promoting the railway received royal assent on 7 July 1856. As a result the Lymington Railway Company was formed with directors drawn from the leading professional and businessmen in the town, namely, Edward Hicks (solicitor), Charles Fluder (surgeon), George Foster St Barbe (banker), Richard Sharp (solicitor), Alfred Mew (brewer) and William Squire. The cutting of the first sod took place on 8 January 1857 and within a year four miles of track had been laid from the main line at Brockenhurst, over the heathland at Setley, through Battramsley and Ampress into Lymington to a point where a temporary wooden station could be erected at Bridge Road. Unfortunately, during construction a 12-year old lad, James Pressey, had been playing on the line despite warnings not to do so, and was crushed to

The earliest known photograph of Lymington railway station, probably about 1870.

death by a wagon on 9 February 1858.[47] The site for the permanent terminal station was to be an old mill pond which needed draining and filling; work that was going to take some time. Great celebrations were planned for the opening in May but no doubt the delays dampened the promoters' enthusiasm so when the line did open it did so with

Lymington railway station. This modern photograph shows the imposing brick-built buildings of Lymington station. The two gable ends and flat roof extension to the right were added later in the nineteenth century.

'no demonstrations of any kind'[48]

The Lymington branch line opened officially on 12 July 1858. The new town station was opened 14 months later and a short street, aptly named Station Street, constructed eastwards from Gosport Street to link with it.

The line was continued beyond the station to a jetty, which was opened in 1861 allowing Isle of Wight ferry steamers to berth alongside. However, the paddle steamers could not use the jetty at all tides and there were some other difficulties. It was soon realised that a more drastic solution was needed. So in August 1881 the London and South Western Railway Company, who had taken over the running of the Lymington branch, received parliamentary authority to extend the line across the river to a deep water berth on the eastern side. A 70-yard long viaduct, supported on steel piles, was constructed to carry the line over the Lymington River to its new terminus to be named Lymington Pier. This was opened officially on 1 May 1884.

After a slow start the financial viability of the branch line was vindicated and profits enabled dividends to be paid regularly to its shareholders; the rate of return in 1877 was 3½%.[49]

The regularity and reliability of the Lymington-Yarmouth ferry service had been much enhanced

Above This engraving, made about 1860, is a view from the Walhampton side looking across to the railway and the jetty in the centre of the picture. The rowing boat in the foreground is the Lymington-Walhampton ferry.

Below The railway bridge, opened in 1884, which carried the extended line across the river to a new terminal and landing stage.

Lymington Harbour with the 1884 railway bridge in the foreground, and the *Mayflower* moored between the bridge and the quay.

when steam powered boats were introduced in 1830 with the *Glasgow*, a 16 h.p. paddler. By 1839 she was making four return trips daily departing from Lymington at 9 a.m., 11 a.m., 3 p.m. and 5 p.m.[50]

The Solent Sea Steam Packet Company of Lymington was founded to run the Lymington-Isle of Wight Ferry services and by 1840 it was able to commission its own vessel. An agreement was drawn up on 30 January, 1841 between William Alltoft Summers, John Thomas Groves and Charles Arthur Day of Mill Place Ironworks on the Itchen at Southampton and John Blakiston and Richard Galpine of Lymington and William Squire of Yarmouth, all members of the Solent Sea Steam Packet Co. The Ironworks was to build a steamship, with engine of 25 h.p., on or before the 10 April, 1841, for the sum of £2,275 with a two month

guarantee following delivery. The agreement contained a penalty clause whereby the Solent company could withhold payment at the rate of £10 a day for each day the vessel was delayed in delivery after the 10 April 1841. It was, in fact, not launched until 10 May! This all-iron ship was fitted with paddles and drew only 3 feet 4 inches. Water closets for men were fitted by the paddle box and for the ladies in their cabin. There was no specification for any life-saving equipment.[51] Building on the success of this ship a second, named the *Solent*, was constructed. After entering service the *Solent* mainly served the Lymington-Southampton and Lymington-Portsmouth routes while the *Glasgow* maintained the Lymington-Yarmouth ferry service. The *Red Lion*, a wooden paddler, joined the small fleet in June 1858[52] arriving in time to serve the railway connection from the jetty. The *Solent* was withdrawn from service in 1861 and replaced by a second vessel bearing the same name which was constructed by the Lymington ship and yacht builders, G. & J. Inman, in 1863. She was timber-built and had sleek lines reminiscent of a yacht. In service she was first skippered by Captain J.M. Cribb and continued her working life until 1901.

In 1866 a fine iron-built paddler, the *Mayflower*, was added to the fleet of the Solent company and brought a touch of Victorian luxury with wood-panelled cabins lit by stained glass windows. She served as a ferry until 1912.[53] She made a small but immensely significant contribution to radio communication when, in December 1897 Guglielmo Marconi (1874-1937) chartered the *Mayflower* to expand his experiments in transmitting wireless signals. The vessel was fitted with a receiving apparatus, the first in the world to be so equipped, while the transmitter, sited on a hill behind Totland Bay, broadcast signals. The success was considerable, representing the first major step in shore to ship communication, as contact was maintained for a distance of 18 miles.[54]

In July 1884 the Solent Sea Steam Packet Co. was purchased for £2,750 by the London and South-Western Railway Company.[55]

In the 1850s steam paddlers were running from Lymington to Cowes, Portsmouth, Ryde and Southampton on Tuesdays and Fridays each week, but this service was abandoned once the railway network became established leaving the Yarmouth to Lymington ferry as the only route.

A popular maritime activity provided by the paddlers and much enjoyed by the people of Lymington and the surrounding area were occasional moonlight cruises. On one such excursion to the Needles in the summer of 1886 'the steamer was crowded. The weather was beautifully fine, and the trip was much enjoyed'.[56]

YACHT BUILDING

The once important salt industry had died by the mid-nineteenth century so it was fortunate that the conjunction of two influential figures should usher in an alternative industry of lasting commercial importance to replace it, that of yacht building. The first of these was Joseph Weld (1777-1863), a substantial landowner, who had been given Pylewell Park estate lying two miles east of Lymington, as a wedding present by his father in 1801, probably

The *Mayflower* paddle steamer with a barge in tow, leaving for the Isle of Wight.

with the idea of enabling him to indulge his enthusiasm for yachting.[57] The second was Thomas Inman (1787-1870), a boat builder from Hastings, who on a visit to the Solent saw the potential of Lymington as a yacht building centre. Inman established himself first at Pylewell Hard and then, by 1820, on the Lymington River.

Another event which gave impetus to the industry was the foundation of the Yacht Club in 1815 which was later to become the Royal Yacht Squadron, with both Joseph Weld and his brother,

Joseph Weld (1777-1863) owned Pylewell estate from 1801 to 1850. He was a passionate yachtsman and an enthusiastic farmer.

An engraving shows the *Alarm* winning the Ladies Challenge Cup in 1830.

James, as founder members. Inman's first boat, the 20-ton *Hind*, built for N. Polhill, was completed the same year as he arrived. The much more ambitious 85-ton cutter, *Arrow*, was constructed for Joseph Weld in the following year and, in 1830, the magnificent *Alarm*, a 193-ton cutter, costing around £30,000. In racing these vessels were to achieve great success; a fact poignantly recognised in the following comment: 'A hope has been expressed that the old *Arrow* like the *Alarm* will retire from future contests with all the honours they have so

Thomas Inman, boat builder.

A pencil drawing of *The Alarm Inn* at the bottom of Quay Hill by Ruth Collingridge in about 1925. The inn was named after Joseph Weld's racing yacht, the *Alarm*.

nobly won, and leave the field open to other yachts who might thereby be induced to enter'.[58] Large sums of money were spent by Joseph Weld on his Inman-built yachts, for example the *Lulworth*, a 127-ton cutter, built in 1828, cost over £14,000 but in addition to this he was paying Inman about £1,200 annually for yacht maintenance. His lifetime winnings of about £3,000 pale into insignificance when compared with the outlay.

In view of Weld's patronage of the Inman boat yard it is easy to understand why, on the completion of the *Lulworth*, Lymington tradesmen, in acknowledgement of the business he had brought to the town, should have sent him the following letter:

We the undersigned inhabitants of Lymington beg your acceptance of the accompanying Flag for the use of your Yacht *Lulworth* and we must sincerely hope she will prove a successful competitor.
To yourself, sir, and all your family, we offer our hearty good wishes – may health and happiness, be your constant attendant.

Joseph Skeats [carpenter], John Upwards, William Hibberd [brewer], William Suffield [plumber], Edward May [builder, stone mason], William Norris [draper], R.A. Grove [grocer], Thos. Skeats [surgeon], Jos. Gatrell [chemist], Jas. Brown, Jr. [Town Clerk], Jon(?) Rutter [wine merchant], Charles Brown, Henry Mew [brewer], Benjn. Baskett[59]

The largest yacht built by the Inman's shipyard was the 366-ton *Fortuna* for Adrian Hope in 1876. The founder of the business, Thomas Inman, retired in 1845 and was succeeded by his sons George and James. They traded under the name G. & J. Inman, though after two years the mentally unstable James ceased to have any direct connection. Between its foundation and 1889 the yard built 118 yachts.[60] It is salutary to realise that work on yachts extended beyond the immediate yacht building yards to the building trade as Rashley and Co., founded in 1859 with premises in the High Street, often carried out work on their superstructure.[61] In 1891 Elgars, William Le Roy and H.L. Swatridge were all engaged in plumbing and decorating yachts in addition to their more usual work on houses.

Thomas Inman's yard was so successful that he was able to extend this by purchasing land lying between the river and Bath Road and King's Saltern

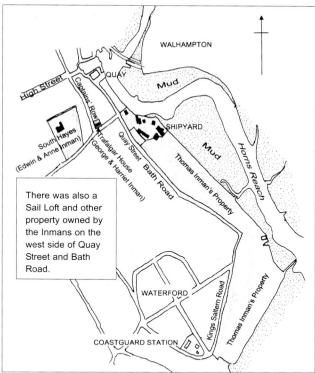

The principal properties of the Inman family in Lymington.

Road (see map above).

Thomas Inman also constructed much smaller boats as is revealed in the comment made by the enthusiastic wildfowler, Col. Peter Hawker, 'The punt, built by a man of great celebrity, Mr Thomas Inman, appears to be the neatest and best I ever had'.[62] Not all boat builders aspired to the standards of Inman if we are to believe a letter written by Hawker to the press:

I beg, through the medium of your paper to publish the inclosed Receipt to a bill of Mr Cooper, boat-builder, in Lymington for *"repairs"* (done in such a bungling manner, as to be, the day after delivery, quite unserviceable) to a small canoe, which with oars complete was *made*, at Poole, expressly to my order, *for three pounds*.

I should have left for some one else to expose such Lymington boat-builders' charges to gentlemen, had not this man treated me with the greatest impertinence, and with no other provocation than my offering to bet him the price of his bill, which he refused to accept . . . (Mr Cooper is, I understand a METHODIST! one of the ELECT!) . . .

Captains' Row still retains a splendid array of late eighteenth century houses, once much used as the residences of families connected with maritime life.

The appropriately named Nelson Place, a terrace of fine houses close to the quay area, many once occupied by sailors.

The receipt, signed by D. Cooper, came to £2 16s. 11d. and what had so incensed Hawker was the fact that a Milford boat-builder, Mr Ireland, could have done the job 'most perfectly' for £1 10s.[63]

Other notable Lymington yachtsmen of the period were George Alexander Fullerton[64] and Col. Shedden. King recites an intriguing anecdote concerning the former when sailing the yacht, *Zephyr*:

> Somewhere about the year 1806, Mr Fullerton, accompanied by his friend, Mr Weld, of Lulworth Castle, and by two other friends, was sailing outside the Needles, when to their consternation, they espied a French privateer bearing down upon them. This was an awkward position, indeed, for at that time we were at war with France, and to be taken prisoner by the French conveyed anything but pleasant thoughts to the minds of the occupants of the gallant little yacht: with all speed therefore they sailed away, and were fortunate in reaching Hurst Castle, and thus escaping the threatened danger . . .[65]

White's *Hampshire Directory* of 1878 records that 'Mr Inman employs here about 70 men and boys[66] in building and repairing yachts, schooners, etc., and is celebrated for his "improved sterns and afterbodies"'. A press report stated that 'the shipbuilding yard will be fully employed during the winter. At Messrs. Inman's yard full time was commenced on Monday and at Watkins,[67] activity is displayed in executing orders in hand'.[68] Allingham, referring to the Solent, stated that 'There are at least 7000 men and boys, all picked, engaged in Yachts', which, if true, reinforces its economic importance. However, he was extremely critical of the privileges granted to these owners: 'They pay no lighthouse dues, no Port or Harbour Dues, no fees on engaging or discharging men, all of which must be paid by every merchant vessel . . . Why should rich owners of Pleasure Yachts be thus favoured? The only reason I have heard given is that yachting is a "nursery for the Navy". Is it?'[69]

The Inman family, particularly George and his son Edwin, according to Jones 'became far too easy going in business, and the habits of both him and his son were not conducive to success'[70] consequently the yards were sold in 1887 and passed through a succession of owners, including Watkins, until bought by Frank Aubrey May, then owner of the Berthon Boat Company, in 1918.

The maritime role of Lymington remained

A view down a crowded Quay Hill, with the Solent Inn in the background.

important throughout Victorian times. By the 1850s there was a Customs House[71] and a harbour master's office near the Quay and of the 16 insurance companies represented through agents in the town one, the National Mercantile was specifically maritime. Twelve master mariners were recorded as resident in the town, eight, perhaps not unexpectedly, living either in Nelson Place or Captains' Row, three in Bath Road and only one much further out in Southampton Buildings. In 1851 William D. Murray was the river pilot with his base at the Quay.

The maritime life was closely integrated with that of the wider town. In 1891 there are recorded 31 residents engaged as mariners, sailors and seamen; three yacht captains and two ship's engineers. A sail loft in Bath Road (later to become the Drill Hall) and the Spar Loft in Quay Street were part of the Inman boatbuilding enterprise.

The Drill Hall in Bath Rd, originally Inman's sail loft.

TRADE & RETAILING

Throughout the nineteenth the Saturday markets attracted produce and customers from the surrounding areas. The liveliness of these in around 1840 is recounted by a resident:

> Saturday was the day, and a busy day it was. The underpart or ground floor of the Town Hall was well supplied with fish, vegetables and dairy produce, and farmers' daughters did not think it beneath them to attend and sell their poultry, butter, eggs, etc. Outside the Market House was a row of butchers' shambles supplied with excellent meat by butchers from Milford, Brockenhurst and Lymington, and housekeepers made it a rule to go to market and buy what they wanted.[72]

Before the Magistrate by George Elgar Hicks.

A rather fine example of life connected with the nineteenth century market comes from the painting by the Lymington born artist, George Elgar Hicks (1824-1914).[73] In a large oil painting, executed in 1865-6, he shows the magistrates' court (Petty Sessions) held in a room in the *Anchor & Hope* inn with portraits of the four presiding JPs: William Peere Williams Freeman of Pylewell, Edward Hicks the artist's father and chairman of the magistrates, Sir George Burrard of Walhampton and Captain William Lindsey Shedden of Delaware Cottage. The clerk of the court, Edward Horatio Moore, stands with notes in his hand. The plaintiff standing is Mrs Elizabeth Hampton, a furniture broker of the High Street.[74] She is evidently being arraigned for striking a woman whose bandaged head bears witness to the attack. Even before the court Mrs Hampton is continuing to threaten her accuser with a furled umbrella while the policeman, Constable Wisdom, restrains her with his arm. The details of the audience in the courtroom are quite splendidly captured and show clearly the case is being tried on market day.[75] A basket containing two geese stands on the floor whilst other local folk gaze attentively at the drama unfolding before them. The crux of the case appears to be a bonnet, removed from a hat box, which is being held up by the constable as an exhibit. Above the large table at which the magistrates sit is a fishtail gas lamp, there is a bundle of documents stacked in the clerk's top hat, which stands on the floor, and details of the case are being noted down with a quill pen. On the wall of the courtroom are a number of posters, one advertising 'Randall's Soda Water, Lemonade, Ginger Beer', another proclaims the advantages of artificial manure shipped in at Deptford Creek, whilst a third, hanging askew, announces the programme of London's 'Royal' theatre.[76]

Increasingly the role of the retail shops grew, outpacing the weekly markets by providing a more consistent and reliable form of trading. The High Street, gravelled and with paved drains on either side, in 1851 boasted a wide variety of shops, as did the streets and lanes immediately adjoining it. Sensibly, the luxury retailers were concentrated in the High Street, amongst them the solitary jeweller and watchmaker, Charles Padbury at 33, adjoining the *Nags Head;* three china and glass dealers, four booksellers, stationers and printers, two of whom ran circulating libraries, and two gunsmiths, John Jeffery and Alfred Clayton. The latter's services were much used by Col. Peter Hawker who on one occasion referred to 'my new ignition' guns which

A solitary boy stands nonchalantly in the centre of the High Street at 10 am on what seems to be a very quiet day sometime in the early years of the twentieth century. It is not a Sunday as the sunblinds are erected outside the shops on the north side of the street.

Clayton was making.77 Richard Galpine's circulating library at 88 High Street, bore the name of Lymington Book Society and numbered amongst its 25 members, Charles St Barbe, William Towsey, Percival Lewis, Sir Harry Neale and the Rev. Henry Comyn. Books could be borrowed for seven days. The three chemists and druggists were also sited in the High Street.

Grocers, butchers, haberdashers and iron-mongers, though well represented in the High Street, also had premises spread around the side streets. For example, out of 13 milliners and dressmakers only four had High Street premises and of the 14 grocery and sundry dealers there were only two with shops in the High Street. Those engaged in craft and workshop activities such as

Topp the Butchers at 20 High Street sets out a magnificent display of carcasses. The butcher stands proudly at the door. Note the gas standard to the left.

Three family businesses in the High Street: Francis Dale, tailor, G. Elliott, outfitters, later to move to the other side of the High Street, and R.J. Klitz, music saloon.

saddlery, coach and gig builders, cabinet makers and coopers were also spread throughout the borough with relatively few represented in the main thoroughfare.

One notable business, that of King's the booksellers, printers and stationers, is well documented. Charles King arrived early in the nineteenth century from Dorchester and in 1817

Edward King (1821-85), succeeded his father successfully continuing the business of bookseller, stationer and printer. He was three times mayor of Lymington.

was joined by his nephew, Richard from Yeovil, who was a hard working and astute businessman. He became a substantial property owner and his daughter, Harriett, married George Inman the shipbuilder.[78]

The importance of the High Street meant that it was where the professional occupations such as banking, law and insurance were predominantly represented. The first bank had been established as early as 1788 by Charles St Barbe (1750-1826); in the 1850s it was designated as a partnership with Charles, Samuel and George St Barbe and by 1878 it was trading as Daniel, St Barbe, Edmonds and Co., later to be absorbed by the Capital and Counties Bank which was, in turn, taken over by Lloyds. Charles St Barbe, eldest son of the founder, now a prosperous banker, moved into his fine mansion, Belle Vue House (48 High Street) on Lady Day, 1828.[79] The Wilts and Dorset Bank also had a branch in the High Street in the mid-nineteenth century.

Banking played a vital role in the economic well-being of the town as the handling of money, including the raising of loans, meant trade and

A £5 note issued for St Barbe's bank in Lymington (mid-19th century). As was normal commercial practice at that time the note could also be drawn on a London bank.

Above The tall building on the left was still called 'The Old Bank House' recalling the time that it was St Barbe's Lymington Bank, before it transferred to 48 High Street, on the opposite side.

Below Bellevue House built in 1786 became the home of Charles St Barbe the banker in 1828. Later it was to be the Noake sisters' girls' boarding school.

business could run more successfully. It was thought that even those on lowly incomes, such as labourers, artisans and small tradesmen, could benefit by being given access to a bank and in February 1818 a savings bank called The Lymington Provident Institution was founded. By about 1850 there were nearly a thousand depositors with well over £38,000 invested. It had excessively restricted opening times, being only open for business on Saturday, market day, between 1 and 2 o'clock.

A detailed glimpse into aspects of retailing may be obtained from the letters of Henry Hapgood (1810-90), the Lymington Registrar and London and South-Western Railway delivery agent. In April 1849 he wrote to his fiancée, Leah Barrow of Newtown Farm, stating that 'if the pair of Shoes I have sent you should not suit you return them by the servant this evening and I will get some from Whitchells . . . the pair of shoes I sent today are from Burton; he had no more of that size on hand, the price is 4s. 6d. – don't keep unless they suit both as to fit and price.' The shoemakers referred to are James Whitchell and James Burton, both with premises in the High Street.

In November he referred to George Clark and Sons, wholesale grocers and tallow chandlers in the High Street, when he wrote, 'I could get no bacon at Clark's under 7½d. a pound that was new home cured, they have some now, just ready, of Mr Milner's fattening and I intend sending you a small piece tomorrow for trial. The pieces I sent yesterday were from Mr Gibbs' shop, the largest piece is 7d. and the smaller piece 5½d. a lb., by the score, the

first mentioned is Irish the latter American'.[80] Richard Gibbs was another grocer with premises in the High Street, opposite the church on the corner of Church Lane.

Interestingly, neither Clark or Gibbs was in business by 1878, which illustrates how some enterprises operated as family concerns for generations (such as Elliotts, Kings, Klitzes and Rands) whilst others, seemingly just as viable, changed hands on a regular, and often short-term, basis.

Though the local gentry did much of their shopping in London they nevertheless patronised

Above Fords furnishings shop at 62 High Street was formerly Richard Gibbs' grocery stores. Today it is Burwoods, and still sells furniture and domestic fittings.

Below The advertising card of Hewlett, saddlers and harness makers, established in Lymington in about 1795, representing one of the many practitioners of this important occupation when horse transport for both social and commercial purposes was dominant.

many Lymington shops, as we can see for example from bills sent in 1858 to the Honourable Lady Henrietta Morant of Brockenhurst from dealers such as Frederick Watson, book and music seller, printer, binder and stationer who also ran Galpine's Library, and William Good a linen and woollen draper.[81]

The central importance of horses for riding and as draught animals is revealed in the establishment of the Lymington Stud sometime in the early 1850s and continuing through to the 1870s. It was a large establishment situated at the southern end of Southampton Road, founded by Teesdale and Chamberlayne but run for about 20 years by Henry Thorne, who lived in 26 Southampton Buildings. It was very well appointed with 40 roomy boxes described as being '18 ft square, padded all round, well-ventilated, and as sweet and clean as a drawing room'. There was attached to the stud 40 acres of land where now is Eastern and Middle Roads. In the mid-1860s one of the stallions was an Arabian horse belonging to Lord George Gordon Lennox, the MP for Lymington. This animal was lodged at the stud for the benefit of poor people having ponies on the forest, the object being to improve the breed. In addition to the stallions the stud was home for

Press advertisement for William Good and Son with their premises at 55 High Street.

many breeding mares.

Press advertisements, too, throw light on trading in the town. Good and Son ask rhetorically of readers of *The Lymington Chronicle* 'Why do Black Silks wear so badly?' No answer is actually given but it is a problem whose solution we are assured lies in the purchase of black silks from Goods, who have negotiated special deals with eminent silk weavers in Lyons and Spitalfields.[82] Other businesses acted as agents for London firms, demonstrating the growing importance of the large manufacturers and dealers in supplying provincial outlets. For example, Isaac Archer, tailor and habit maker, of Regents Street, London, 'Begs most respectfully to return his sincere Thanks to the Nobility and Gentry of Lymington and its Vicinity, who have honored him with their Commands and trusts that by a strict Attention to those Orders with which he may be favored, to merit their Patronage and Support and begs to inform them of his intention to be at Lymington' on Friday, 8 January 1841.

Coal continued to be delivered directly to the quays in Lymington, mainly from collier vessels trading from Sunderland. Alfred Cole, the Milford sub-postmaster, recalls, 'Our coal was obtained from Lymington, most being brought there in sailing ships. When a cargo arrived, the coal merchants sent out notices that a cargo was being discharged at the Town Quay and quoting the price,

which was lower if loaded from a ship than if obtained from the store. My grandfather sold coal and I have often been with him in with the cart and watched the unloading. One brig, the *Laura*, I particularly remember; I should think she must have been a hundred years old and had probably been trading between Lymington and Sunderland during the whole of her existence'.[83]

The number of inns and public houses in the borough at any one time varied but in 1859 there were 20 of which three made provision for posting and travellers, namely, *The Angel* (earlier *The George*), *The Anchor and Hope* and *The Nag's Head. The Travellers' Rest* at 129 High Street was a lodging house for men and women in search of work. Of the others no fewer than six were clustered around the river. Beer and ale were still brewed locally and we find five breweries operating in the mid-nineteenth century.[84] Contrasting with the position revealed in an advertisement of 1776 for selling the lease on a 'convenient common brewhouse, situated near the Quay' it was stated that 'the copper boils five hogsheads, and there is no other common brewhouse in the town of Lymington'.[85]

FARMING & THE AGRICULTURAL RIOTS

Farming within the parish of Lymington remained an important economic element in the life of the community. The parish covered approximately 1,200 acres of which about 1,150 were devoted to farming.

In 1799 the Lymington Agricultural Society had been formed with John Richman as secretary and Charles St Barbe as treasurer. Its aim was to improve agricultural practice on the Lymington farms and those in the adjoining parishes. Various premiums or prizes were authorized and awarded to agricultural workers who attained a certain standard. Amongst the founding members were Sir Harry Neale, Sir Matthew Blakiston, the Rev. Ellis Jones, curate of Lymington, and William Rooke of Woodside.[86]

The society appears to have become moribund and a call was made in a letter in 1869 to re-establish the Lymington Agricultural Society. It

A harvest scene on an unidentified Lymington farm in 1905, probably at Woodside.

came from a large landowner, William Cornwallis-West of Newlands, Milford, in which he stated that he had been for some years connected with the Milton, Milford and Hordle Society but suggested the new one he was advocating should comprise all the parishes of the Lymington Union. He concluded his letter by stating: 'If the present active secretary (Mr Hayward) of the Milford and Milton Society will act cordially with some other agriculturists connected with Lymington, there is no reason why we should not have a very flourishing society'.[87]

A rare surviving medal issued for ploughing prowess by the Lymington Agricultural Society in 1846. It was presented by R. Jennins of Carrington Farm in Milford.

In Lymington itself the main farms lay to the north and south of the town. The 53 acres of Ampress Farm were largely devoted to arable crops, but the farm was hard hit when the railway arrived in 1858, constructing an embankment over its fields. Samuel Perry, the tenant farmer, received £105 compensation from the railway company although he had asked initially for £150.[88] The lord of the manor, John Pulteney, maintained the larger farm of Buckland. To the south lay Woodside and Normandy farms, whilst Belmore Farm is now only recalled in Old Farm Walk, off Belmore Lane. As the salterns closed so the land was gradually reclaimed and turned into rough pasture for grazing. A few of the more easily drained parts were developed as arable and some laid out as asparagus beds.

The farms and smallholdings in the surrounding rural parishes made use of Lymington's markets as an outlet for their produce, while the town's fairs had a reputation for the quality of the cheese sold in the High Street and for the cattle auctioned in New Lane.

Although nearly 19 acres of Barfields, owned by the Burrard family, were still devoted to allotments in the mid-nineteenth century and other portions, totalling about 12 acres, were leased as pasture and meadow, the increasing expansion of the town

gradually ate into the available land.

Henry Hapgood's letters indirectly allude to the role of agriculture and reflect its declining importance in Lymington's economic life. When he wrote to farmer J. Sabine when he left Newtown Park Farm to return to his brother's farm at Ripley, south of Ringwood, he stated:

> The Furniture has sold off to day I think tolerably well, but I cannot say that with regard to the other things, neither the Wagons or Carts are sold, not a single bidding was made for either, nor even a bidding for the Horse. The red and white Heifer sold for £4, the black and White Heifer is not sold, the highest bidding was £3 10s., the light color pig fetched 23s., the other because of his snoring, was not liked and consequently did not fetch a bidding above 16s. I bought it in at 16s. 6d. and if you like I will keep it at that price or I will keep it till your carts and Wagons are sent to Ripley and then send the Pig to you.[89]

An indication of the intimate relationship between and town and country, so much a feature of all market towns, is revealed by a Mr Gatrell when giving an account of his childhood, 'my grandfather had two cows, and he rented the ground — the land that is now the Council Ground, where the Royal Yacht Club is, and his cows were there and he had a cowshed in the centre of it'.[90] This was probably William Gatrell, who in the Tithe Schedule of 1840 is recorded as leasing 67½ acres of arable land from the Rev. Thomas Beckley.[91]

The agricultural riots of 1830, provoked by the harvest failure of 1829 and the widespread introduction of the threshing machine, had little impact on Lymington but, nevertheless, reports indicate that the town was sympathetic to the labourers' appalling conditions.[92] Despite the fact that the usual threatening letters had been sent to all the farmers in the neighbourhood the mayor, the Rev. Ellis Jones, held a public meeting in which a resolution recommending an increase of wages was adopted. 'The aim was "that every labourer might receive not less than 9s. per week, and those with families a gallon of bread and 6d. per week additional for each child that is unable to work." It was believed this would be acted upon in all the surrounding parishes.'[93] Shortly after the meeting a group of about 50 labourers from Boldre came to Lymington and marched quietly to the Town Hall. Here they were met by the Rev. George Burrard, Col. John Shedden and the Rev. Peyton Blakiston who informed them that their wages would be increased immediately, on hearing this 'they gave three hearty cheers and returned peaceably to their homes.'[94]

As previously mentioned, by the mid-nineteenth century there were several agents of insurance companies established in Lymington who provided

By the river side a forest pony wanders freely where Gatrell's two cows once grazed. Photographed by T.A. Heath in 1957.

Above left Part of Southampton Row terrace of brick houses photographed by T.A. Heath in 1956.

Above The mix of mid to late nineteenth and early twentieth centuries' houses in King's Saltern Road illustrates the inexorable expansion of the town into the suburbs.

Left The red brick house is Temple Bar Cottage. The house next door (No. 6) has decoratively carved gables and a delightful tented roof to the porch with fretwork side panels. Probably built in the 1820s.

Below The whole extent of Buckland Terrace is shown in this early twentieth century photograph. From the bay of No. 1 then occupied by Eliza Fry to No. 11, then the home of Alfred Covill, medical assistant.

appropriate facilities such as fire insurance to the local farmers. One of these, the banker Charles St Barbe, acted for the Royal Exchange Insurance Company and was responsible for collecting the premiums on insured agricultural properties such as £120 on Vinings Farm at East End and £100 on Carters Farm at Norley Wood, both belonging to Joseph Weld of Pylewell.[95]

NEW BUILDING & THE 'PROPOSED SUSPENSION BRIDGE'

A certain amount of new building took place throughout the nineteenth century, mainly at the western end of the town. This started in the 1830s with the building of the Stanford Row terrace, but more substantial was the long terrace of middle-class houses, known as Southampton Buildings with its continuation of Buckland Terrace, which together ran for about 180 yards along the west side of Upper Buckland Road (now Southampton Road); these were finally completed in the early 1840s. Many were the homes of small trades people, such as carpenters, milliners, mariners and shopkeepers, some of whom ran their business from their homes, others were occupied by retired or independent men and women of modest means. Rather grander were the still existing fine houses at Highfield, overlooking the meadows of Stanford Brook, developed by Robert Lillington Rice on his own land and built in about 1830 by George Banks. Here lived annuitants, clergy, doctors and bankers,

Above Pardey's Terrace, a short row of cottages in Lower Buckland Road built by George Pardey, some of which were to provide accommodation for those employed in his nearby brickworks.

Below The row of brick houses in Priestlands Place.

Bottom Looking south along Gosport street. The Methodist Church is on the left.

The granite obelisk commemorating the life of Sir Harry Burrard Neale, sited at Walhampton but visible from Lymington High Street. The cost was met by public subscription.

all of whom had two or more servants living in. Between these developments an area of new roads, namely, Eastern, Western, Southern and Middle was laid out. George Banks also constructed the great granite monument at Walhampton, to the designs of George Draper, commemorating the life and services of Sir Harry Burrard Neale, both to the nation and his native town of Lymington, which was completed in 1841 at a cost of £1,482 3s.[96]

During the period some of the town's older buildings were demolished, as happened in 1842 to a group of three late sixteenth century cottages, including a bow windowed shop, in the High Street at the corner of Ashley Lane. In the central one Henry Hapgood had been born in 1810. In their place was erected a four-storied brick-built block which for a number of years bore the sobriquet of 'Gibraltar' from the rather gaunt way it dominated the High Street.[97] High Street numbering was adopted in 1858 and these buildings still survive as numbers 40, 41, and 42.

The population of the borough increased by over 1,000 between 1821 and 1851, many accommodated in the new terraces mentioned above and also in Newington Place, New Lane, and Rosetta Place, Buckland, both of which were constructed in this period.

Richard Grove wrote in 1832 that 'Lymington has evinced a considerable spirit of improvement . . . Many of the old and unsightly houses in the street have been taken down, and replaced by handsome modern buildings . . . The *Angel Hotel* has undergone a complete repair; and is become an ornament to the street'.[98]

Richard Andrew Grove was a member of a small but influential group of townsfolk who saw in the Industrial Revolution the key to progress and development. His most dramatic proposal, made in 1834, was for constructing a suspension bridge across the Lymington River as a continuation of the High Street. In the prospectus issued he declared:

> To remove all obstructions to an uninterrupted intercourse between the Town and a highly respectable portion of the Neighbourhood and thereby relieve the Inhabitants of a Tax exceeding £1000 a year, will, it is hoped, prove a sufficient recommendation to the Public to induce their ready support of a plan for erecting a FREE BRIDGE in the eligible situation pointed out in the above sketch.

The bridge span was to be 300 feet with two solid causeways, 130 feet long, on either side each 'faced with stone'. The carriageway, including two pathways, was to be 26 feet wide, leaving a clearance beneath the bridge of 7 feet at high water so allowing 'boats and lighters to pass under it to any part of the harbour'. In order to widen and straighten Quay Hill it would be necessary to buy property to the value of £3,000. Even with the inclusion of that cost Grove estimated the total expense for the whole project to be a very reasonable £6,000.

He pointed out that the Lymington-Yarmouth 'Steam-Packet would be enabled to land her passengers on the west causeway, at any time of the

tide'. Grove's prospectus was couched in the most persuasive language, with a powerful and altruistic appeal, 'To erect a Free Bridge by voluntary contributions, is not to make a profit of vested capital with a view to the enriching of a few persons to the loss of others – but is solely for the advantage of the community at large'.[99] An artist's impression, reproduced as a picturesque lithograph of this bridge, designed by the Christchurch-born architect, Benjamin Ferrey (1810-78),[100] illustrated the head of the prospectus. Despite support, some from influential quarters, the scheme foundered and Lymington's communication with the east was ever afterwards restricted either to the toll bridge, which continued to charge a toll until freed in 1967, or to the ferry to Walhampton.

THEATRES

For centuries strolling players had visited towns throughout the country, bringing a range of performers from singers and musicians to jugglers and conjurers. In Lymington their performances took place in a barn at the back of the *Angel Inn*. This was described by the Rev. Richard Boucher when he visited Lymington in 1789, 'In the yard is an old Barn turn'd into a playhouse, the only Evening amusement for the company. When we were there Jonas the Conjuror display'd his slight [*sic*] of hand'.[101]

Amongst many of the townsfolk these players were often thought to encourage, at best, bad behaviour and, at worse, vice. The corporation imposed certain restrictions, stating that 'all common players of Interludes or other entertainment of the stage...not being authorised by law, shall be prosecuted as vagrants if they presume to act in any part of the town'.[102] In 1764 several of these strolling players had been imprisoned in the fire engine shed overnight, but only after the engine had been taken out![103]

In the market streets many violent 'entertainments' were enacted including bear and bull baiting, cock-fighting and bare-knuckle fist fights. Charles Colborne (1690-1747), a well-known and popular local barrister, had been an early exponent of these 'sports' which continued into the early nineteenth century. Gradually public opinion changed, and parliament brought in legislation banning such 'sports'.[104]

The establishment of a permanent theatre provided a more sophisticated place of entertainment. Lymington's first theatre[105] was built in New Lane in about 1798. James Shatford, already established as a manager owning theatres in Blandford, Poole and Salisbury, became the first proprietor and often took part in stage performances, together with his wife.

Many of the performances reflected the maritime character of the town. *Thomas and Sally or The Sailor's Return* by the Irish playwright Isaac Bickerstaffe (1735-1812) set to music by Thomas

Lymington Literary Institute was built on the site of the Lymington Theatre after its closure in 1847 and partial demolition.

Arne, *True Blue or The Press Gang* by Charles Dibdin (1745-1814) and *The Purse or The Benevolent Tar* by J.C. Cross (fl.1796-1805) were all much enjoyed and loudly applauded. The foreign troops based in the town are recorded as being great patrons of the theatre.

After Shatford's death in 1809 his widow continued to manage his theatres until 1818, when they passed into the control of John Penson, a leading actor and comedian, remaining under his management until 1832. The theatre continued to flourish but was not well supported for every performance:

> Generally speaking, the Season has not to boast of having crowded houses, but on this evening [the last of the season] Mrs George Sloper bespoke a play for the benefit of Mr J. Penson and this occasion Mr George Sloper, Junr. with great kindness and good nature offered to undertake the character he had previously performed in Private Theatricals; so every part of the house was crammed to overflow. We hope next season we shall have to offer our congratulations on a more abundant harvest which talent and unceasing exertions to please deservedly merit.[106]

Mrs Sloper was the wife of the Rev. George Sloper who lived at Bowling Green House (now Eagle House) close to the theatre in New Lane.[107]

The *Salisbury and Winchester Journal* on 4 September, 1829 reported:

> Lymington. Our theatrical season is rapidly drawing to a close. On Monday evening the provincial comedian, Mr John Penson, took his benefit and we were most happy to see so crowded a house as a just testimonial of appreciation to him and so deserving a performance.

The performances by Master William Robert Grossmith, 'The Infant Roscius', aged only ten, in 1828 attracted tremendous acclaim.

The Lymington Theatre, together with those at Blandford and Salisbury, was sold in 1832 and bought by John Bedford, former manager of the Garrick and other London theatres. The opening night under his management was announced as follows:

> The Nobility, Gentry, and Inhabitants of Lymington and its Vicinity are respectfully informed that this elegant little theatre will be re-opened for the season with an entire New and Talented Company from London, under the management of Mr Bedford . . . [who] being determined to spare no pains in rendering the Theatre attractive, begs leave to announce that he has, at considerable expense, had the Apparatus laid on in the interior of the House, and that in future THE THEATRE WILL BE BRILLIANTLY LIGHTED WITH GAS.

Performances were given on Mondays, Wednesdays and Fridays and admission cost 1s. to the gallery, 1s. 6d. to the pit and 3s. to the boxes.

In 1834 a new manager, Mr Harris, took over, but attendances were declining. A newspaper commented that the theatre 'is "well aired" through the medium of chinks and crevices, etc.' the irony of which suggests it was falling into disrepair. It seems to have remained empty and unused until 1844 when it was taken over by E.D. Davies, a 'well-known and enterprising manager'. Although in the next two or three years the entertainments were acclaimed it seems that audiences were ebbing away. In 1847 the theatre closed and the building was partly demolished.

Itinerant players continued to make visits to the town, putting on plays and entertainments in the assembly rooms of the *Angel Hotel*, rather as the strolling players had done a century and more earlier in the outbuildings of the inn. This was the time of the Victorian melodramas and Lymington audiences thrilled to such epics as *Sweeny Todd*, *The Murder in the Red Barn* and *The Face at the Window*.

The lack of a permanent theatre was remedied when in 1890 Major George Jobling built a replacement on the eastern side of the river, inaugurating his own ferry service to carry his customers. But those already operating the cross-river ferry objected so that Jobling had to stop. This undoubtedly was a blow and although the theatre flourished for a while it evidently could not sustain its audiences and was closed.[108] The building was then purchased by Lymington Model Laundry which operated well into the twentieth century.

THE ASSEMBLY ROOMS & BALLS

The Assembly Rooms were constructed in 1805 as an addition to the *Angel Inn* and became a popular venue for all kinds of entertainment, most particularly for balls.

An intriguing description of one of these balls is contained in a letter penned by Henry Hapgood to his fiancée, Leah Barrow, in February 1848.

> I suppose you will expect to hear how the Ball went off last evening, I therefore will endeavour to give you a somewhat & detailed account of it, the Party consisted of about 60 in number, rather more Gentlemen than Ladies so that those Gents who were not favorites stood a poor chance with the best of the Ladies (I, of course, was among the unfortunates) as no Lady will ever care to dance her hair out of curl with an engaged Gentleman, the party was an agreeable one and I think all enjoyed themselves exceedingly well...[109]

These balls had a universal appeal and drew in participants from the surrounding countryside. They arrived in their carriages outside the inn and on stepping down were escorted into the brightly illuminated rooms, from where the strains of music would be playing. These balls were reported in some detail in the local press as the following example shows:

> The Lymington Ball took place on 2 January 1885 at the Assembly Rooms when there was a very large attendance of the neighbouring gentry. Targett's Band was in attendance, and dancing was kept up with spirit until an early hour. The Ball proved a most pleasant and successful one.[110]

These rooms continued in use for balls and dances until the middle of the twentieth century.

Lymington Model Laundry operated from Jobling's theatre (the flat roofed building on the left) until well into the twentieth century.

CIRCUSES

Circuses visited the town once or twice a year, as is revealed by Henry Hapgood in letters to his fiancée: one, dated 4 August 1848, states, 'Wombwells Collection of Wild Beasts etc will be here for exhibition to morrow, if you would like to come in and see it, and will let me know I will fetch you, enclosed is a Bill of Particulars'.

Three months later he tackles the subject again remarking that had he not been so busy 'I would have taken you to the Circus' but cannot resist commenting, 'but if once seen there is no great treat in seeing it a second time.'[111]

School children were sometimes given a half-day holiday when the circus was in town as happened at the National School in 1893.[112]

Lymington was offered a spectacular circus show for one day only, Friday 19 July 1872, when a menagerie with 'Fifteen huge caravans drawn by sixty magnificent draught horses' was to form a great procession – as well it might, if the advertisement describing it as 'The finest travelling menagerie in the world!!!' is to be believed.[113]

SEA BATHING & THE BATHS

A detail from *Mrs Beeston's Baths at Lymington*, by Thomas Rowlandson.

The vogue for sea-bathing, primarily for health reasons, began in the mid-eighteenth century and soon many coastal towns began promoting themselves as watering places. Lymington jumped on the bandwagon and in 1789 the Rev. Richard Boucher, on visiting Lymington with his wife, makes a reference to the 'Baths'.[114] The first bath house was built in 1777[115] and Rowlandson depicts it in about 1784 when he produced a delightful sketch of Mrs Beeston's Baths at Lymington.[116] However, the attractions and facilities offered cannot have been very highly regarded for a guide to watering places published in 1806 says of the town 'considered solely as a watering place, *Lymington* has little that can recommend it....'

Perhaps it was because of such observations that a more systematic approach was adopted and which, in 1833, led to the foundation of the Lymington Bath Improvement Company. Close on £6,000 was raised for a venture committed to erecting more commodious baths and improving access to them. The charming main building (which survives today as the Lymington Town Sailing Club headquarters) was designed by William Bartlett. There was machinery for pumping and heating, hot, cold and vapour baths, separate accommodation for both sexes, and a 'commodious' circular room on the upper floor for social gatherings. Outside a large open-air seawater swimming bath was constructed,

whilst the surrounding grounds provided space for genteel sports such as archery, which became very popular in the mid-nineteenth century. Some visitors evidently thought highly of the facilities, one remarking,

> The air of Lymington was wonderfully beneficial to me together with frequently taking a warm bath I don't think I have looked so well for ten years as I did while I was there, the improvement to my health, and the kindnesses of my friends induced me to stay a week longer there than I intended . . .[117]

Despite the investment of cash and the development of the baths Lymington never really succeeded as a watering place. When Dr A.B. Granville published his voluminous and highly respected *Spas of England and Principal Sea-Bathing Places* in 1841 Lymington received no mention.

Because of lack of support the company running the baths was soon in difficulties and, despite a generous boost from the Lymington MPs, they were obliged in the end to sell them for a fraction of their cost to George Inman in about 1855. After several further changes in ownership they were acquired in 1929 by the Lymington Corporation, which has run them ever since. The 1931 guide described them as being 'well appointed, entirely up-to-date . . . [and] being over an acre in extent the largest on the South

The Bath House from an engraving of about 1840.

Coast'. However, the baths were an amenity retained for the benefit of the residents and visitors since they never made a profit. It was a blow to ratepayers when in 1990 the assessment was raised from £400 to £7,500.[118] However, the baths, now known as the 'Open Air Swimming Pool', are open annually between mid-May and mid-September and form an attractive centre for relaxation with facilities for boats and canoes and a paddling pool for children.

Children enjoy the paddling pool against the backdrop of the Bath House in about 1930.

Below The Bath House as it appears today (now the headquarters of the Lymington Town Sailing Club).

CRICKET, FOOTBALL & CYCLING

Outdoor sports became increasingly popular during the nineteenth century and most towns boasted their own cricket and football clubs.[119] Lymington Cricket Club was founded as early as 1807. Brian Down records that 'one inhabitant of the town expressed the wish that, on his burial in the adjoining churchyard, his grave be so placed that boys might stand on the stone to watch the cricket'[120] – leading to the suspicion that this is the kind of thing he did as a boy. A delightful example of the popularity of the game is revealed in the following report:

Lymington, 20th July [1820].
The admirers of the manly game of cricket were highly gratified on Monday last by a match, between this town and Milford, which was played on Pennington Common.

So great an assemblage of company was never remembered and the Common bore the appearance of a pleasure fair. Betting, on the outset was 5 – 3 on Milford which varied after the second innings of the Lymington club to even, and afterwards, from the Milford [side] having 15 runs to get and four wickets to go down, 5 – 1 was fairly even throughout the field. Lymington was victorious by 6 runs.[121]

The Lymington Football Club was founded in 1876 and was fortunate in having as its first president Sir Harry Burrard, who owned the former open fields and allotments lying to the north of St Thomas Street, known as Barfields. He allowed the club to use part of this land for its pitch. When Barfields was later purchased by John Lane Shrubb of Boldre Grange he ensured that an area was set aside for use as playing fields for both the football and cricket clubs. Later in the century Lymington cricket benefited by having in its team an amateur player of exceptional skill, Christopher Heseltine (1870-1944) of Walhampton, a regular for Hampshire County Cricket Club and who even played for England in the 1895-6 Test Matches against South Africa.

Lymington also had its own bicycling club, which competed with those of neighbouring towns. A report in June 1879 records that 11 members, under a Capt. Purchase, attended a 'meet' at Christchurch.

It seems likely that the cycling club leader was Isaac Bentley Purchase, the proprietor of the large grocery emporium in the High Street (later to become Willis & Sons and subsequently Tesco). The active Christchurch club often cycled to Lymington, as in 1877 when a party set out from Purewell at 6 o'clock on a May evening and arrived at Lymington 'shortly after seven' spending an hour strolling around the town before heading homewards. The roads then had gravel surfaces and the going must have been quite tough at times.[122]

For the sedentary there was the Lazy Club, founded in the late eighteenth century, so delightfully described by Edward King, where members' activities, such as working, must not be engaged in. Even when standing in the street, the member must support himself against 'a House, a Post, or other convenient Thing'. Even those members engaged in the seafaring life had to be careful 'not, on any Pretence row in the Heat of the Day. It will be far more honourable to lay down and sleep'. Membership was addressed 'TO THE FREE AND EASY and such as are desirous of attaining A GOOD OLD AGE!'[123]

There seems to be a curious example of these principles spreading to the inmates of the union workhouse. A satirical letter, written in a semi-literate and vernacular style, by a man signing himself 'Luke Lazy', observes, 'Well, has I was saing, we wos just got kumfrtable, an laffin lyke at sum of hour stewped kwaintences has doant like the Hunyon, an' stopps houtsides, an pays raites and txes – wen sum coave among the gardyens hups an says we fellers ought 2 worke. Ought 2 worke, indede, wy, that's the very thing we went inter the Hunyuon to get away from . . . '[124]

The Lymington Town Band was founded in 1883 and became so accomplished that it took part in many national competitions, winning several prizes. When the Lymington Football Club achieved a victory 2-1 over Andover the band played *See the Conquering Heroes Come* to welcome the team back on 8 March 1913.[125] The band had several changes of name but always flourished, surviving today and still providing concerts, many in the bandstand in the recreation ground in Bath Road.

CRIMEAN GUN FOR THE TOWN

Patriotic feeling ran high in time of war, of which the Crimean War was the first major conflict since the defeat of Napoleon in 1815. When it finally ended in 1856 the corporation felt a durable symbol should be provided and the mayor, John Hayward, made a request of Lord Panmure, Secretary of State for War, for one of the Russian guns captured in the Crimea to be given to the town.

The request was granted and a cast-iron carriage to support it was made at Woolwich Arsenal, and paid for by public subscription. The gun was set up at the north end of New Street at its junction with Union Hill.

In due course an even greater conflict was to see its removal, in 1941 when it was taken as scrap to aid the war effort.[126]

ADULT LEARNING

As with many Victorian towns Lymington established a society intended to promote the cultural and educational 'improvement' of its citizens, often known as mechanics or literary institutes. In Lymington the Literary Society was

Children enjoy playing on the Russian gun captured during the Crimean War (1853-6) and given to Lymington to commemorate the British success.

formed in 1846 in Mr Banks's house 77 High Street, later purchasing for £440 (of which £205 came from public subscription) the defunct theatre building in New Street. This was converted into a Literary Institute with the provision of a library, reading and lecture rooms. Within five years it had 190 male and 38 female members, and 520 books[127] in a library whose shelves were kept stocked by its librarian, George Milledge. Subscriptions were payable quarterly; 2s. 6d. for the men and 1s. 6d. for the ladies and youths. Lectures on scientific and literary subjects were held weekly throughout the winter. It was often the local gentry who provided loyal support for the Institution, John Morant, the lord of the manors of Brockenhurst and Ringwood, was president in the 1870s and two William Ingham Whitakers, father and son, of Pylewell successively, were presidents from 1901 to 1988.[128]

The poet William Allingham was an early member of the Literary Institute for he writes in his diary:

Left Buckland Cottage once the home of Caroline Bowles (1786-1854) who was a poet and literary aficionado. In 1839 she married the Poet Laureate, Robert Southey, at Boldre and moved to the Lake District but following his death in 1843 returned to her beloved cottage. She was the great-granddaughter of Sir Paul Burrard, MP for Lymington, who built the Lymington Town Hall 1710.

Below Left Prospect Place, a semi-detached pair of town houses situated at the southern end of Ashley Lane. In one lived William Allingham, the renowned poet and customs house officer for Lymington. Here he entertained such figures as William Barnes, the Dorset dialect poet, and Edward Burne-Jones, the pre-Raphaelite artist.

Tuesday, November 1 [1864]. – Rev. Wm. Barnes [the Dorset dialect poet] comes on my invitation to give a lecture at the Literary Institution. He duly arrives by train at 3, and I gladly welcome the good old poet. We walk about the Town and he shows much interest in the Furniture Brokers' shops, old china, pictures, etc. – and bargains for a little oil painting . . . then dinner at my lodging and we moved to the Lecture Room. Mr Barnes lectured on 'West of England Speech', and read some of his own poems. What the audience liked best was 'A Bit o' Sly Coortin', which he gave at my particular request . . . [on returning to Allingham's lodging] Barnes and I chatted till near 1.

Barnes was invited back in the following year:

Tuesday, October 31.– . . . Rev. William Barnes comes to me by invitation. I go up from the Custom-House and find him sitting by my fire in Prospect Place. We dine at 6.30: to the Literary Institution, where B. lectures on *House and House-Life* – caves, huts, tents, etc., Wives (laughter), Praise of the good wife, – Odd lecture, rather puzzled everybody . . . [129]

The Literary Institute sought also to provide popular entertainment, as in an undated poster of about 1902 when Lieut. Walter Cole, the 'Famous Ventriloquist with his great London Company, gave a performance enlivened with animated pictures of Edward VII's coronation'

Allingham, as a member of the literary circle, received many visitors of renown including the Poet Laureate, Alfred Lord Tennyson, who lived on the Isle of Wight and made frequent journeys to Lymington. Indeed, Tennyson was inspired to write his contemplative *Crossing the Bar* whilst entering Lymington River on a ferry.

Other literary figures connected with Lymington included Coventry Patmore, who died in 1896 having spent the last five years of his life in Blake's Lodge, near Lymington Pier Station.[130] His widow and son then moved to live in Lymington High Street.

Paul Verlaine, the French poet, who had come to teach in a private school in Bournemouth in May 1876, left in September 1877[131] to join the staff of William Murdock's school in Lymington High Street as French teacher. However, his stay here was brief for he was back in his homeland before the year's end.

NEWSPAPERS

The establishment of provincial newspapers represented a significant advance in the dissemination of news and information. They were an organ for advertisements for local trade and commerce and offered a vehicle for readers' correspondence. Lymingtonians had to rely on either the *Hampshire Chronicle* (1772), the *Salisbury and Winchester Journal* (1729) or the *Sherborne Journal*, forerunner of the *Western Gazette* (1737) until, in 1858, the *Lymington Chronicle* (first issue 11 November 1858 at 2d.) was founded. Like so many provincial newspapers, it bore several mastheads appropriate to the areas in which its readers resided. For example, in the 1860s it was published as the *Lymington and Isle of Wight Chronicle, Ringwood and Fordingbridge Times, and Christchurch Advertiser* and was printed by Henry Penney of Poole for the proprietors James Tribbett and William Mate. In the 1870s it became *The Poole and Bournemouth Herald, Wareham, Purbeck, Wimborne and Blandford Gazette, Lymington and South Hants Chronicle, Ringwood, Christchurch and Fordingbridge Times*. Its local offices were in the High Street, nearly opposite the Post Office. The paper survived until 1934.

The *New Milton Advertiser* was established in 1928 by Mr Kirby Wynne who two years later sold it to Conrad L. Davis who, in turn, went into a short-lived partnership with Charles T. Curry, father of the present editor. On the closure of the *Lymington Chronicle* in 1934, Curry purchased the copyright and published it as the *Lymington Times*. From 1932 the masthead has included 'incorporating *Lymington and Milton Chronicle*'. Later this paper, too, appeared in two editions as the *New Milton Advertiser* and the *Lymington Times*, with some variation on news coverage to suit either end of the borough though it trades as the *Advertiser and Times*. With a readership of around 22,000 it has flourished and successfully survived the establishment of two free weeklies of which only one, *The New Forest Post*, continues.

The Popular Advertiser had been founded in 1891 as a free newspaper by Charles Thomas King and 1,000 copies were circulated monthly. Though, as its name suggests, it was primarily an advertising paper it did contain snippets of local news and dedicated articles, including a long running series of biographies of Lymingtonians. This paper ceased publication before the outbreak of the first World War.

BRIGHT'S
LYMINGTON COURIER,
AND
ISLE OF WIGHT ADVERTISER;
OR
GENERAL AND LOCAL INTELLIGENCER
FOR
Lymington, South Hampshire, and the Isle of Wight.

NOVEMBER, 1866.   Circulation 1,100 Monthly.

Bright's Lymington Courier. The banner of one of the free newspapers, November 1866.

SCHOOLS

The Fulford's School seems to have ceased functioning in the early years of the nineteenth century, though there is no clear documentation to explain why.

There were a number of private schools operating in the second half of the eighteenth century[132] and in 1803 there is reference to a girls' school in Captain's Row run by a Mrs Young. An advertisement for the school revealed the following: 'four-six years 6s. per quarter; six-nine years 8s. per quarter; nine years 9s. per quarter; plus writing extra 7s.; embroidery and print work included for 9s. Plus a footnote stating, 'strictest attention is paid to their morals'.[133]

Most of the Lymington schools were small privately run institutions catering for both boarding and day pupils. They have various titles including academies, seminaries (seemed to be a popular designation from about 1865) and schools. Generally they seem to bear the names of the proprietors. Most of the information compiled below is abstracted from trade directories and the first to mention 'academies' is the *Pigot & Co Directory* for 1824.

There is a reference in 1828 to a school in Church Lane, 'run entirely at the expense of Mr Wall', which made provision for 80 boys and 80 girls, but details have proved elusive. From the 1840s to the end of the century we find a number of privately run schools such as those established by Charles Domine, Jane Elizabeth Ford, Mary Galpine, Mary and Sarah Perress, Jane Pittis, the sisters Frances Louisa and Harriet Salome Noake, William

The young ladies demurely exercising in the gardens of Bellevue House when it was the school or seminary run by the two Noake sisters. Photographed in about 1870.

Above A docket issued to a Frenchman, Jaques Teilleul, permitting him to teach in Rev. Anthony Davidson's academy, dated 20 July 1798. Undoubtedly he had come over with the French émigrés escaping from Republican France.

Below Caricature of William Murdock from a political poster.

Murdoch and Sarah Barton who all took boarders. There were also a few ephemeral establishments which might perhaps be described best as 'dame's schools'.

The Noake sisters' school, which started in Gosport Street, was finally accommodated in Bellevue House, 48 High Street. It aspired to high standards and took in young ladies from 11 to 17 years of age, which it 'finished' as well as taught. By the later nineteenth century there were six teachers, including the Noake sisters, and 34 boarding students, a ratio of five pupils to each teacher. A newspaper report in 1885 stated that 'For half a century Miss Noake and her sister conducted an important ladies' school in this town, one of the most important in the county, with great success'.[134] William Murdoch (1835-1903), a university educated Scotsman, set up the Solent Collegiate School for boys in 63-64 High Street in about 1865 and had among his early pupils two of the Burrard boys,[135] sons of Sidney Burrard, author of *Annals of Walhampton* (1875). Both Charles Thomas King and his son, Edward, were pupils of William Murdock. The latter described his master as 'a fierce venerable old gentleman with long white whiskers...Here I lived a life of terror as he kept a huge bundle of canes in the corner and was extremely free with them...I once saw a big boy thrashed with extreme force and much to my admiration he took it without wincing'.[136]

Murdock demonstrates the esteem in which the proprietors of these schools were regarded by the community when he became much involved in the town's affairs being elected councillor, alderman and, on three occasions, mayor.

The children with their teachers in the garden of Southend House, a girls' boarding school in Church Lane. Possibly at the time the Perress sisters ran the establishment.

About this time Mrs Eliza Grant ran a small 'ladies school' at 6 Priestlands Place and Maria Johnson and Annie Taylor ran a somewhat larger establishment at Stanwell House in the High Street.[137]

The boarding pupils in these schools numbered over 100 in 1871, having an impact on the economic life of the town. The high number of private schools in a small market town is an indication of Lymington's significance as a favoured location, as pupils came from many parts of the kingdom as well as from abroad.

But it was the churches, both the non-conformist and the established, that ushered in organised schooling. The National Society for Promoting the Education of the Poor in the Principles of the Established Church throughout England and Wales (a long-winded title) was the sponsor for the new school, called a National School. It was housed in a purpose-built brick building, started in 1835, having segregated class rooms for 160 boys and 120 girls and a common hall. This was situated in New Lane and is now the home of the St Barbe Museum and Art Gallery. There survives an intriguing drawing of a school inscribed, 'Sketch School for Lymington, Hants' which shows a rather Italianate building, and the central part of the surviving school certainly has an architectural affinity with the one in the drawing. The building was enlarged in 1871 at the cost of £500. Mrs St Barbe had given £220 for the purchase of ½ acre of land for the original school and had met the costs of the houses for the master and mistress. A stone lintel bears the following inscription commemorating her generosity:

Mrs Ann St Barbe widow of Samuel St Barbe Esqr of Ridgway in this parish, during her lifetime gave the site, and enclosed it, built the dwelling-houses and contributed largely to the erection of the school rooms. The trustees since her decease on the 17th June 1840 have caused this record of her benevolence to be here inscribed.

The school was vested in The Official Trustee of Charity Lands in 1870 under a provision of the Endowed Schools Act of 1869. The name National School was retained until 1909 when it formally became the Church of England School.

Richard King (1796-1877), the printer and stationer whose grandfather, John King, had been a teacher in Yeovil, waxed philosophical on the benefits of education when he wrote that these new schools provided an important improvement,

in the worse condition of the rising generation, and though it is readily admitted, that there are not wanting instances, in which a good education has only prepared

Left The central block of the first National School with a date plaque of 1835 set above the central window in the gable end. Compare with the central portion of the architect's drawing above; though not identical it does have striking similarities.

Above An architect's provisional drawing for the National School at Lymington. The centre portion is very similar to the surviving centre of the St Barbe Museum but it is evident the wings were never built in the style indicated in the drawing.

a man for the practice of every species of vice and immorality; yet it is equally true that the diffusion of useful knowledge among the poorer classes is calculated to make them better members of society, and to prepare them for those situations in life to which they may be called to move; whether it be considered in reference to the character of a servant, a master, a husband or a parent.[138]

The school was intended to give a basic education, with moral and religious instruction to the children of the working and lower middle classes. Some financial contributions were expected from the children and in 1872 it was agreed that children in standards 4, 5 and 6 should pay 2d. a week instead of the 1d. formerly charged. As with most comparable schools attendance could be erratic: absences sometimes caused by enterprises such as blackberry and potato picking and sometimes by

Inside a classroom in the National (Church of England) School.

children's illnesses which often attained epidemic proportions, as in 1900 when the school was closed for six weeks because of an outbreak of the then virulent scarlet fever.

A school for infants had been founded in 1859 in Ashley Lane, but eventually became too small and a new school to replace it was erected immediately opposite the National School in School Lane in 1888 and the former building sold. The late Mr Gatrell, who was born in 1870, recalled his schooldays:

My first school was the Infants' School – [in Ashley Lane] – and I paid a penny a week. The schoolmistress was an elderly spinster, Miss Perry, and the best behaved boys she would allow to go out for half-an-hour in the morning – winter time especially, and gather the twigs and dry sticks from The Grove to light the school fires.[139]

Gatrell attended school with a boy who was later to become renowned as a boat-builder, Dan Bran (1867-1950), who learnt his craft under Gatrell's uncle, the foreman boat builder with Inman's.[140]

A non-denominational County Junior School was built in Cannon Street in 1911. The Church of England Junior School and the infants' school opposite were closed in 1991, some 44 years after the schools inspectorate had declared it 'wholly unsuitable and unacceptable for modern teaching'. The new school, in Avenue Road, built at a cost of over £1.1 million, was opened by the town mayor, Ben Baker, in July 1992.

The Baptists established a school in the basement of their newly erected chapel in New Lane in 1834, but it appears to have closed following the opening of the National School just a few yards away on the opposite side of the road.

The British School, the name given by non-conformists to their schools, opened behind the Congregational chapel in January 1848. A committee reported that,

> A school conducted on such liberal principles as this institution was needed in the town. It is open to all, without any party or sectarian test, and parents of all denominations have availed themselves of the superior advantages proving at once that religious bigotry is on the decline, and that the benefits of a liberal education are becoming generally appreciated.[141]

At the end of the first year on the register there were 161 Congregationalists (or Independents), 64 Baptists, 29 Anglicans, 4 Roman Catholics and one Wesleyan Methodist. A financial record for the school in its first year survives showing that income was £140 16s. 4½d. while running costs exceeded this by just over £4. The school appears to have flourished for a number of years but closed in 1877. It reopened in 1888 only to close finally in 1911.

Both the Congregationalists and the Baptists continued to run their Sunday Schools independently from the British School. The Congregationalists are recorded as having 268 children attending in 1884 whilst the Baptist numbers were put at between 300 and 400. William Robinson, Sunday school teacher and superintendent, served the Baptists for 50 years from 1820-70.[142]

The Catholic children got their first school in 1860 when Joseph Weld, junior, provided the finance for the building and for the teacher's salary; the first was a Miss Murphy. The school was enlarged, or rebuilt, in 1885 to the designs of Leonard Stokes, building work being carried out by the Lymington firm, Rashleys. The Weld family

The façade of the Baptist church in New Lane. The cement rendered classical front was added in 1866 and the modern porch was added in the 1980s.

motto, *Nil sine numine* (Nothing without God), is carved near the school entrance.

RELIGIOUS LIFE & THE CHURCHES

As the schools show most towns developed strong links with non-conformity. Throughout the nineteenth century the dissenting churches flourished and expanded their influence into the surrounding countryside. Lymington was no exception. In 1834 the Baptists had a new commodious chapel built in New Lane with its own graveyard adjoining the theatre. The cost of the new building was £1,625: the classical front which survives to the present day was added in 1866. Sadly, the graveyard is now a car park for the church but an inscribed brass memorial plaque (now gone) reminded those who read it of the support given to dissent by many of the business folk and craftsmen. It stated:

IN CHRIST
Benjamin Wickenden
who died Octr 6th 1798. Aged 34 years
Sophia, his wife
who died April 24th 1848. Aged 86 years

An engraving of the Independent (Congregational) Chapel in Lymington High Street.

After its demolition the Irvingite church was replaced with this pair of terraced houses. Southampton Row lies to the left and Buckland Terrace to the right.

Benjamin Wickenden had been a brick maker and at his early death in 1798 his wife Sophia, took over the business and ran it for many years.[143]

The Congregational (Independent) chapel was built in the High Street in 1847 at the cost of £4,000 of which £1,000 was donated by Robert Lillington Rice, a wealthy Lymington businessman.

Evidently there was an Independent Methodist chapel in the town by 1851[144] though details of where it stood have not been discovered. The Wesleyan Methodists were relatively late in becoming established but they had a chapel built in Gosport Street in 1859.

The Roman Catholic presbytery and the entrance to the church and school.

The Catholic Apostolic Church (the Irvingites)[145] had a modest chapel built towards the northern end of Southampton Buildings in 1838 at a cost of £853.

The Roman Catholics, seem to have all but disappeared in the years following the Reformation and indeed, judging by the puritan support of the townsfolk, would not perhaps have been welcome. By 1725 there were no more than a dozen Catholics in Lymington.[146]

It was the arrival of Joseph Weld at Pylewell in 1801, a member of a long-established Catholic family whose base was at Lulworth Castle in Dorset, which paved the way for a revival of Catholicism in Lymington. At first they worshipped in chapels founded by the Welds in Pylewell House, later at East End and at Walhampton. The great step forward was made when Joseph Weld purchased properties in the High Street known as Mitchells House, and Nos. 133 and 134 together with their grounds for 1,000 guineas in 1857. Joseph Aloysius Hansom, a well-known architect of Catholic churches, who is more celebrated today as the designer of the Hansom cab, was commissioned to design it. His account, submitted on 7 February 1859, is of some interest:

To design, making plans, specifications and personal superintendence of the new church at Lymington, Hants –

5% of the outlay of £1,240	£62
Travelling expenses, postage and pencils	£15
Total	£77

Another benefactor of the new church was James Brown, junior, town clerk and a Catholic convert, who gave £48 10s. for the construction of 28 benches.[147]

The foundation stone was laid by Bishop Thomas Grant of Southwark who returned on 18 May 1859 to consecrate and open the finished building,[148] which was dedicated to Our Lady of Mercy and St Joseph. The first priest was the Rev. John Milner, SJ., who had already served at the Walhampton chapel since 1854.

During the construction, which was carried out by a local builder, Mr Richman, a workman named Preston died from the effects of poisonous fumes released on the opening of old vaults on the site and several other workmen were overcome and became ill. The firm of Elgar, with premises almost opposite the church, renovated the imposing Georgian Mitchells House and converted it for use by the resident priest.

The parish church of St Thomas continued in its central role as the Anglican church for Lymington. Extensive work was carried out between 1792 and 1811 which transformed the interior. To provide additional accommodation fine galleries were added, supported on pairs of Tuscan columns. The Royal Arms were remounted on the front of the west gallery. Some years later the churchwarden, Henry Figg (a Lymington glazier and plumber), decided to amend these arms so that they displayed those of George IV. Those of Charles I, painted on a large canvas, had merely been amended earlier to display (inaccurately) the Hanoverian arms. This curiosity happily still survives at the head of the stairs in the narthex. The church vestry was however, not pleased with Figg's decision (presumably taken without its authority) and announced on 20 April 1824 that the churchwarden should not be paid 'in any way by the Parish for the Coat of Arms . . . as a wholesome example to all future Churchwardens'. No doubt, feeling this was

Above The interior of St Thomas's parish church in Lymington, looking towards the east window. The large eighteenth century galleries are supported on pairs of Tuscan columns. The nave roof has a wagon roof which was replaced in the major restoration of 1911, largely financed by Mrs Martha Earley.

Below The north side of the parish church in about 1905. This view is now to some extent screened by the construction of the church hall.

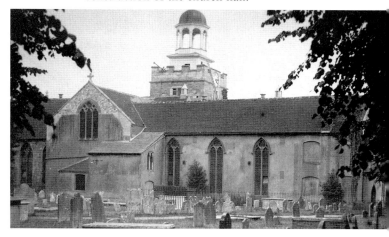

rather hard on Figg, the vestry members had second and, indeed, third thoughts about the matter agreeing in the end to allow him £7![149] Recent research has suggested that these royal arms were, in fact, an otherwise unrecorded adaptation of William III's arms[150] so perhaps Figg, in turn, was trying to be economical.

The churchyard which had served the parish

131

Two Victorian clergymen.

Top The Rev. Henry Chicheley Michell (1804-51) was curate at Lymington from 1831 to 1850, also performing the office of incumbent to South Baddesley for 18 of those years.

Bottom An early photograph of the Rev. Benjamin Maturin (1816-1905), who was vicar for 53 years.

portion of the churchyard which projected into the street (diminishing the road to nearly half its present width,) and by placing iron railings round the church, with handsome folding gates to the entrances of the churchyard'.[152]

An entry in the parish burial register for 1796 relates an anecdote concerning John Tout, aged 74, for many years to the Corporation Mace Bearer:

> When his Majesty George the Third in the year 17[89] was staying at Lyndhurst, he graciously visited this Town. Mr Tout as Mace-bearer did not fail to attrack [*sic*] the notice of His Majesty. Particularly when His Majesty entered the Town Hall, Mr T. dressed in all the insignia of his office, fell down on his knees before him, saying (as is said) at the same time "I am like a beast before thee". The whole scene, &c., made such an impression on His Majesty, that he has frequently since enquired of Sir Harry Neale for the old Mace-Bearer of the Corporation.[153]

The vicarage which had been in the gift of the Bishop of Bristol since the Reformation, as part of its endowment when the diocese was created, was transferred to the Ecclesiastical Commissioners in 1857. For nearly two centuries it had only been served by a curate. Recognition of the proper ecclesiastical status of Lymington was overdue and a long legal struggle ensued, culminating in the issuing of an order by Queen Victoria in 1869 whereby Lymington was declared an independent vicarage, vested in the Bishop of Winchester.[154] The clergyman who saw through these changes was the redoubtable Rev. Benjamin Maturin (1816-1905) who, during an incumbency of 53, years became an institution in the town. Indeed, when he had completed 25 years in 1877 a collection was made in the parish on his behalf which realised nearly £167, part of which was spent on an engraved silver salver, and 125 guineas given in a 'purse'.[155]

The traditional provision of church music by the players of the church orchestra, whose instruments had been a constant though relatively small cost to the church rates, was superseded by an organ purchased by public subscription in 1831. This fine instrument was played at the opening ceremony on 13 October 1831 by Philip Klitz, the first of three successive members of the family who were to be church organists until the death of Robert Augustus

unchanged for about eight centuries was enlarged to the north in 1821 through the gift of about three-quarters of an acre made by Sir Harry Neale.[151] Earlier, the part lying to the south of the church, which had so constricted the junction between the High Street and St Thomas Street, was closed and removed, enabling the road to be widened, leading Richard Grove to comment, 'Within the last twelve years, Lymington has evinced a considerable spirit for improvement. It commenced by removing a

Klitz in 1887.[156]

The religious census held on Sunday 30 March 1851 gave the following information in relation to Lymington's places of worship. The parish church is recorded as having seating for 2,000. The morning service was attended by 964, that held in the afternoon by 420 whilst the evening service had 1,040 in attendance. The Baptist chapel with seating for 600 had attendances of 350, 277 and 262 respectively. The Independent (Congregational) with seating for 500 had 429, 262 and 303, the Independent Methodist chapel with seats for only 192 had 72, 65 and 170. The Holy Catholic and Apostolic Church (the Irvingites, not to be confused with the Roman Catholic Church) had seats for 192 with 36 at the morning service and 44 in the evening. Lymington had no R.C. church at the time of this census so the Catholics would most likely have attended the chapel at East End where the morning and afternoon services had congregations of 30 and 12.[157]

CHARITIES

Two charities were instituted in the nineteenth century. That of Rear Admiral Thomas Rogers was created by a bequest of £1,000, made at his death in 1814. The capital was invested and administered by the minister and churchwardens, whilst the income was divided annually into ten equal shares for the benefit of five men and five women described as 'old and indigent'. The dividends were payable through St Barbe's Bank in the High Street.[158]

In 1868 Commander Thomas Rogers bequeathed £2,100 pounds in 3% stock, the proceeds annually were to be used to buy 20 'good strong great or Overcoats to the value of 30s. each' for 20 poor men of Lymington and also 20 'good strong Cloaks of the value of 30s. each' for 20 poor women of the parish. Amongst the list of conditions, so often found in charitable endowments, was one debarring the residents of the Union workhouse. This charity did not bear the Rogers name but was known as 'How's Charity', in memory of his wife, Ann, the daughter of John and Eleanor How of Lymington.[159]

Above This polished granite drinking fountain presented to the town by the widow of William Wowen Rooke of Woodside in 1885. It first stood at the western end of St Thomas Street but was later moved to Bath Road recreation ground.

Below The Cottage Convalescent Home, as it was first known, located at Waterford, was built in 1876 at the expense of Adeline and Margaret Harding of Grove House. It was financed by patients' fees and voluntary contributions.

A fine late nineteenth century view west along the whole length of St Thomas Street. The monumental gas standard is on the right on which the commemorative panels can be clearly seen. Ford's first shop, established in 1840, can be seen behind the gas column. Two horse-drawn brewer's drays are delivering to the *Six Bells Inn*.

THE GREAT BLIZZARD, 1881

The greatest blizzard of the nineteenth century occurred on the night of 17-18 January 1881. Many of the surrounding villages were completely cut off from Lymington by huge snowdrifts and in Lymington itself the snow lay many feet deep. Paths had to be cut for pedestrians and traffic. Near the Post Office a snow house or grotto large enough to accommodate a dozen people who 'might imagine themselves Laplanders or Esquimaux' was carved out from the bank of snow. Alfred Cole, the Milford sub-postmaster, described this curiosity, 'A house was built of snow in the Lymington High Street, and a charge made for admission with which coal and other comforts were purchased for the poorer inhabitants; quite a good sum I believe was so obtained . . .'[160]

Outside the town's streets, where some clearance was possible, the drifts were a considerable hazard. *The Lymington Chronicle* recorded the situation by stating, 'that the suburbs of Lymington may almost as well be a hundred miles away; it was only by incessant digging, that anything like communication could be maintained . . .'

The blizzard was followed by an extended hard frost so that the snow hardly thawed for many days. No train was able to travel along the branch line from Brockenhurst so for days no newspapers or letters arrived in the town.

Above It still appears to be snowing in this historic photograph of the High Street at the time of the Great Blizzard of 1881.

Below The little terrace of cottages at Woodside that were inundated when the snows thawed and swelled the streams. The census of 1881, taken only about nine weeks after the flooding, shows only eight residents remained occupying the cottages. The cottages were demolished in 1906 and never replaced.

When the thaw at last came there was flooding in the low lying parts of the town and those living in the cottages by the stream at Woodside suffered from an inundation containing a mixture of sewage and water.[161]

FIVE

Into Modern Times

WELLWORTHY ARRIVES

In the census of 1901 the population of the Borough of Lymington stood at 4,165, an increase of 43% over the course of the nineteenth century. Change had been considerable, and was to be even greater in the coming decades. But as the new century began the town's innate suspicion of progress had left it in the doldrums and in danger of being bypassed by a fast changing world. A contemporary report revealed a sense of disquiet:

LYMINGTON IN 1901: A RETROSPECT – Lymington has certainly not made much progress in the matter of trade, and the almost deserted state of the once famous shipyard is a sorry spectacle to those who remember what a busy hive of industry this was only a few years since. The projected tunnel under the Solent, it is thought by some, will in a measure make Lymington a busier place, and that much building will ensue. Others fear – and not without good reason – that the new [railway] line will materially decrease the trade of the town from the fact that the present railway communication will almost cease. The new line has not yet been commenced; when it is there is sure to be a large addition of trade, as was the case during the construction of the Bournemouth District [*sic*, Direct] line, and it will be imperative that our local authorities should leave nothing undone in striving to secure for the town quite as many advantages in railway transit as at present exist, with a station much nearer the town than that at present proposed.[1]

The Solent tunnel referred to was a proposal to create a direct line from Brockenhurst to the Isle of Wight with a railway tunnel under the Solent from Keyhaven marshes to near Freshwater on the Island. The route suggested departed from the Lymington branch railway a little north of Ampress, traversing Lymington to the west to reach Keyhaven. The fear was that this would leave the stretch of railway from Ampress to Lymington Pier as a spur serving

Above left Edward Henry Pember, QC (1833-1911) whose home was at Vicars Hill, Boldre, held the office of mayor at the turn of the century. He was in office to proclaim the accession of Edward VII from the balcony of the *Angel Inn* in 1901.

Above right Villiers Francis Dent (1846-1909), whose home was in Buckland Manor, was elected mayor to succeed Pember, thus serving a third time as mayor.

Below Flooding and blizzards weren't restricted to the nineteenth century. Here residents gaze out from the upstairs windows on a flooded Waterloo Road in 1909.

The newly built All Saints Church at Woodside.

nothing, as the tunnel route was expected to take all the railway trade destined for the Isle of Wight. If such a route was constructed a new Lymington railway station somewhere to the west of the town would be required. Although an act of Parliament for creating this railway was passed funds were insufficient to enable work to begin and in due course the scheme lapsed.[2]

Despite the apparent stagnation of the town it was considered worthwhile, at least in spiritual terms, to invest in an additional place of worship. In 1909 the large Anglican church of All Saints was built at Woodside to serve the population in the southern part of the parish, which had grown considerably in the last quarter of the nineteenth century, particularly around the Waterford roads of Westfield, Stanley, Brook and Spring. Its construction was made possible through the generous bequest of two sisters, Harriet Spike and Fanny Haldane whose premises, Holme Mead[3] (since demolished; the Lymington Post Office now stands on the site) was sold for £4,000 and added to other monies which realised a total of £18,000. Its architect was W.H. Romaine-Walker[4] who designed the new church in the then admired decorated Gothic style. Its first minister was a curate, the Rev. Edwin Ernest S. Utterton.[5] All Saints still fulfils its role but now ecumenically shares its space for Sunday worship with the Methodist congregation.[6]

Much more significant for the economic fortunes of the town was the arrival on Easter Monday, 8 April 1912, of 29-year old John Howlett. The loss of the *Titanic* a week later overshadowed his arrival which went largely unnoticed. Howlett had qualified as a mechanical engineer by studying at evening classes at Battersea and Woolwich Polytechnics and had come to Lymington to take up a post as manager for South Coast Garages, which had showrooms in the High Street and workshops at the top of Stanford Road.

His first impressions of the town, as he humped his luggage from the town station up the steep High Street, are very revealing:

> I passed a great number of public houses – there must have been over thirty in the town – and several butchers' shops which gave evidence of slaughtering animals on their back premises. I passed many great houses, with pillars and gardens and windows which looked down the High Street with more than enough aristocratic disdain to ignore the presence of butchers and pubs . . .

The principal owner of South Coast Garages was Hamilton Henry Montague Dent (known as Henry) of Buckland Manor.[8] The enterprise was inefficiently run and constantly in debt. Howlett

Advertisement for the South Coast Garages where John Howlett had applied for employment. The firm had two premises: the works in Stanford Road (later to become the Wellworthy factory) and showrooms in 76 High Street.

Standard 11·9

South Coast Garages Ltd.
LYMINGTON.

For Hire: Luxurious Cars, Careful Drivers. Any Distance, Day or Night. Trains met at Lymington or Brockenhurst Stations by appointment. Service Depot replete with Covers, Tubes and other Accessories, is always at your command. Full Repairs by competent Mechanics at our works, equipped with the latest machinery. Estimates given. Agents for Austin, Albert. Bayliss-Thomas, Gwynne, Rhode, Standard & Sunbeam Cars. Any make of Car Supplied.

The High Street much as it was when Howlett made his
trek from the station to the South Coast Garages.

was hard-working and enthusiastic, and soon won
the respect of the handful of pioneering car owners
using the garage's services, but he could not make
the business pay its way, due mainly to its profits
being squandered by Henry Dent. As a consequence
the banks were unwilling to advance loans and
Howlett came close to resigning and looking for a
new job.

Eventually, after many financial struggles and
disappointments, Howlett, with the help of bank
loans, was able to take the majority of shares so he
became owner and M.D.

Although war broke out in August 1914 it was
not until the appointment of Lloyd George as
Minister of Munitions in 1915 that small
engineering firms were placed under contract by the
Ministry so that their equipment and skills could be
employed in support of the war effort. Under these
changed circumstances Howlett was able to borrow
money to purchase lathes to manufacture shell
cases. He also received help from St George
Caulfeild of Vicars Hill, whose well-equipped

workshops operated in tandem with the Stanford
Road garage.

As Howlett noted in his autobiography, 'We
worked round the clock on shifts, we worked
Saturdays and Sundays alike, and we soon
overhauled the 100 shells a week that we had been
asked for and began to make our way towards
much higher targets'.[9] After a while South Coast
Garages was producing 500 shell cases each week,
but the price paid fell sharply due to improved mass
production by manufacturers elsewhere. To offset
the loss of income, Howlett installed machinery for
making piston rings which, as it happened, were to
prove more profitable than shell cases and yet just
as necessary for the war effort.

Howlett benefited from the expertise and advice
of two leading engineers, William Gray and George
Lanchester, the latter having gained his engineering
knowledge at the Hartley Institute, later
Southampton University. These two men provided
the vital technical knowledge that allowed the
fledgling company to overcome the initial design
problems and become a leading manufacturer of
piston rings.[10] Of the total sales of £21,542 made
by South Coast Garages in the year starting

September 1918 no less a sum than £9,766 was for piston rings.

The name South Coast Garages no longer seemed appropriate for this burgeoning industry and in the summer after the end of the First World War the name Wellworthy Limited was adopted. John Howlett borrowed additional money from the bank, enabling him to initiate a private company with a modest flotation of £1,000, in which the principal shareholders, in addition to Howlett, were William Gray, J.B. Perkins and C.E. Jones.[11] Within a few years this name became, if not quite a household word, certainly one well known throughout the whole motor industry. By 1921 the firm was employing just over 30, and although manufacturing in the 1920s was badly affected by the Depression the enterprise shown by John Howlett and his team of engineers, managers and workers ensured that, despite adverse trading conditions, between 1923 and 1929 profits rose from £1,913 a year to £20,999 and sales quadrupled. Then in 1936 the firm became a public company and the name was changed to Wellworthy Piston Rings Ltd.

To meet increasing demand the company expanded its factory space by purchasing properties around the original site. Despite these additions, by the late 1930s yet more space was required and Ampress Farm, a mile to the north, was purchased and a factory built on what was then a green field site. The foundry was opened in January 1939 and

A photograph of the Wellworthy premises in the early 1920s.

Ampress Farm was bought by Wellworthy in 1938 as a site for a factory. This photograph of the farmhouse was taken by Ian Hodges in 1957 shortly before its demolition.

the machine shop six months later. In 1943, at the peak of manufacturing for the war effort, when the company had close on 4,000 employees, the large Ringwood foundries of J.J. Armfield were acquired which, at that time, were linked to the railway network. It is not directly part of Lymington's story but it should nevertheless be noted that Wellworthy in the ensuing years also established factories in Salisbury, Bridgwater, Weymouth, Plymouth and Waterford, Eire. During the Second World War the factories diversified and manufactured a variety of pistons, liners and other engine parts for Rolls-Royce, Bristol and other aircraft manufacturers. Ironically, an industry so important to the war effort escaped the attention of enemy bombers.

Inevitably its economic muscle and size meant that Wellworthy had a great influence on the social and economic life of Lymington. It was by far the largest employer and also the largest single ratepayer. In 1936 the firm bought 16 houses to accommodate some of its employees and their families and in the following year six more; these properties were earmarked specifically for managerial staff. With so large a workforce the

John Howlett in his mayoral robes in 1930.

Once John Howlett had become successful he was able to purchase land and build himself a considerable house at Buckland which he named Ravenscourt. He later sold this property and moved to Newtown Park. Ravenscourt was demolished and a housing estate built in the grounds.

social facilities in the town were inadequate, so Wellworthy established its own social and sports clubs and, like many other large industrial concerns, its own band. A large sports field was provided by the firm at the Ampress factory site.

Some insight into the importance of the firm may be gained from comments such as those of Jim Arnold who, referring to the early 1920s said, 'I earned 2½*d.* an hour when I started. You had to go there as there was nothing else except the Berthon and the Berthon was only a seasonal job'.[12]

Despite its success during the Twenties and Thirties, the business was far less fortunate in the recession of the 1980s and was forced to close its operation in Lymington. The local paper summed up the position poignantly:

This is a sad week indeed for Lymington, as the last remnants of the Wellworthy piston firm finally vacated the town of its birth, with former managing-director Dr Bob Munro locking the doors for the last time. Fourteen years ago the company employed no fewer that 1,800 people in Lymington, contributing greatly to the prosperity of the town – but since the recession of the early 'eighties, and takeover bids by larger groups, that number has been drastically reduced so that, in the end, just 40 employees were transferred to the Ringwood branch and four to Bradford in Yorkshire. The remainder were made redundant or took early retirement.[13]

In hindsight the fate of the firm seems strangely ironical, for when Wellworthy first merged with its former competitors to become Associated Engineering Holdings it was to ensure survival in an increasingly competitive world. This was expressed clearly when John Howlett in 1947 signed the agreement for this merger:

What use would it be to the firm, what use would it be to the town, if I lorded it for a few more years and then, after my day, Wellworthy collapsed so that I left the men of Lymington with empty bellies and no means of filling them? What sort of memorial would it be to me if my workers stood on street corners with that shame-faced restless look . . . ? Wellworthy had become all that I'd ever dreamed of and it was ready to grow into something bigger than me and beyond me, and I knew that for the town's sake – and the dream's sake – that it wasn't for me to say no.[14]

John Howlett's influence in the town was considerable. He was elected a councillor in 1921, and later made alderman, and then in 1930 he became mayor. He was one of the principal protagonists favouring the enlargement of the borough. New Milton, with its urban district council and a strong sense of self-government, resisted to the end for, as Howlett remarked, it is 'governed by a Council which out-classed the rest of us in experience, knowledge and sheer capacity for work. They had been masters in their own house since 1926 ...'[15] However, the anticipated benefits to be derived from enlargement finally carried the day and in 1932 the borough of Lymington expanded to include Pennington, Milford-on-Sea, Hordle and New Milton. The new borough had nine aldermen and 27 councillors. Howlett, appropriately, continued his term as mayor of the enlarged borough and, in 1955, he was honoured by being made a Freeman of the Borough, just five years after being appointed to the Order of the British Empire.[16]

Edward King had remarked in about 1879, when describing the modern town, that 'We have no manufactures located here; a fact which, while it detracts from the wealth, adds to the quiet, the comfort and the respectability of the place; there being no crowded back-slums, and no large body of squalid artificers, to form the nest or the food of epidemics in unhealthy seasons'.[17] Wellworthy proved how ill-founded his fears of industry had been.

Laying the foundation stone of
the Town Hall, February 1913.

NEW TOWN HALLS & LOCAL POLITICS

In his first year or two in Lymington Howlett witnessed the construction of a new Town Hall on the site of 117/118 High Street. Mrs Martha Earley bequeathed the two properties to the town for the purpose of erecting municipal offices while her sister, Mrs Ellen Hewitt, who laid the foundation stone on 12 February 1913, gave the money for the building. This new Town Hall was to serve the enlarged borough for fifty years.

By the late 1950s it was no longer large enough and the quest for new accommodation was initiated. In April 1962 the borough council confirmed a decision to build on a site in Avenue Road, but the Minister for Housing and Local Government, after an initial promise of support, refused permission for the new hall. This was possibly a political decision reached in the face of criticism, coming mainly from the western side of the borough and co-ordinated by Councillor Frank Jeans of Pennington, about the new building and its cost. Councillor F.C. Price, the mayor-elect, described the decision as 'a bombshell'. The New Forest MP, Col. Sir Oliver Crosthwaite-Eyre,[18] took

The first large council house development at Flushards.

up cudgels on behalf of the council and with the backing of the County Council, was able to have the Minister's decision reversed.

Tenders for the new Town Hall were announced at the end of July 1963 to a total of £114,000 and the scheme was approved by 22 votes to 8.[19] With support democratically vested in the proposal work went ahead. Despite cries of 'ugly building' and 'more like a barracks than a Town Hall' work progressed so that by 25 May 1966 the building was ready to be opened ceremonially by Queen Elizabeth II accompanied by the mayor, Alderman R.H. Alderson.

The enlarged borough continued until 1974 when local government reorganization led to it being merged into the New Forest District Council. The town, comprising the area of the old manor of Lymington, amalgamated with Pennington (which in many ways had become a suburb of Lymington) to form the Lymington and Pennington Town Council.

What Wellworthy and the other light industries ushered in was a workforce drawn from many parts of the United Kingdom; many of whom had grown up in conditions quite unfamiliar to those of a small market town. They perhaps gave it a social mix that provided the foundations for a more radical approach to politics, and was at least partly responsible for the establishment of a branch of the Labour Party by a redoubtable farmer who lived on the east side of the river, Herbert 'Herbie' Goodall. During the First World War he gathered together a group of sympathisers to form the Lymington Labour Party and during the 1920s his enthusiasm for socialism, based on a firm Christian faith, inspired him to give soapbox meetings in Lymington High Street in the evenings: sometimes with crowds of up to one hundred attending.[20] Probably the early relative success of the Labour Party was due more to incomers than the local people, who were essentially conservative in outlook. As nationally, in the Sixties and Seventies, the party became more in the thrall of the 'loony left' so support in Lymington faded and radical opinion found its outlet in support for the Liberal Democrats, where it seems to have remained ever since.

When John Howlett was elected to the council in 1921 there were already two serving Labour councillors both of whom fought, with Howlett's independent backing, for the first council houses for the borough, not, it must be said, without a little controversy about the provision of parlours in the houses. The first group of eight were built in Bridge Road in 1935-6 at the cost of £2,150, but the major development between the war years was at Flushards, near the river, where, in the same year, plans were adopted for the erection of 24 houses at a cost of £7,320. Howlett's extremely cogent remarks throw much light on the innate conservatism of the Lymington people, or at least of those in authority, 'As a reforming measure it was not of course to everyone's liking, and word went round that I had promoted it for my own benefit, to bring strangers to work at my factory . . . this suspicious fear of strangers went very deep and warped opinions on all sorts of matters. The inhabitants of New Milton, or Hordle which was all of five miles away, were strangers not to be trusted.'[21]

THE IMPACT OF THE WARS

As elsewhere, many Lymington men were swept up by patriotic fervour when the call to arms came in 1914. One of these was Percy Blunt who had moved to Lymington when his father was appointed coastguard at Pitts Deep in 1906; Percy attended the Church of England school in New Street. He served in the Royal Navy for 35 years seeing action on the

Edward King (1893-1974) in his army uniform.

Above Convalescent soldiers, mainly from New Zealand, pose with the nursing staff in the grounds of Home Mead, used then as an army hospital.

Below The Home Mead military hospital in the High Street.

battleship *King George V* at the Battle of Jutland, and was among eight of the eleven survivors of the battle who attended the 75th anniversary ceremony on board HMS *Belfast* in 1991. He was also directly engaged in the evacuation of Dunkirk in 1940. Percy married in Lymington in 1919 and on demobilisation in 1945 made his home in the town, where he died in 1992.[22]

Edward King, the bookseller, joined the army in 1915 at the age of 22 and kept a diary of his war service from the time of his initial training on Salisbury Plain, through action on the Western Front and from thence to the Balkans and finally to Palestine. Lymington men fought in all theatres of the First World War and more than 80 'gave their lives for their country'. Their names are inscribed on a war memorial cross which stands by the parish church. This was unveiled by the Rev. Charles Bostock on Easter Sunday 1921 before a gathering of several hundred people, including the mayor, E.A.G. Stone, and members of the council.

It is quite extraordinary that no memorial to those who fell in the Second World War was created until 1990, some 45 years after the end of hostilities. In order to remedy this deficiency Keith McDonell collected 41 names of servicemen killed in the war and, with the aid of the Royal British Legion, successfully sought to place a panel inscribed with their names onto the existing War Memorial.[23]

Home (or Holme) Mead, the site of the present Post Office, was requisitioned during the First World War and turned into a convalescent home for wounded soldiers, mainly from New Zealand.

Many of these servicemen had come from the New Zealand No. 1 General Hospital at Brockenhurst, where they had first received treatment for their wounds. A large number of Lymington women were members of the Voluntary Aid Detachment (VAD) which was based at Home Mead under the superintendence of Mrs E.F. Chinery, wife of one of the local doctors. The recently formed Boy Scouts were described as 'giving useful help' at the convalescent centre.[24]

Schoolgirls, responding in their own way to the material needs of the serving men, collected money to purchase them socks. In 1916 schoolboys in the town collected six hundredweight of horse chestnuts, not for playing conkers but to be used to make fine charcoal for gasmask filters. Sphagnum moss was also gathered in large quantities from the

Peace Thanksgiving Sunday, 17 November 1918. A long phalanx of soldiers followed by Boy Scouts and behind them the mayor, mace-bearer and corporation line up outside the Town Hall prior to marching to the parish church.

nearby New Forest heathland which, after sterilising, formed a useful absorbent in wound dressings.

However, the civilian population was much more involved in the Second World War. A few days previous to the war being declared in September 1939 children were evacuated from perceived local danger areas to the relative safety of Lymington, where the junior school became the collecting point for children evacuated from Southampton and Portsmouth. Some of the older children were from poor, slum areas and behaved in an entirely alien manner to that which Lymington was accustomed. Because of their disruptive behaviour many were known as 'unbilletables'. A few were tempted by nature's bounty and some boy evacuees housed in New Milton helped themselves to chickens' eggs. As Eric Gadd, a schoolmaster who had accompanied some of the children, noted in his diary, 'My first experience of a juvenile court, at Lymington. A little more impressive than I had been led to believe: the police were in uniform, after all. The leader of the gang of egg-thieves was placed on 12-months probation – not unexpectedly'.[25] Most of the

'unbilletables' and had to be housed in requisitioned buildings in Lymington.

'One young fellow of 19 was found four jobs at Lymington and refused them all. All the able-bodied men who were sent to Lymington to do manual work returned in a body to state that the work was unsuitable for them . . . '[26].

Children had to take their gas masks to school. Air raid shelters were built in playgrounds and precautions taken against incendiary bombs and flying glass. The Congregational Church bought a stirrup pump, 12 bags of sand, 6 water buckets and 6 rakes as a precaution against fires, and its lower school room was taken over by the YMCA, at a rent of 25s. a week, to be used as a canteen for troops billeted in the district.

As in most other towns Lymington formed a detachment of Land Defence Volunteers (LDV) largely comprising older ex-servicemen who had served in what was then still referred to as 'The Great War'. This body became the Home Guard and regularly trained in the Drill Hall. The town was also home to an active and well-supported Air Training Corps, many of whose youthful members went on to join the Royal Air Force and a few, such as Sergeant Terence 'Terry' Frogley (1924-44) and Flying Officer Clive 'Curly' Lewington (1925-45), lost their lives in action.[27]

Fortunately the town suffered no aerial

bombardment in the First World War nor was it deliberately targeted in the Second. Of the two stray bombs dropped over the borough one found a target in Ford's shop next to the church, which was destroyed, and the other, happily, fell harmlessly in the river mud close to the Royal Yacht Club.[28] In 1940 the Lymington Corporation entered into an agreement with the fire brigades of Bournemouth, Christchurch, Poole, Wimborne and Ringwood and Fordingbridge so that in the event of large fires caused by enemy action the services of other brigades could be called upon.[29]

Group portrait of the Lymington Home Guard, about 1940. There was also a separate Wellworthy Home Guard at Ampress.

TRADE, TRANSPORT & UTILITIES

The town's shops remained an important part of its economic life and were a major attraction for the inhabitants of the surrounding villages. The coming of the railway had improved links with the town but the omnibus services widened this still further. The first service, operating from 1905, was steam-powered,[30] but as early as 1908 motor buses were making five regular journeys each day from the railway station to Pennington and Milford. The journey time to Milford village was 25 minutes and the single fare was 6d., 2d. was charged for small packages and 4d. for bulky items. These early bus days were recalled by Robert Hole, 'The bus to Milford ran twice a day. It was an old red steam bus

with a delicious smell and was owned by the Brothers Coffin and its conductor was Mr Death'.[31]

In 1920 the buses began to compete directly with the railway with the opening of the first direct Lymington to Southampton bus service operated by Hants and Dorset Motor Services Ltd. By the late Twenties there were four firms offering regular bus services, of which the largest was Hants and Dorset. Edward Gray of Hordle ran the Oakleigh bus service; the first driver was 'Budgie' Stride (later to

In 1902 a motor bus, a 4-cylinder Thorneycroft, chugs up Town Hill having come from the railway station. On the level it could attain a speed of 14 mph.

Dawson's Garage was situated in the High Street, taking over in 1926-7 the premises formerly occupied by South Coast Garages. They also had a garage in Emsworth Road. This advertisement shows the popular Austin 7 at £130.

become a chauffeur for John Howlett) who drove a Model-T 14-seater bus from New Milton to Lymington.[32]

There were also Morton's coaches based at Stanley Road, Lymington, and Billies' Coaches operating from the *Anchor and Hope* in the High Street.

In many ways the bus services were successors to the old carriers in that they transported 'sides of beef for the butcher, iron and timber for the blacksmith/undertaker, flour for the baker, ice for the large houses, large laundry baskets, etc.'[33]

However, it was the Hants and Dorset company which eventually absorbed the smaller operations to create a monopoly of public passenger transport. Its depôt was established in the yard of the *Londesborough Hotel* (formerly the *Nag's Head*) and at its peak in the 1950s was employing more than 90 drivers and conductors, many of whom were women, and who, unlike in many industries, received equal pay. The buses played a vital role in carrying the Wellworthy workforce to and from the factories and, with the massive enlargement of the Esso refinery at Fawley between 1949-51, fleets of buses took a large number of the 5,000 workmen to Foster Wheeler Ltd. the main contractors. During the war, when private transport was severely restricted, the local buses filled with servicemen based on the nearby airfield at Beaulieu Heath eager for a pint in one of Lymington's many pubs or to enjoy the local dances.

The arrival of the motor car, the first in Lymington being said to belong to Dr Alexander Pithie with a registration number of AA4,[34] gradually changed many aspects of everyday life but were too few in numbers to adversely affect public transport. It was only with the popularisation of the motor car and its much wider availability during the later 1950s that the public transport system suffered a reverse in its fortunes. Two-man crews became uneconomic and the principle of one-man buses was adopted. Routes were also gradually curtailed and the once extensive service cut down to the profitable few.

As motor car ownership increased the borough council was faced with the need to provide car parks and adopt parking restrictions on the busier roads. Initially they introduced charges but as early as 1932 Councillor S. Jones was pleading for the abolition of parking fees as a means of encouraging trade.[35] Even today, early in the twenty-first century, the problem of adequate parking is far from solved – although the town now has more car parks than ever before.[36]

The advent of the motor car necessitated vastly improved facilities for the Lymington-Yarmouth ferry service. In the early twentieth century barges laden with a few cars had been pulled by the paddle steamer *Solent* or a hired tug, *Jumsey*. Just before the outbreak of the First World War a LSW Railway poster announced:

Motoring in the Isle of Wight
Special passages can be arranged on Sundays upon arrangement being made with the Station Master, Lymington (telephone No. 7) not later than the previous day, the extra charge being £1 per car above the ordinary rates, which are 9s. for cars not exceeding half a ton, and 14s. for cars above 10 cwts., including wharfage and porterage at Lymington and Yarmouth.

The *P.S. Freshwater* was built for the Southern Railway in 1927 but even then she was not designed for carrying vehicles and it was not for another ten years that a purpose-built vehicle ferry, the *Lymington*, was constructed with a capacity for 16 cars and 516 passengers. In 1947, the *Lymington* was supplemented by the *Farringford*, able to carry 36 cars and 800 passengers. In 1959 a new *Freshwater*

was added to the fleet with a capacity for 26 cars and 620 passengers. In the early Seventies around £1¼ million was expended on the larger and more comfortable *Cenred* and *Cenwulf*, each capable of carrying 76 cars on two decks and 756 passengers.

In 1979 one and a third million passengers were carried in addition to over 230,000 cars, 33,000 lorries and 2,000 coaches. The pressure for car parking at the embarkation point became so great that nearby fields were pressed into use as an overflow facility and land reclaimed at the ferry terminal to greatly enlarge the hard standing car park.[37]

Electricity came to Lymington at first as a purely private venture when E.R. Badcock installed a small generator at the back of his premises to light his shop.[38] In June 1898 the Lymington Electric Light and Power Company Ltd., was formed with G.R. Masters of the estate agent firm of Jackman and Masters as its secretary. Its premises were situated in Bath Road, adjoining what is now the Berthon boatbuilding yard. A year later the company was able to announce 'The plans for the works are complete . . . Light expected to be available next autumn'.[39] The plant was equipped with two 75 kilowatt steam-driven generators providing direct current (DC). This supply was changed in 1931 to alternating current (AC), which is much more suitable for distribution; this was delivered by 560 kilowatt alternators driven by diesel engines. The station remained operational until 1961.

In 1900, following the establishment of the

The *Farringford* was launched in 1947 and was then the larger of the two ferries carrying vehicles. The older *Lymington* had entered service before the war.

electrical supply company, the borough council became interested in providing the town with electric street lighting not solely, it must be said, to show they were in the forefront in the application of technology to social needs but because of increasing difficulties in dealings with the gas company. Quite exceptionally, in 1933, owing to the high costs of electricity the borough council authorised a return to gas street lighting and this system was maintained for a further 20 years.[40]

Small private generating companies, such as

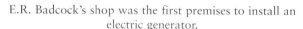

E.R. Badcock's shop was the first premises to install an electric generator.

Lymington's, were quite incapable of supplying the increasing demands for electricity made both by industry and domestic users so that they were obliged to obtain additional power from larger concerns. Indeed for many years Wellworthy had had to supply its own electric power.

The Lymington company contracted with the West Hampshire Electricity Company and the Bournemouth and Poole Company for its extra electricity and in 1935 the Wessex Electricity Company took over the Lymington firm.[41] Initially, electricity was used in domestic buildings for light only, followed by heating with electric fires and then used to power machines such as vacuum cleaners, refrigerators and a range of other tools which greatly increased demand and consumption. On nationalisation in 1948 the company was absorbed into the Southern Electricity Board.

The telegraph had been introduced into Lymington in 1852 with its station at the Solent Bath building at Waterford, but it seems to have been underused and ran into debt closing five years later. The borough council then negotiated an arrangement with the railway company to use its telegraphic facilities once the branch line was opened.

The telephone arrived in the late nineteenth century. The Western Counties and South Wales Telephone Company, founded in 1886, had within three years of its establishment services running to Southampton and Bournemouth. When the National Telephone Company took over in 1892 it began a more active campaign to seek new subscribers.

By the early years of the twentieth century a 25-line telephone exchange was fitted up in the backroom of the Lymington post office, operated by the counter attendant.[42] Lymington No. 1 was a Mr J. Miller, who lived at 'Tolosa', Grove Road; gradually a handful of businesses, such as G.T. Vince at the 'Invincible' Motor Repairing Works and Garage in the High Street (number 190) and the High Street chemist, George H. Gare (number 197) were also connected.

HEALTH CARE & THE HOSPITAL

It was the many visits made to the area by royalty, and in particular by Edward VII, that provided the impetus to opening a hospital in Lymington. The local gentry and other families who entertained the king decided that his visits should be commemorated by the building of a memorial hospital. A committee was formed under the chairmanship of Lord Arthur Cecil of Passford House, whose daughter later married Dr Pitt, and a public subscription was initiated 'for the cost of building and endowing a hospital'. The estimate for the initial building was a modest £600 and work started immediately. Both the architect, Bernton Benjamin, and the builder, Stone and St John, were local. The site, part of a large field belonging to Buckland Farm, was the gift of the lord of the manor, Keppel Pulteney.

The Lymington Cottage Hospital opened in 1913 and was typical of the then popular 'cottage hospitals', consisting of two four-bedded wards and a single bed emergency ward, all heated with open coal fires, with a centrally-heated operating theatre, an X-ray room and dispensary. The X-ray machine was the gift of Mr Caulfeild, of Delawarr House, the gifted amateur engineer and supporter of John Howlett. There was a kitchen to prepare and cook meals for the patients and also accommodation for the matron and two nurses. The first matron was a Miss D.K. Lynch, whose sister, Miss E. Lynch, and an Irish nurse made up the residential medical staff. The medical expertise was provided by all the local GPs, backed by Dr Belben and Mr Ramsey of Bournemouth, who acted as consultants.

In due course the hospital was extended. In 1919 the number of patients treated was 167 and operations performed 49; in 1928, just nine years later, 800 patients were treated. Such use required greater numbers of nursing staff and in 1929 a £2,500 nurses' home was built in the newly made King's Road. One extraordinary aspect of the hospital was that until 1933 all administrative work was carried out by volunteers.

The Second World War saw the addition of two hutted wards, given by the government, which remained in use until the hospital closed in January

Nurse Elizabeth Wood (1851-1915) was for 30 years the
Lymington district nurse. She was a Lancashire girl and
had trained at the Infirmary in Derby.

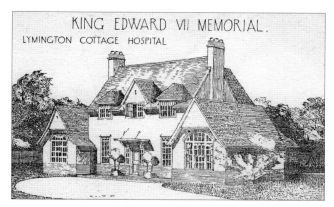

A contemporary drawing by the architect H. Bernton
Benjamin, of the first Lymington cottage hospital, issued as
a promotional postcard.

2007. With the establishment of the National
Health Service in 1947 Lymington Hospital became
part of the Southampton Group of Hospitals. Many
developments have taken place since (in 1966
nearly 10,000 out-patients and well over 2,000 in-
patients) and an increasingly sophisticated service,
such as the Pathology Laboratory built as a
memorial to Dr de Mowbray, with a highly praised
staff. Nurses' training had become an important
part of the hospital's wider role and its nursing
school enjoys a high reputation.

Voluntary support has always been important and
the League of Friends of Lymington Hospital have
raised prodigious sums for a whole range of
facilities, some directly medical and some social.
John Howlett was a great benefactor, promoting the
Annual Hospital Ball and encouraging other fund-
raising events.43 For many years Walter Symons
was the active and inspirational chairman of the
Friends, who encouraged such people as Dennis and
the late Joan Knight to participate in organising and
sponsoring activities such as their open-air vintage
car events, staged at Buckland, which raised many
thousands of pounds. As a former matron, Miss
Marion Buckeridge, remarked, the hospital 'was

started by Lymington people, belonged to
Lymington people, and served Lymington people'.44

The Lymington Union Workhouse continued to
maintain a hospital for sick inmates and in 1927 a
maternity unit was added. Because of the stigma
still attached to being an inmate in a workhouse the
children born there had the address on their birth
certificates recorded merely as 'New Street'.
However, its role gradually changed and legislation
in 192945 altered the status of all such buildings. In
1947 it became an infirmary for geriatric cases and
was amalgamated with Lymington Hospital in
1955. It closed in 2002 and the building's future is
uncertain at the present time.

Although proposals for a replacement hospital
had been under review since 1983 it was not until
1995 that firm plans to construct a new hospital to
serve Lymington and the New Forest District were
first mooted. Eventually land was purchased at
Ampress on the former Wellworthy factory site and
a new hospital constructed at a cost of £36 million.
It opened on 2 January 2007. On the occasion of
the official opening by the Princess Royal on 6
February 2007 the League of Friends made a
donation of £400,000 towards the cost of a new CT
scanner. The last of its donations from the 'new
hospital appeal' started in 1983 which raised in
total over £3m.

The modern hospice movement, founded by
Dame Cicely Saunders in London in 1967,46 soon
had an impact in Lymington and has become one of

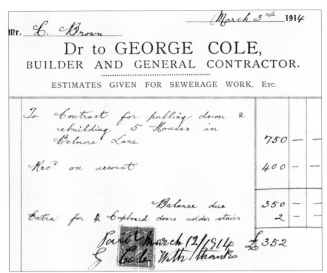

the town's most strongly and consistently supported charities by businesses, institutions and individuals. The initial drive for the foundation of a hospice for Lymington came from Phoebe Coates (1915-2006) in the late 1980s. Her generosity and enthusiasm were the essential catalysts in this humane enterprise. The grounds of her property in Lower Pennington Lane became the site for the construction of a purpose built hospice which was opened officially by the Duchess of Kent in 1992, though it had already been operating for two years. It serves not only Lymington but the whole New Forest district and was given the name of Oakhaven Hospice.47 It was founded as and remains a charity but with close links to the NHS and local doctors and hospitals.

FIRES & THE FIRE SERVICE

Many provincial towns have suffered dreadfully destructive fires through the centuries. In this respect Lymington is a fortunate exception as there is no record of a serious conflagration. However the churchwardens at first, and later the corporation, have always made provision for fire fighting. Eighteenth century churchwardens' accounts mention fire hooks, leather buckets and payment to men maintaining the engine. References are also made to the town pump, as when Mr Basted was paid 9s. 7d. in 1739 for 'putting the town pump in order in case of fire'.

The corporation took responsibility for the fire service in 1889 and provided a horse drawn pump: a year later the firemen were issued with uniforms and helmets. The fire station was situated in Southampton Road, with its engine shed between the water tower and the playing fields. The horses for the engine were stabled in the yard of the *Angel Inn*. A new fire warning bell was attached to the water tower, the old one being fitted outside the police station in Gosport Street where it could be used to give warnings of fires in the lower part of the town.

The former town clerk, Aubrey Slater noted, 'Practice call outs seem to have been rare, but there is one case on record where the fire engine had left the station within 25 minutes of the call, and this was thought to be an excellent result!' The part-time brigade had a complement of 15, who were paid 2s. 6d. for the first hour fighting a fire and 1s. for any subsequent hour. The men attended one unpaid drill every month and those who failed to turn up without good reason were fined 6d.

The charges paid by the council for attending fires were at the rate of two guineas (£2 2s.) if under one mile, three guineas for one to two miles and four guineas for two to four miles. For a false alarm the charge was 10s. 6d. In 1919 the engine was replaced with a horse-drawn steam powered pump which remained in use until 1928 when a motorised engine was purchased. Two serious, though localised, fires occurred in the twentieth century: in 1905 the old *Anchor and Hope Inn* was burnt down and in May 1913 a terrace of five thatched cottages and a pub, *The Millwrights' Arms*, in Belmore Lane were so severely damaged by fire that they had to be demolished.[48] They were rebuilt in the following year at a total cost of £750.

SHOPPING

The changing pattern of shopping began to be felt in Lymington from about 1880 onwards and accelerated during the twentieth century. The impact of these changes is reflected in the recollections of Sydney Edward Prichard, who was born in St Thomas Street in 1874 and for many years had his butcher's business there. The hours were long: from Monday to Friday from 6 a.m. to 8 p.m. and up to 11 p.m. on Saturdays. Before the days of refrigeration, two hundredweight ice blocks chilled the meat, but all meat remaining on Saturday was sold off to avoid keeping it over the Sunday. The Rev. Charles Bostock, interviewing Sydney Prichard, asked 'did some people come along late on Saturday night and get a big joint for very little?' 'Not in my shop', he quickly responded. Home produced meat was quite dear in the early years of the century but imported lamb was from

Glass bottles bearing the names of Lymington traders and manufacturers. The stoneware bottles contained ginger beer produced by Henry Badcock, the chemist (left) and the Lymington Mineral Water Company (Lance & Son) in North Close.

8d. to a top price of 10d. a pound. In search of economy many Lymington shoppers used to take the train to Southampton to buy cheaper cuts.

Sydney Prichard also recalled coal being brought into Lymington: 'coaling was done at the Quay. There were five public houses on the Quay [including] the *Dolphin*, the *Yacht*, the *Ship*, and they were full up soon after 6 o'clock in the morning with coal heavers'. Apparently they started their working day with a drink when beer was 2d. a pint![49]

The greatest changes came in the decades after the Second World War when many long-established businesses disappeared. Rands once renowned as having the largest supplies of cloth and material in the south of England, all set out on shelves redolent of a quieter age, finally succumbed to the new more aggressive climate. The Badcocks, an influential trading family with various retailing interests whose members had often filled civic appointments, also closed. R. Klitz, the reputable music instrument suppliers founded in 1789, although modernising with the advent of the wireless, gramophones and radiograms, finally closed in 1981. Kings, the long-established booksellers, printers and stationers, lost its direct family connection and was taken over by a staff buy-out: it was later purchased by Ottakers

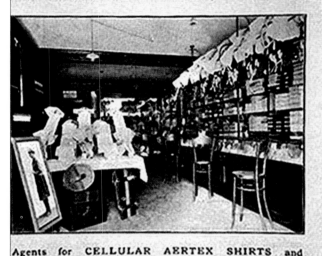

Above left An advertisement of 1920 for Elliott's.

Above Plumbly's Stores was a grocer's at 116 High Street. It opened at the end of Victoria's reign and closed in the 1960s.

Left Advertisement for Klitz's Music Warehouse at 88 High Street.

Below Advertisement of Lincoln-born George F. Saul, the ironmonger, who had come from Caterham in 1880 to set up business in Lymington. The premises were on the corner of New Street where Boots' shop now is. His second son, John, became an articled clerk to Moore and Rawlins, the solicitors.

Above Six are employed in Elliott's tailors' shop behind their High Street premises. Note the treadle sewing machine operated by a young woman.

Left A hand propelled dairy float belonging to Aldridge's Dairy of 46 St Thomas' Street. Milk was served directly from the churns into the jugs customers brought to the milkmaid. Photographed in about 1930.

Below Waterford Post Office and general stores run by Wyndham H. Dyer from the mid-1920s to about 1930.

and subsequently Waterstones. H.E. Figgures, founded by Herbert Figgures as a cycle business in 1904, later diversifying into electrical goods, closed in 2006.[50]

Other businesses flourished and seemed as if they would go on for ever; an example is G.F. Saul the ironmongers. Few old businesses survive. One is Elliotts, 'Clothiers, Hatters & Outfitters', established in 1873.

The arrival of chain stores brought some changes to old business practices and those that failed to adapt to the changing retailing climate ultimately closed their doors. The International Tea Company, trading as International Stores, established an outlet in the High Street in the late 1880s. Timothy, White

Above & above right The Home and Colonial Stores, one of the earlier chain stores to become established in Lymington at 83 High Street in the late 1920s.

& Taylor established premises on what had been Saul's, just before the outbreak of the Second World War, to be superseded in turn by Boots the Chemist, whose first premises had been at 24 High Street. From the mid-twenties Macfisheries, on the south side of the High Street, set out its display of fish on cold marble slabs. Among the first post war incomers was Woolworth, which opened in 1952[51] on a large High Street site that had been formerly Barrow's garage and Rowland Hill's grocery shop. Though, at that date, no longer trading as the renowned 3d. and 6d. store, it was still able to offer a wide range of relatively cheap goods.

A particular sadness was the disappearance of Willis and Son of the South Coast stores, a high class family grocery business which had been founded in 1829 by Robert Bentley Purchase. The

A date stone set into the wall of Robert Bentley Purchase's grocery shop at 25 High Street.

façade, of gilded lettering behind glass panels, was a perfect example of a Victorian shop front, which, despite protests, did not survive after the shop was purchased by Oakshotts and shortly afterwards by Tesco. Porter and Clark, suppliers of gardening and agricultural goods, purchased the Lyric cinema which they converted into a large store but this closed and their business was concentrated in New Milton. These premises were then taken over by Waitrose, who built a small supermarket on the site and later, to some local dismay, absorbed Mark's old-established bakery shop next door. The large Wellworthy factory site proved ideal for the construction of Lymington's largest purpose-built superstore, Safeway,[52] with its own huge car park.

Some of the smaller shops, due to the special niche they filled, usually because of quality and service to customers, survived the changes. One such example is A. Jennings, the baker and confectionery business, founded in 1930 and still flourishing.

The *Londesborough* Hotel, once one of the largest residential hotels in Lymington and which in its heyday had provided accommodation for guests such as William Morris, Dante Gabriel Rosetti and Andrew Thomas Turton Peterson, builder of Sway Tower, was reduced to a single bar and the front divided into two parts – one taken by an optician and the other by the wine merchants, Oddbins. Fords, a much patronised dealer in furniture and household goods, had large premises on the corner of Church Lane and the High Street which were closed in 1992 and the business retrenched in their original premises, opened in 1840, adjoining the churchyard until, in due course that too closed. Henry Doman, who had established his business in 1851, specialised in drapery, haberdashery and related products; the shop remained a family concern until it closed in the 1970s. Doman was an ardent supporter of the Literary Institution, a close friend of Henry Allingham and a poet in his own right who published several slim volumes of verse.53 Like many businessmen he was a freemason and became treasurer of the New Forest Lodge.54

The recession of the 1980s badly hit retailing and Andrew Ross writing in the *New Forest Post* stated:

> Lymington High Street is at a figurative crossroads with the future of shops and small businesses in the town at the centre of a growing row between traders and landlords. The traders claim high rents are pushing them to the wall while the landlords assert they are only charging the going rate. But all residents and tourists see is a lot of empty shops.

Ross estimated that 10% of the business premises in the town were closed. Peter Edwards, treasurer of the Chamber of Trade, said the root of the problem lay in 'the fact that Lymington became too fashionable when the town became a sailing and

Right An interior view of the packed shelves of the Markwell family's large grocery business. It was established by Thomas Markwell in the late nineteenth century and was situated in a prominent location at 1 Gosport Street facing the High Street.

Like most businesses, especially the grocery trade, Markwell maintained an extensive delivery service to the residents of the town and the surrounding villages. Note the motor van and bicycle.

tourism centre'. The adoption in 1990 of the Uniform Business Rate dramatically increased the amount shop keepers had to pay and led to widespread protests. The Lymington Town Council was not immune to these changes, as when calculations showed that the rateable value of the ancient street market had 'increased 84 times, from £325 to £27,000'. Allen Clark, the Town Clerk, is reported to have said, 'I knew the market assessment would go up, but when I went round to see the figures I nearly fell through the floor. It's crazy'.55 Happily, the problems facing commerce and industry following the long-lasting recession gradually faded as the retailing boom gathered momentum from the late 1990s. Despite the

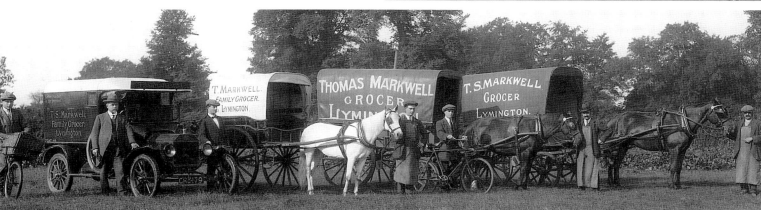

Lymington River in the 1930s, with the Walhampton ferry arriving at the quay while just beyond can be seen the shipyards.

economic problems some light industries in the town showed commercial buoyancy and achieved success, such as Gill Electronics which won a contract for supplying gas meters to the value of £300,000 in 1989.[56]

The very successful manufacturing company Lymington Precision Engineering (LPE) was founded by Leon Crouch in 1981.[57]

YATCHING & BOATING

The river remains a dominant feature in the life of Lymington. Its early commercial and economic roles were expanded by the interest in boating for pleasure. Joseph Weld and others pioneered yachting as a popular pastime for the wealthy, but it took the more egalitarian twentieth century for the river and Solent to be enjoyed by a wider cross-section of the townsfolk.

The yacht building and servicing industries remain important both economically and socially. The town became the base for John Laurent Giles, a gifted and able naval architect specialising in yacht design, who established himself in Captain's Row in 1927, later moving to Quay Hill, and continuing in business until his death in 1969. The

Berthon Boatyard continued to turn out fine vessels, such as the 71-foot schooner, *Vera Mary*, built in 1932 at a cost of over £5,500. The company, founded in 1877, had its origins in Romsey where the Rev. Edward Lyon Berthon (1813-99) designed the first, and highly successful, collapsible lifeboat (tested in the River Test). The business passed to his son, Edward, but on his death in 1917 it was sold to Frank Aubrey May whose brother Harry became a partner. In the following year the Lymington yard, formerly Inman's, was purchased and the Berthon Boat Company relocated there. In due course the firm passed to his grandson, David (1935-2007), and subsequently to his sons, Brian and Dominic, who continue to supervise and run an important industry. During the war naval vessels were constructed. In 1993 the firm was awarded the contract to build a new patrol boat for Associated British Ports in Southampton. Such work ensures local employment for at least a 100.

Another boatbuilding firm, founded as recently as 1979, is Blondecell, which expanded its premises in 1993. In 1983 Bill Green founded Green Marine, a successful company which has built hulls for many vessels. Successful firms sometimes fall into the doldrums as happened to Hood Sail makers, founded in Lymington in 1966, who for most of that time manufactured sails of high quality but by the turn of the century high rents and overheads led to closure.

Dan Bran (1869-1950), was renowned as a skilful boat builder, working largely on his own account. Amongst his many achievements was the designing and building of the Lymington Prams.

Early in 1914 the Lymington River Sailing Club was founded with 14 members. Captain H.H. Nicholson was the club's captain. The 'club was really a racing club for 'prams', although between the weekly races (held annually between May 15th and August 15th) members cruised about the river, and the Solent, and when the weather was suitable, going as far afield as Yarmouth and Newtown in the Isle of Wight'.[58] The subscription was a manageable 10s. a year and the harbour dues were 5s. annually.

The outbreak of the First World War led to the

Above Boats frozen in the ice during the bitterly cold winter of 1962/1963. (Photo: Myles Cooper)

Below A drawing of Dan Bran's boat shed.

The ever-popular Lymington Regatta continues to draw the crowds. This photograph dates to about 1900.

club's closure but the idea had taken root and in 1921 Major Cyril Potter, himself a member of the Royal Yacht Squadron, called a meeting which led to the re-founding of the Lymington River Sailing Club. Another club formed shortly afterwards, known as the Solent Sea Birds, competed with the boats of the LRSC. Participation of the various clubs in the Lymington Town Regatta, established in 1875, in August 1921 brought much interest to the activities on the river.[59] Membership of the LRSC was raised to 2 guineas (or half that for non-boat owners) but by that time they had established a clubhouse in the old coastguard boat house near Dan Bran's famous shed.

A view of the many pleasure craft moored in the river near the Royal Lymington Yacht Club.

The club, perhaps inevitably, attracted the wealthy as larger vessels became popular and in 1926 its name was changed to The Lymington Yacht Club. In 1931 the Duke of Gloucester became patron, which in turn led in 1938 to the grant of a royal warrant, enabling the club to become the Royal Lymington Yacht Club. The club closed during the Second World War but by 1946 was back in operation and has continued to flourish to the present day.[60] The RLYC also held its own annual regatta, complementing that of the town.

The raised status of the club led to the exclusion of many of those for whom it had originally catered. Consequently, a public meeting was held in 1946 which 'because it was thought that there was room

This aerial view of about 1960 shows the Royal Lymington Yacht Club in the centre with the houses of Bath and King's Saltern Roads in the background.

for a club for people who were shipwrights, builders and shopkeepers who might not wish to join the Royal or possibly they could not anyway!'[61] led to formation of the Lymington Town Sailing Club. The club was able to obtain use of the old Bath House as its clubhouse, thanks largely to the efforts of Stan Lamb, a Labour councillor.[62]

The Lymington Rowing Club was founded in 1881, over the years it enjoyed a number of successes in rowing competitions and is still well patronised.

The popularity of Lymington as a yachting centre has led to the opening of chandleries and other marine businesses situated mainly around the Quay. During the post-war years the demand for mooring space in the river led the Berthon Boat Company to construct a large marina.[63] Jonathan Raban on arriving by boat commented:

> I was in no position to rail against the craze for owning boats, and the Lymington marinas were simply the inevitable consequence of a lot of people sharing my own dream of making an escape from an overcrowded country in a private ark. They were a perfectly fair reminder that the dream was not an innocent one: it violated the landscape and the wild things that lived there; as with so many dreams, there was an ugly twist to the idyll.[64]

LEISURE & ENTERTAINMENT

Ewart Read, born in Southampton Road in 1901, recalled some of the entertainments of Lymington in the early years of the twentieth century when he wrote:

> What lovely times they were: The Hospital Sunday Procession with the Town Band, a well-drilled marching band, leading, High Street illuminations on Regatta Night, Empire Day parades in the Cricket Field; exciting six-a-side football tournaments on Easter Monday, Minstrel Shows at the Literary Institute, roller skating in the old malthouse, (now part of the Community Centre), with the weighbridge outside . . . [65]

The church, too, made provision for the community by the construction in 1926 of a Parish Hall costing £3,700, which became widely used for social events such as musical recitals, promoted, no

The well-supported Hospital Sunday parade in 1906 with good contingents of sailors and soldiers represented amongst the many townsfolk and the clergy.

doubt, by the honorary secretary and church organist, Harry Wakeford. Saturday evening dances were particularly popular with the younger folk of the town and surrounding areas: the accomplished and popular band of Ronnie Horler (1920-2005) frequently providing the rhythm. This hall was later sold by the church and the site developed for modern housing while a new, well-equipped parish hall adjoining the church, was constructed in 1981. This attractive building, an enhancement to the town, was the last work of the famous local architect Roger Pinckney (1900-90), whose ashes lie nearby.[66] The fine red-brick Masonic Hall in the High Street was built in 1927.

The Assembly Rooms, adjoining the *Angel Hotel*, were popular for dancing and on Saturdays throughout the Second World War were much patronised by visiting soldiers, sailors and airmen and, of course, the local girls.

Lymington's first cinema, *The Lyric*, built by Rashleys on the site of a garden called Woodlands in St Thomas Street, was opened in 1913 with Cecil Elgar as the first manager.[67] Seats cost 3d., 6d., 1s. and 1s. 6d., and despite disappointing trading figures in the first few years the cinema soon began to flourish, especially after the advent of 'talkies' and the fitting of what was claimed to be the best audio equipment in the south. The new go-ahead manager, Hector McCullie, had much to do with

Above New Forest ponies wander nonchalantly by the serpentine wall in Church Lane. Photographed by T.A. Heath in 1958.

Left In this advertisement the Lyric cinema proudly offers the finest talking film system in the south.

CONSERVATION, HERITAGE & CONFLICT

Until the passing of the New Forest Act in 1964 the commoners' animals wandered far and wide beyond the forest perambulation. As a consequence, ponies often ambled through the streets of Lymington and were regarded by many visitors as an additional attractive feature to the townscape. They were not popular with residents, as they entered gardens, devouring flowers and vegetables and generally causing minor but irritating damage. A newspaper report summed this up very neatly, 'The amazing sagacity of Forest ponies who come into the Borough, open garden gates, eat all the crops, and latch the gates as they leave, undo other gates and entice councillors' ponies away, commit sacrilege by eating the flowers from church yard graves . . . '[69] They also posed a hazard to motorised traffic, especially on the roads leading in and out of the town. The 1964 Act initiated the fencing of the forest and the gridding of all the roads at the boundary, so forcing the animals to remain within the perambulation.

In considering the changes he had witnessed since his boyhood in the town Raban[70] unerringly captures the mood of change:

'Yet somehow between 1959 and 1982, Lymington had been sacked by the barbarians of the new. The saltings had been quarried out to make marinas. Where the herons used to fish was now a solid mile of car parks, catwalks and pontoons. The clink and jangle of steel

this success and he was himself a composer of some distinction.[68] During and after the Second World War queues gathered for nearly every evening performance. But as happened elsewhere the spread and availability of television caused a decline in attendance and its seats were increasingly empty from about the mid-Fifties onwards. The cinema struggled on for a few more years, finally succumbing to the inevitable closure in 1963.

The Lymington Carnival became a major event following the drab years of the war. Many businesses provided decorated vehicles to make up the parade, which traversed the High Street. John Howlett was a considerable supporter and on one occasion his glamorous film star niece, Ann Crawford (1920-56), attended. A local carnival queen, with her entourage, was chosen each year and took a leading position travelling on a float in the parade.

Above A cyclist freewheeling down Priestlands Place, formerly known as Soapy Lane, a constricted passage linking the main road (A337) to St Thomas Street.

Above left The narrow entrance into Priestlands Place between Priestlands Dairy and a house in Belmore Lane.

Left In the late 1950s the shops were demolished and Priestlands Place widened.

rigging against alloy masts rang out over Lymington like the bells of a demented herd of alpine cows. The boats themselves wedged into slots like bits of gigantic Lego kit, appeared identical. Shark-nosed and white, their slit-eyed windows of smoked perspex gave them an air of an army of mobsters in shades. They loafed sulkily in their berths, their white plastic fenders sighing a little as they grazed the pontoons.'[71]

The 'barbarians of the new', in the form of developers Chilworth Estates Co. Ltd., sought planning permission in 1986 to erect 160 houses, a hotel and sports amenities on, in and around the Buckland Rings Iron Age hillfort, the last truly rural part of Lymington. The New Forest District Council threw the scheme out with an unanimous vote – an incensed public sent over 250 letters of protest supported by such prestigious bodies as the Royal Commission on Historic Monuments, English Heritage, the Council for the Protection of Rural England, The Hampshire Field Club and

Archaeological Society, the Lymington Naturalists' Society, The Lymington Society and even the Chamber of Trade. Chilworth responded by appealing against the NFDC and an inquiry lasting 13 days took place in the Lymington Town Hall with witnesses being called on both sides. The inspector, Mr M. Cross, issued a 70-page report, which came down clearly against the developers. The local paper noted, 'The combined forces of the New Forest District Council have seen off the Buckland Rings invasion by Chilworth Estates . . . The Secretary of State has ruled that part of the company's scheme was unreasonable and has awarded the Council half of its costs . . . '

Two happy events resulted from the engagement; firstly, Hampshire County Council purchased the Buckland Rings site for £200,000 and dedicated it as public open space; secondly, one of the stalwart defenders of the 'Rings', Edward 'Ted' Marsh (1923-95), spurred by events connected with the struggle to save Buckland, set in motion the process towards the establishment of a Lymington and District Museum. This came to fruition when, in 1999, the St Barbe Museum and Art Gallery was

Above Looking north along Queens Street in about 1955 before Priestlands Dairy and Millers butcher shop (on left) had been demolished to create the new road.

Left No. 52 High Street (Grosvenor House). Only the classical façade of this fine town house remains. It was once the home of James Monro, mayor of Lymington in 1831 and 1836, later becoming a boarding school run by Jane Smith and then home, successively, of three doctors, the first of whom, William Robinson Hill, was also mayor in 1891 and 1892.

officially opened in the former Church of England School. Since its foundation in 1951 the Lymington and District Historical Society (as the Lymington Historical Record Society) had held three successful exhibitions about various aspects of the town's history, which had finally borne fruit in the founding of the museum.

The volume and intensity of threats, or perceived threats, to the town's environment and history led to protests being better focussed and organized. All this increased public awareness of Lymington's natural and historic heritage led to the formation of the Lymington Society, an influential amenity organisation which has been particularly active over planning matters. For example, concern about the introduction of much larger ferries because of the possible damage they might cause to the marshes, as well as to other river users. In 1992 the reed beds immediately to the north of the bridge across the river were saved for posterity when purchased by the Hampshire Wildlife Trust with money raised by a public appeal.[72] Happily, both the Hampshire County Council and the New Forest District Council have been, in most cases, sympathetic to the aesthetic quality of the environment and conservation areas have been designated in Lymington. Nevertheless, many concerns remain about both the pace and the extent of residential development and protests against schemes are constantly being voiced by residents.

Even in the realms of commercial development anxieties were expressed following the closure of the Wellworthy Ampress factory. Uncertainty about the best use for the site meant it lay vacant. Eventually a proposal was put forward to turn it into a large retail base with firms such as Marks and Spencer, Tesco, Texas Homecare and others showing an interest. Many expressed fears that such a development would 'kill Lymington'. Traders in the town stated that 'It would destroy jobs in the centre of the town, which will become dead like Christchurch'. But John Farmer, for the developers, stated the opposite view when he said, 'We are convinced this would bring trade back into Lymington. I think generally local traders fear the unknown', a charge resented and rebutted by the Vice-president of the Chamber of Commerce who stated 300 commercial and retail businesses were opposed to the scheme.[73] The site has now developed a mixed use, partly commercial and industrial, partly residential and significantly providing a location for the brand new hospital.

A rather sadder indication of adverse conditions in the early 1990s, some think due at least in part to high unemployment, was growing teenage and youth violence in the town. Vandalism and burglaries increased and the police were accused of 'inaction'. The Lymington Police Inspector, Ron Godden, promised to increase foot patrols stating, 'I do recognise the very real problem caused by a small minority of youths in the town. It is intolerable that people should be frightened to go out in Lymington in the evenings . . .'[74] *The Times* reported on 29 October, 1992, 'Four people, including a girl aged 12, were arrested after a fight with police in Lymington on Monday night. Four police were hurt in the fight which began when they tried to arrest a teenager for a public order offence'. On the same day the headlines in *The New Forest Post* declared: 'TIME BOMB! Town's night of shame must prompt action to beat yobs'. Its report went on to record a scene of mob violence when '60 youths went on the rampage'. Inspector Godden responded with the observation 'For some time youngsters have been allowed to do what they like, but the police are now in control of the streets'.

Episodes such as these have flared up in Lymington, as in many other towns, from time to time over the centuries, and, distressing though they are, they should not be seen as the harbinger of a decline into lawlessness. One example comes from more than a century before when in 1869 a group of young men 'not composed principally of what is called "the Lymington roughs," but of what is called "the respectable young men of the town" set light to a bonfire in the middle of New Lane. 'The young men composing the mob were very insolent to the police, and did as much as they could to provoke a row."[75]

Unfortunately, there is a continuing problem with youth harassment and some vandalism, though since the installation of CCTV cameras in 2001 there has been an easing of the situation.

SOCIETIES, CLUBS & OTHER COMMUNITY GROUPS

The first Freemasons[76] in Lymington formed a lodge in 1764 which had its first meetings at the *Crown Inn*, Buckland, moving later to the more central location of the *Nag's Head* in the High Street. It seems that subsequently membership dwindled until William Hebbard initiated a revival in 1814 when a new body was formed designated The New Forest Lodge. They then met in a building in Quay Street which became known as the Masonic Hall but when the lodge became dormant it was hired by the Rev. Benjamin Maturin as a mission chapel, known as The Seamen's Bethel, in which regular Sunday services were held. Later the Masons reformed and continued to use the building for their meetings. Jones remarks, 'In 1838, the Lodge, after experiencing fluctuating fortune, "dwindled to nothing" and finally was extinguished in that year, Masonry remained in abeyance in the town for 22 years'.[77]

It was revived in 1860 but fell again into abeyance until 1874 when the lodge held its meetings at the *Bugle* in the High Street. In 1898 the Freemasons acquired premises in Ashley Lane which formed their meeting place until they were able to purchase land at 10 High Street where they erected a brand new large brick hall opened in May 1927 and which still stands.

The Oddfellows founded a lodge, the Bud of Hope, in Lymington in 1845 which had its headquarters at the *Anchor and Hope* but sadly its records were destroyed when the pub burned down in 1905. However, the lodge continued to survive.

The malt house which became the Lymington Community Centre in 1946 and since then has gone from strength to strength. The latest addition being the 200-seater Fuller-McLellan Hall, opened in June 2007.

The friendly society, the Ancient Order of Foresters established Court Yelverton in Lymington in 1851. One of the founder members was the brewer, William Knight. Other Lymingtonians amongst the early members were Benjamin James Croucher, tinsmith, and John James, cabinet maker. Margaret Knight, great-granddaughter of William Knight, recalled her own involvement, 'when aged about 10, [she used] a huge, dilapidated, antique typewriter to address membership cards'.[78] Despite a few ups and downs Court Yelverton is flourishing and, to commemorate the 150th year of its foundation, donated a public seat which is positioned in the Bath Road Recreation Ground with a pleasing prospect overlooking the river.

Royal British Legion, founded as the British Legion in 1921 to provide aid and support to all ex-servicemen and women, established a branch in Lymington in 1924 and by 1931 was able to establish a permanent base for its club at Haig House, 22A High Street which, despite some vicissitudes, continues to thrive to the present day. The Women's Section was founded in February 1926.

The Rotary Club was established in the town in 1938 one of the founder members, Dr Basil Thornton (1913-2000), surviving to celebrate the club's fiftieth anniversary in July 1998. Among those at the foundation were Noel Cowper (solicitor), John Humphreys (hairdresser), Edward King (bookseller, printer and stationer), who for

many years was secretary, Herbie Rand (draper), and Joseph Walsh (registrar).

The Lymington Round Table held its inaugural meeting in the *Angel Hotel* in 1951 and within a year was raising funds for many deserving causes, which included aid to those who had suffered in the great flood disaster at Lynton and Lynmouth in 1952 and also for the victims of the worst natural disaster to strike England in the twentieth century, the overwhelming East Coast Floods of 1953. Over the ensuing years it continued to raise funds to support many activities and projects in the locality. Sadly, membership gradually declined and the club was wound up in April 2000. At the final meeting the only founding member present was Geoff Isted (1923-2007), whose great-grandfather had founded Fords in Lymington.

The Boy Scout movement had been started by Sir Robert Baden-Powell in 1908. And in the same year Francis, son of Coventry Patmore, established a troop in Lymington and became its first scoutmaster. It was one of the earliest in England and was visited at its opening by Baden-Powell.

The Sea Scouts were founded by Robert Hole in 1921 and 12 years later were sufficiently well-established to have their permanent headquarters in King's Saltern Road, designed by the well-known Lymington architect, Roger Pinckney.[79]

EDUCATION WIDENED & FACILITIES BROADENED

The development of the Lymington Community Centre must be seen as one of the town's great social and cultural successes. The Lymington Community Association was founded in 1946, capitalising on the post-war comradely spirit, and it was able to secure the old malt house in New Street and start converting it to community use. The success of the venture was due to a team of enthusiasts inspired by the vision, hard work and commitment of Robert H. Hole (1897-1963), who is rightly commemorated as the founder of the Community Centre.[80] The Evening Institute classes were transferred there following its opening in 1949, providing a more appropriate venue for adults than in the schools where formerly they had met. By 1952 several extensions had been added, making it one of the most advanced community centres in the country. By the mid-Sixties over 100 classes a week were provided during the autumn and spring terms by the Local Education Authority, Southampton University Extra-Mural Department (as it then was) and the Workers' Educational Association. Many local organisations also used its facilities such as the gardening and travellers' clubs, bridge and chess clubs, historical and music societies. Drama was an important and popular feature of the centre and the Malt Hall provided a satisfactory theatre. The Lymington Players provided plays of all kinds from classics to comedies and thrillers, which continue to be supported and enjoyed by the public to the present day.

The centre catered for young children in several ways including play groups. Accommodation was available for meetings of political parties and trades unions. By 1993 the membership stood at nearly 2,900 and 117 organizations were affiliated. Practically every cultural aspect of Lymington's life found some provision in the Community Centre. Many thousands of pounds in support of the centre have been raised over many years through the sale of books donated by the public and originally organized by the late Walter Simmonds, who is commemorated in the gallery named after him.

Importantly, since 1979 the centre has provided the only cinema in the whole area with a regular programme of feature films. The centre also provided accommodation for the Citizen's Advice Bureau, which has given a valuable service to the community since its inception.

Lymington had to rely on commercial lending libraries attached to businesses in the town for its supply of reading matter and further provision was made in the mid-nineteenth century with the Literary Institute, so it is perhaps surprising that a branch of the County Library was not established until 1952 when a purpose built library, designed by Roger Pinckney, was constructed adjoining the Community Centre and which soon had to be enlarged. In 2002 a large modern library was constructed on a nearby site and the former library premises were demolished. This enabled the building of a major extension to the Community Centre in the form of a 200-seater hall built in 2006-7 at the cost of £700,000 provided almost entirely from the Centre's own funds.[81]

Secondary education for non-fee paying children only arrived in 1949. The County Secondary School for Lymington was built between 1955 and 1957 in the grounds of the 25-acre estate of Priestlands House at Pennington. Prior to that date Lymington children received secondary education at Brockenhurst County Secondary School. Even after Priestlands was opened pupils attended both schools, being transferred by buses as required. For example, in 1957 three classes spent two days at one school and three days at the other. By 1967 the combined common room numbered 52 teachers (some teaching at both schools). In 1970 the school became a Comprehensive and with new buildings it became feasible to make all provision on the one site. Interestingly enough during the decade 1957-67 the biggest single source for employment of boy school leavers was in agriculture, horticulture and forestry (17%) while 11% were taken by industry. By far the biggest number of girls, 34%, went into retailing and shop work whilst nearly 20% found employment in clerical and secretarial work.[82] By 2007 the school had 235 pupils.[83]

Priestlands House itself, built in the late eighteenth century, was retained as the Gurney-Dixon Residential Centre by Hampshire County Council's adult education service. Following its closure in 1993 as a result of economies the house was renovated and incorporated into the main school.

During the nineteenth century Lymington had provided a large number of private schools, mainly for boarding pupils. Whilst the number gradually diminished a few continued to survive in an increasingly difficult climate for privately funded education. Ridgeway Preparatory School, founded by Miss E.E. Twine, in 1946, provided for both day pupils and boarding girls and continued successfully for a number of years at Woodside. Most famously (though just outside the borough), Walhampton School,[84] sited in the former home of the Burrard family was founded in 1948 and continues to provide good quality and innovative private education for both boarding and day pupils.

LARGE HOUSES IN
THE TWENTIETH CENTURY

Lymington had its share of substantial mansions. One of these, first known as Ropewalk House, built by George Burrard around 1715, was for some years the residence of a branch of the family. It was later purchased for £3,500 by Captain Joseph Bingham, who extended the grounds by further land purchases, then changed the name to Grove House. The novelist Dennis Wheatley bought this property in 1944 for £6,400 and wrote 30 of his popular novels whilst living there. For relaxation Wheatley, like Winston Churchill, did bricklaying and has left one visible piece of his work in the form of a serpentine (or crinkle-crankle) wall along Church Lane. He sold the property in 1968 for £29,000. The house was demolished in 1969[85] and the site developed to provide a neo-Georgian housing estate.

Another fine house standing in extensive grounds was at Woodside, the home of the Rooke family from 1830. William Rooke, brother of Sir Giles Rooke, who purchased the property had married in 1831 Marianne Burrard, sister of Sir Harry Burrard Neale, who bore him two sons and two daughters. It was his grandson, Colonel Henry Douglas Rooke, who bequeathed to the Lymington Corporation his

Top The mansion of the Rooke family at Woodside set in attractive grounds later to be bequeathed to the town by Col. Douglas Henry Rooke in 1925. Unfortunately, during the war the house fell into disrepair and later had to be demolished.

Above Fairfield House photographed shortly before demolition. At one time it was hoped this might become the Town Hall.

Author Dennis Wheatley (1897-1977) building a serpentine wall in the grounds of his home, Grove House, in 1947-8.

mansion and grounds in 1925. In 1938 it was hoped this building might become a museum for the borough but the war intervened and the uncared for house became dilapidated and was demolished in about 1960, though the grounds, known as Woodside Gardens, are well-maintained as a public park and are the home of the limestone pillars that once supported Lymington's late seventeenth century Town Hall.[86]

Yet another of these fine houses, also to suffer demolition, was Fairfield. For a time it was considered as a potential site for a new Town Hall but this idea was abandoned.

Probably the oldest complete domestic building in the town, Monmouth House, dating to the late

166

Above Two views of Quadrille Court. The second photograph shows it after being rebuilt in 1911.

Below The mansion called South Hayes first built by Edwin Inman and greatly extended by Thomas J.D. Rawlins. It later fell into decay and was demolished.

seventeenth or very early eighteenth century, was extensively repaired in the late 1980s. In the early 20th century it had been the home of Dr F.H. Maturin, grandson of the Rev. Benjamin Maturin. It is now a rest home for the elderly. Nearby, Quadrille Court, the most attractive architectural ensemble in St Thomas Street, was built in 1911 incorporating materials from the original building,[87] once a base for the foreign troops in the early nineteenth century.

Home (or Holme) Mead, a large house in the High Street, after being a fine residential property throughout the nineteenth century, became a military hospital and convalescent home during the First World War and was afterwards ignominiously reduced to a furniture store and, because of its dilapidations, finally demolished in 1959 to make way for the new Post Office. Part of its extensive grounds, extending to Church Lane, was used as the site on which to construct an old people's rest home known as Solent Mead.

Edwin Inman, grandson of Thomas the shipbuilder, built a large house just to the south of the High Street in Grove Gardens. After Edwin's death 1885 it was purchased by Thomas Joseph Davis Rawlins, manager of the Wilts and Dorset Bank, and greatly enlarged and a tower added. Following his death it could not be sold as a residence and it gradually fell into disrepair and was eventually demolished. Part of its grounds became

the open public space called Grove Gardens, lying within a minute's walk of the High Street, which was given to the town by a building developer, Charles Webb, who constructed a number of quality houses on adjoining land in the 1930s. William Whitaker of Pylewell donated a fine brick-built pavilion for the gardens but because of misuse and vandalism during the 1980s it had to be demolished and has not been replaced.

Epilogue

ALTHOUGH there is everywhere the intrusion of modern architecture, note for example the Police Station in Southampton Road built in 1952, the Post Office built in 1960, and the numerous industrial premises built along the riverside, these structures reflect the changes that all dynamic towns undergo. As the old becomes redundant and unsuitable, for whatever reason, so it is swept away. However, from about the early 1970s there has grown an increasing awareness of the aesthetic qualities of past townscapes rather than just individual buildings and this has led to a treatment more in scale and sympathy with the past.

Stark concrete street lamp standards were introduced along St Thomas Street and in the High Street in the brave new world of the Fifties; the Eighties saw them replaced with more traditional wrought iron standards. The New Forest District Council created a Conservation Area covering much of the urban townscape. It was then described as 'the most important conservation area in the District'. Its importance lay in the essentially unchanged medieval street pattern, as described earlier in this book, of both the High Street and St Thomas Street, with the remarkable addition of many high quality buildings largely belonging to the period 1780 to 1910.

An urban community exists for trade, commerce and social intercourse in all its wide variety, a fact reinforced by the story of the past. If it is to flourish, economically and socially, it must change to accommodate increasing population and the aspirations of people in their domestic life. New roads, like Station Street, Avenue Road and Marsh Lane, have been laid out at different times to meet new needs. Additional housing for a growing population, new factory and workshop buildings for industry, new retail shops, more car park provision, expanded health care facilities, new schools – all are responses to change dictated by changing aspirations and expectations of the people and to the application of modern technology and administration.

Despite these many changes Lymington has retained a special and distinctive character and charm, and the town and its immediate environs has

Below and below right The gardens of Home Mead in the High Street are now occupied by Lymington Post Office, built in 1960.

A view from the church tower looking west along St Thomas Street. This is a conservation area. Monmouth house can be seen on the far left and Quadrille Court next to it. Beyond, just visible is the roof of the now demolished Lyric Cinema.

long been favoured as a place of retirement. Yachting, charming coastal and river scenery and the proximity of the New Forest have attracted people for more than two centuries and those elements still retain a magnetic fascination for those who can afford to buy properties in the select parts of the town and surrounding area. Amongst the many famous people to have settled here in recent times are Robert E. Groves (1869-1948), marine and topographical artist; Lord Donaldson of Lymington (1920-2005), Master of the Rolls; Sqdn-Ldr Neville Duke (1922-2007), much-decorated wartime air ace and test pilot; Leslie Thomas (b.1931), renowned author; Clare Francis, famous yachtswoman and author, also lived here for a few years.

The town grew rapidly in the twentieth century and by 2001, Lymington and Pennington (Town Council area), had 14,329 residents.[88] That census revealed that about 60% were in employment (including part-time and self-employed) while nearly 22% of the total population was retired. No fewer than 74% of properties were owner-occupied and less than 20% had no car. The pressures on the landscape, the infrastructure and on communities created by population increase means sensitive and innovative responses are required by the elected members of the planning authorities if the town is not to completely lose its character by being subsumed in extensive residential development. Inevitably, there are strong opinions about the effectiveness of the District Council's responses to these pressures and bodies, such as the Lymington Society, play an active role as watchdogs for the community.

What is important is that the inevitable changes should always fall within the context of the needs of the people, and wherever possible should be designed to enhance and enrich the life of residents and visitors alike. It will no doubt always be an unequal battle between those who seek to retain what they perceive to be the historic and landscape character of Lymington and those, at the other extreme, who believe the future lies in unrestricted development.

Our history is a record of changes and by setting these down an opportunity is provided of measuring those we are undergoing now against the challenges faced in the past. It is important that we should try to understand the legacy our forebears have left in carrying out the changes they saw as necessary or expedient or beneficial. If this book in telling the story of the town and its people has helped to provide that kind of perspective it will have made a small contribution to Lymington and its residents.

Ownership of the Manor of Lymington

Note: the manor of Lymington, though subject to various definitions from time to time, appears to comprise both Old Lymington and the borough of New Lymington. From the time of the charter granted by William de Redvers (*c.*1200) this is taken to be the case in the ownership list below.

1086	Roger of Bêlleme, Earl of Shrewsbury
1090 to 1098	About this date Roger died and the manor passed his son, Hugh Montgomery, Earl of Shrewsbury. On the death of Hugh his brother, Robert, succeeded.
1102	Robert dispossessed and banished by Henry I for supporting Robert Curthose, eldest son of William the Conqueror. Manor then granted to Richard de Redvers.
1107	Baldwin de Redvers, 1st Earl of Devon, son of Richard, succeeded.
1155	Richard, 2nd Earl of Devon succeeded.
1162	Baldwin, 3rd Earl of Devon succeeded.
1182	Richard, Baldwin's younger brother, 4th Earl of Devon succeeded.
1191	William de Redvers 5th Earl of Devon and uncle of Richard and Baldwin (above) succeeded. He granted the first charter to Lymington, created the borough of New Lymington which, however, remained subject to the manor.
1216	Baldwin, 6th Earl of Devon, William's grandson succeeded.
1245	Baldwin, 7th Earl of Devon, Baldwin's son, succeeded. He granted Lymington's second charter enlarging the original borough. He granted the manor to the Priory of Breamore for 7 years.
1262	Isabella, Baldwin's sister, succeeded on her brother's death. She was the wife of William de Fortibus. She disputed the right of Breamore Priory to hold Lymington.
1271	Isabella de Fortibus granted a charter to Lymington confirming those of her grandfather and brother. The Prior of Breamore acknowledged Isabella's right to the manor of Lymington.
1293	Isabella sold the Isle of Wight and Christchurch to Edward I. She died shortly afterwards. Edward then took the manor of Lymington, 'as a member of Christchurch', into his own hands.
1299	Edward I granted Lymington to his wife Queen Margaret as part of her dower.
1302	Hugh Courteney, 9th Earl of Devon, cousin and heir of Isabella, successfully claimed the manor stating that Lymington never had been 'a member' of Christchurch and was therefore not included in the sale to the Crown.
1315	Hugh Courteney was empowered to put his mother, Eleanor, in possession of the manor of Lymington.
1316	Hugh in sole possession of the manor.
1340	Hugh died and was succeeded by his son and heir, Hugh, 10th Earl of Devon.
1377	Hugh died and was succeeded by his grandson, Edward Courteney, 11th Earl.
1419	Edward died and was succeeded by his son, Sir Hugh Courteney, 12th Earl of Devon.
1422	Sir Hugh died, succeeded by his son Thomas, aged 8 years (Lancastrian supporter).
1458	Thomas died, succeeded by his son, Thomas, 14th Earl of Devon, executed 1461 (Lancastrian supporter).
1461	(April) Following Thomas's execution Lymington was confiscated from the Courtney family and reverted to the Crown in the person of Edward IV.
1461	(July) Edward IV issued a licence for Henry Courteney, brother of Thomas, to hold the manor of Lymington.
1465	Lymington 'borough and manor' confirmed to Henry Courteney.
1465	Henry Courteney died. Lymington granted to Walter Blount, Lord Mountjoy.
1474	Lord Mountjoy died, succeeded by his son, 7 years old Edward.
1485	Presumably Lymington reverted to the Crown in the person of Henry VII during Edward's minority.
1489	Henry VII restored Lymington to Edward Courteney, heir of Henry. Edward died childless and Lymington passed to his sister, Joan, wife of William Knyvet, and then to her sister, Elizabeth, wife of Sir Hugh Conway.
1490	Possession of the manor confirmed to Sir Hugh and Elizabeth Conway, who died childless. Manor then reverted to the Crown.

1511   Henry VIII granted the reversion of the manor of Lymington to William Courteney, 18th Earl of Devon, and his wife Katherine (6th daughter of Edward IV). William died the same year.

1512   Manor of Lymington confirmed to Katherine.

1527   Katherine died, succeeded by her son, Henry, Marquis of Exeter and 19th Earl of Devon.

1539   Henry executed and the manor of Lymington confiscated from the family so reverting to the Crown in the person of Henry VIII.

1541   Lymington made part of the jointure of Katherine Howard, then queen of Henry VIII. She was executed and Lymington reverted to the Crown.

1553   Shortly before his death Edward VI granted Lymington to his uncle, Sir Henry Seymour.

1554   Mary I granted Lymington to Edward Courteney, Marquis of Exeter, heir of Henry, 19th Earl of Devon.

1556   Edward died (at Padua) and Lymington again reverted to the Crown.

1589   Manor of Lymington divided up and the portions were leased.

1593   Lymington reunited as a single manor and granted by Elizabeth I to Thomas and William Fortescue and then (in fee) to Nicholas, Lord Zouche and Elizabeth his wife.

1601   Elizabeth, Lady Zouche, conveyed Lymington to Charles, Earl of Nottingham and his wife.

1609   Abraham Campion, cloth-maker of London, lord of the manor of Lymington.

1611   Abraham Campion died (in London), succeeded by his son, Henry Campion.

1665   Bartholomew Bulkeley in possession of the manor of Lymington. He was succeeded by (i) his son, Bartholomew, (ii) his grandson, Thomas and (iii) his great grandson, Bartholomew, successively.

1733   Thomas Missing, lord of the manor of Lymington.

1778   Thomas Missing, Thomas Mardey and James Missing conveyed Lymington to Clewer Stares.

1785   Mrs Elizabeth Guitton lady of the manor of Lymington.

1805   Elizabeth Guitton sold the manor to George Pretyman Tomline, bishop of Lincoln, later bishop of Winchester.

1827   George Tomline died and the manor passed to his son, William Edward Tomline.

1834   William Edward Tomline sold the manor to John Pulteney.

1849   John Pulteney died and the manor passed to his grandson, John Granville Beaumont Pulteney, as a tenant for life.

1875   John Granville Beaumont Pulteney died, succeeded by his son, Keppel Pulteney.

1918   Keppel Pulteney sold the manor of Lymington to the Keyhaven Syndicate.

1937   Mr Nientsky purchased the manor of Lymington from the Keyhaven Syndicate following the death of its main promoter, Frank Aman.

1945   Manor of Lymington purchased by Lymington Borough Council for £800.

Appendices

Charter of Baldwin de Redvers, Earl of Devon, confirming the liberties granted by William de Redvers to the Borough of Lymington, *circa*.1256

[The passages in the charters emphasised in bold type may be regarded as of particular importance.]

KNOW ye all men present and to come that I, Baldwin de Redvers, Earl of Devon, have granted and by this my present charter have confirmed to my burgesses of Lymington all liberties and free customs alike from toll and all other customs of which the free burgesses are quit, as far as concerns me, throughout all my land, in towns and villages, by land and by sea, at bridges, ferries and gates, at fairs and markets, in selling and buying, in the borough and without the borough, in all places and in all things. I have granted also to the aforesaid burgesses that they shall be free and quit of suit of shire and hundred court as far as I am concerned. I have also granted them that every plea that arises in the said borough which pertains to me shall be pleaded in the borough. And if any of them be amerced on such a plea and the amercement be made by them, I have also granted that none of them in respect of any amercement that pertains to me shall be amerced at more than 30 pence, and that by the advice and judgement of the burgesses themselves.   I have likewise granted to the aforesaid burgesses that no one shall be prepositus in their borough except him whom they shall elect by common assent and present to me and my heirs, provided that he is one who will serve me faithfully and who will treat my burgesses well and kindly. And the aforesaid burgesses and their heirs shall pay me and my heirs each for his messuage six pence a year in lieu of all service, namely three pence at Easter and three pence at Michaelmas. **And for this service they shall hold their burgages in fee and inheritance and shall have the aforesaid liberties and quittances as is fully provided in the charter of good memory made to the burgesses by William de Redvers, formerly Earl of Devon.** I have also given to the said burgesses and granted the toll of the said borough and of the extension of the borough which I have made on the north side of the church of Lymington, to have and to hold for them and their heirs freely and quietly for ever from me

and my heirs in return for the yearly payment to me and my heirs from them and their heirs of thirty shillings at two terms in the year, namely at Easter fifteen shillings and at the feast of the blessed Michael, in September, fifteen shillings. Also the toll from the tallage of the fair on the feast of the blessed Matthew the apostle together with the pleas and perquisites fully reserved to me and my heirs. But the burgessses shall hold the new burgages of the said extension of the borough and their heirs shall have all the liberties and free customs and quittances which William de Redvers formerly earl of Devon, and I have granted to our burgesses of Lymington. And that this my gift, grant and confirmation of my present charter may be ratified and abiding, I have affirmed this present writing with the protection of my seal. These being witnesses: Andrew abbot of Quarr, N' prior of Christchurch, S' prior of Breamore, John de Insula, John de Campden, Martin de Chanflur', Richard de Affetone, Henry de Trenchard, Walerand Trenchard, Robert de Albemarl', W' Spileman, Eustace Fucher, Nigel of Buckland, S' de Arnewood, J' de Essebir, William Lion et multis aliis.

Charter granted by Edward Courtenay, Earl of Devon, dated Feeast of St Thomas the Apostle, 6 Henry IV [21 December, 1404] with vidimus of the Charter granted by Isabella de Fortibus dated 9 June, 55 Henry III [9 June, 1271]

To all whom the present letter may concern: We, Edward Courtenay by the grace of God earl of Devon, have considered the charter which Lady Isabella de Fortibus, formerly Countess Albemarle of Devon, and Lady of Isle of Wight, granted to our burgesses of Lemyngton in these words:
Let all present and to come understand that **I Isabella de Fortibus, Countess Albemarle and Lady of the Isle of Wight have given, granted and by this my present charter, confirmed for ever to my burgesses of Lemyngton entirely the liberties and free usages** derived from toll with all other usages which the free burgesses have through all my territory in farm lands and roads, ashore and on the sea, in bridges and fords, in harbours and fairs, in markets for selling and

buying within and without the borough in all places and things pertaining to me and my heirs. I have also granted to the said burgesses that they may be free and undisturbed in their shires and hundreds and that all questions that shall arise in the said borough shall be pleaded the borough itself in the presence of our bailiffs for the time being. And if any fine be imposed let it be imposed among the burgesses themselves and by themselves and let no fine as far as concerns me amount to more than 30 pence, and this by counsel and judgement of the burgesses themselves. I have granted likewise to the said burgesses that none of them shall be appointed to any office in the borough unless they elect him by common consent and present him to me and my heirs, it being provided that such person be one who shall serve me faithfully and treat the burgesses reasonably and kindly. **The said burgesses and their heirs shall severally pay to me and my heirs out of their property either in the old [William de Redvers'] borough aforesaid [sic] or from any increase thereof [Baldwin, her brother's extension] 6 pence annually for all dues, 3 pence at Easter and 3 pence at the feast of St Michael, and for that payment they shall hold their rights as burgesses from us and our heirs in trust and inheritance.** And they shall hold the said liberties and rights in perpetuity (except the two districts of the abbey and convent of Beaulieu which shall hold none of the said liberties). **I have given and granted to the same my burgesses** the toll and stallage of the said borough together with the toll and stallage of **that district which Baldwin de Redvers, formerly Earl of Devon, my brother created out of the northern part of the church estate of Lemyngton,** to be held by himself and his heirs free and undisturbed for ever, there being paid out of it annually to me and my heirs 30 shillings sterling at equal periods of the year, namely, at Easter 15 shillings and at Michaelmas 15 shillings with the toll and stallage of the markets or fairs at the feast of St Matthew the apostle together with the fees and perquisites reserved in full to me and my heirs. The burgesses who belong to the borough itself shall hold and their heirs shall have and hold from me and my heirs all whatsoever liberties and free

usages and rights as above mentioned. And that this my gift, grant and confirmation of my present charter with the impression of my seal, these being witnesses: John Lord le Warre, Henry Trenchard, William Spylman, Gordan le Warre, John Lord Rector of the church of Schaldefelde, Gordon de Kyngeston, Gilbert de Chalfhunte, Walter de Rubrigge, Eustace Fucher, Henry N---, Simon de Arnewoode, John de Badesle and others.

We [Edward Courtenay] have ratified and confirmed for ever these present gifts and grants aforesaid, holding them in all respects as above secured and sufficient for us and our heirs. **Moreover, we have given and granted to our said burgesses and their heirs the whole of the Quay with all things belonging to it together with tolls and stallage, anchorage and wharfage of vessels and boats, with the usual perquisites of fairs to be held annually in the same place for ever on the feast of St Matthew the Apostle and out of this to pay to us and our heirs 2 shillings annually at Easter and Michaelmas in equal portions.** Moreover we will and decree that no one in our said borough shall have or enjoy the liberties derived from toll or any established usages except the burgesses so elected or the son of the burgess and that any one appointed in our borough aforesaid (who for the time shall be as one of the burgesses of the same borough) shall cause to be observed the weighing of bread in the aforesaid borough according to the law and custom of the kingdom of England, at all convenient seasons and therefrom pay the fines at two equal legal periods to us and to our heirs in the accustomed manner. We have also given and granted to the same our burgesses the market rights in the High street of the said borough together with the toll and stallage pertaining to the same.

In testimony of which deed we have affixed to this indenture both our seal and the common seal of our said burgesses. These being witnesses: Peter Courtenay and others. Given at Tyverton [Devon] at the feast of St Thomas the apostle in the sixth year of the reign of King Henry the fourth, after the conquest [21 December, 1404].

The de Redvers Family Tree

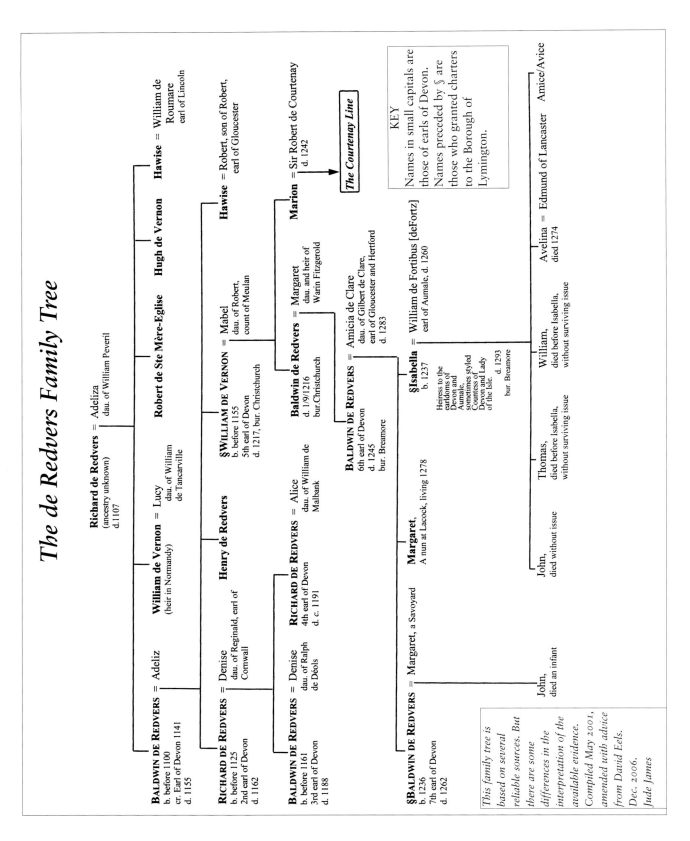

Richard de Redvers = Adeliza
(ancestry unknown)   dau. of William Peveril
d.1107

BALDWIN DE REDVERS = Adeliz
b. before 1100
cr. Earl of Devon 1141
d. 1155

William de Vernon = Lucy
(heir in Normandy)   dau. of William
de Tancarville

Robert de Ste Mère-Eglise

Hugh de Vernon

Hawise = William de
Roumare
earl of Lincoln

RICHARD DE REDVERS = Denise
b. before 1125   dau. of Reginald, earl of
2nd earl of Devon   Cornwall
d. 1162

Henry de Redvers

§WILLIAM DE VERNON = Mabel
b. before 1155   dau. of Robert,
5th earl of Devon   count of Meulan
d. 1217, bur. Christchurch

Hawise = Robert, son of Robert,
earl of Gloucester

BALDWIN DE REDVERS = Denise
b. before 1161   dau. of Ralph
3rd earl of Devon   de Déols
d. 1188

RICHARD DE REDVERS = Alice
4th earl of Devon   dau. of William de
d. c. 1191   Malbank

Baldwin de Redvers = Margaret
d. 1/9/1216   dau. and heir of
bur.Christchurch   Warin Fitzgerold

Marion = Sir Robert de Courtenay
d. 1242

→ **The Courtenay Line**

BALDWIN DE REDVERS = Amicia de Clare
6th earl of Devon   dau. of Gilbert de Clare,
d. 1245   earl of Gloucester and Hertford
bur. Breamore   d. 1283

§BALDWIN DE REDVERS = Margaret, a Savoyard
b.1236
7th earl of Devon
d. 1262

§Isabella = William de Fortibus [deFortz]
b. 1237   earl of Aumale, d. 1260

Heiress to the
earldoms of
Devon and
Aumale,
sometimes styled
Countess of
Devon and Lady
of the Isle.
d. 1293
bur. Breamore

Margaret,
A nun at Lacock, living 1278

John,
died without issue

Thomas,
died before Isabella,
without surviving issue

William,
died before Isabella,
without surviving issue

Avelina = Edmund of Lancaster
died 1274

Amice/Avice

John,
died an infant

This family tree is
based on several
reliable sources. But
there are some
differences in the
interpretation of the
available evidence.
Compiled May 2001,
amended with advice
from David Eels.
Dec. 2006.
Jude James

KEY
Names in small capitals are
those of earls of Devon.
Names preceded by § are
those who granted charters
to the Borough of
Lymington.

Footnotes

Abbreviations and contractions used in Notes (for full bibliographical details see Bibliography).

A&T	*Advertiser & Times (New Milton Advertiser & Lymington Times)*
A Walk	*A Walk through Lymington* (1st edition, King)
Brit. Lib.	The British Library
Cal.	*Calendar*
CIL or *C in L*	*The Church in Lymington* (1912)
DCRO	Dorset County Record Office
DNB	*Dictionary of National Biography*
DRS	Dorset Record Series
HAT	Hampshire Archives Trust
HCC	Hampshire County Council
HFC&AS	Hampshire Field Club & Archaeological Society
HMC	Historical Manuscripts Commission
HRO	Hampshire Record Office
HRS	Hampshire Record Series
ibid.	*ibidem*
Inq. Misc.	*Inquisitions Miscellaneous*
I-o-W	Isle of Wight
Jones	C.P. Jones, *A History of Lymington* (1930)
LHRS	Lymington Historical Record Society
LILH	*Lymington Index of Local History* (1992)
M-o-S Occ. Mag.	*Milford-on-Sea Historical Record Society Occasional Magazine*
NFR	*New Forest Report* (published by HFC&AS)
OTR	*Old Times Revisited, Lymington, Hants*
PRO	Public Record Office (now TNA see below)
Procs	*Proceedings*
SPD	*State Papers Domestic*
SRS	Southampton Record Series
TNA	The National Archives (formerly the Public Record Office)
VCH	*Victoria County History*
WRS	Wiltshire Record Society

CHAPTER ONE

1. The Domesday translation is taken from Round, J.H., 'The Hampshire Domesday', *VCH Hampshire and the Isle of Wight*, Vol. i, 511: J. Munby, editor, *Domesday Book, Hampshire*, 51a, and the facsimile version published by Ordnance Survey in 1862. Parage is here taken as the holding equivalent to a manor, see Finn, R.W., *Domesday Book: a Guide* (1973), 42.

2. Place-name evidence is abstracted from: Ekwall, E., *The Oxford Dictionary of English Place-Names* (4th edition, 1960); Coates, R., *The Place-Names of Hampshire* (1989); Rivett, A.L.F. and Smith, C.C., *The Place-Names of Roman Britain* (1979); Lloyd, A.T., 'Local Place-Names: their interest and meaning', *Papers of LHRS* (6/3/1959). For an early interpretation of the problem see Warner, R., *Topographical Remarks relating to the South-Western parts of Hampshire* (1793), 12 and n.

3. This is a problem that exercised Warner, *ibid.*, 16; but his conclusion was that the entry relates 'not to the *town*, but to the *manor*'.

4. Lloyd, A.T., *Lymington Index* (1962), 97ff. Stagg, D., 'The New Forest in Domesday Book', *NFR*, No. 13 (1974). About the extent of the forest see: Stagg, D., 'New Forest Boundaries in the Thirteenth Century', *NFR*, No. 28 (1990), 10-12.

5. Hawkes, C.F.C., 'The Excavations at Buckland Rings, Lymington', *Procs HFC&AS*, XIII, pt. 2 (1936) and personal communication from Dr J. Close-Brooks, FSA.

6. See Close-Brooks, J., 'A New View of an Old Fort' in *Buckland: An Anthology* (1991), 130.

7. Bede, *A History of the English Church and People*, translated by L. Sherley-Price (revised edition 1968), 56 (author's italics). See also Yorke, B., 'The Jutes of Hampshire and Wight and the origins of Wessex', *The Origins of Anglo-Saxon Kingdoms* (1989) edit. S. Bassett, 84-96.

8. There is some confusion over the title of earls of Devon taken by the de Redvers. *Extinct Peerages* states that Richard was created Earl of Devon by Henry I. He is referred to in the Christchurch Cartulary (Charter 348) as Earl Richard but other sources state the first creation to be that of Baldwin in 1141 (*e.g.* Hockey, F., 'The House of

Redvers and its Monastic Foundations' in *Anglo-Norman Studies*, V, (1982), 147; Round, J.H. 'Family of Redvers' in the *DNB*, 828-9; *Charters of the Redvers Family and the Earldom of Devon 1090-1217* (1994) edited by R. Bearman, 7, and *Handbook of British Chronology* (3rd edition 1986) edited by E.B. Fryde, D.E. Greenway, S. Porter and I. Roy, 459.)

9. William acceded as 5th earl in about 1191 on the death of his nephew, Richard, the 4th earl. It is likely that Lymington's charter dates to that time or only a year or two later.

10. *The Beaulieu Cartulary*, edited by S.F. Hockey (SRS 17, 1974), 294 (243-5) also in Bearman, *op. cit.*, 170-1.

11. The texts of the three medieval charters for Lymington appear in English translation in Appendices 1 and 2.

12. See Bearman, *op. cit.*, 99-100.

13. HRO 29M82/89.

14. Lloyd, A.T., 'The Early Officials of Old Lymington and of the Borough of New Lymington', *NFR*, 13, (1974) 30-2.

15. Lloyd, A., *LILH* (Lymington 1992), Appendix G, 1-110.

16. Granted its charter by Richard de Redvers in about 1180.

17. A convenient reference source for such boroughs is Beresford, M. and Finberg, H.P.R., *English Medieval Boroughs: A Handlist* (1973)

18. HRO 29M82/70.

19. The present day Cannon Street.

20. The *Inquisition Post Mortem*, 47 Henry III, reprinted in King, E., *OTR* (1900), 232-3. The entry for Eberic may be a misprint - 10d instead of 1s. 0d.

21. Other comparable wide-street, planned boroughs near Lymington include: Alresford (*c.*1210), Downton (*c.*1210) and Hindon (*c.*1219).

22. St Barbe, C., *Records of the Corporation of the Borough of New Lymington* (1848), map facing page 3 and map following page 47.

23. This does not cover the whole area of Old Lymington which comprised about 1,000 acres. It is not possible to explain the deficiency.

24. *Charter Roll*, Hen.III, quoted in E. King, *OTR*, 228.

25. John Boucher of Harfleur.

26. *Passagium* = passage over water, ferry: *passarius* = a ferryman. Interestingly, the embassy sent from Beaulieu in 1425 hired a ship called *Passager* at Dover to convey the party to Calais (Hockey, *King John's Abbey* (1976), 135-6).

27. The case was recorded on 18 October when a mandate for reprisals was issued, see: *Cal. Patent Rolls, Hen. IV, 1408-13*.

28. A brief biographical note in Hicks, M., *Who's Who in Late Medieval England* (1991), 12-13, see also Burnett, J., *A History of the Cost of Living* (1969), 25; Powicke, M., *The Thirteenth Century 1216-1307* (1962), 364-5; and

Miller, E. and Hatcher, J., *Medieval England: Rural Society and Economic Change 1986-1348*, (1978),191-2.

29. *VCH Hampshire, op. cit.*, Vol IV, 639.

30. This map is reproduced in St Barbe, *op. cit.*, facing page 27.

31. King, E., *OTR*, map facing p. 3. Importantly, see comments in Lloyd, A., *LILH* (Lymington 1992), 2-3.

32. The salt industry will be more fully dealt with later (see pp.71-4). Information from Lloyd, A.T., 'The Salterns of the Lymington Area', *Procs. HFC&AS*, XXIV (1967), 86-102 and the same author's *The Salterns of the Lymington Area* (Buckland Trust 1996) and Keen, L., 'Coastal Salt Production in Norman England', *Anglo-Norman Studies*, XI (1988), 133-179.

33. *New Forest Documents 1244-1334*, edited by D.J. Stagg (Hants Record Series, vol. II, HCC 1979), 509, p.190.

34. Hockey, F., *Beaulieu King John's Abbey* (Beaulieu 1976), 20.

35. *The Beaulieu Cartulary, op. cit.*, No. 148, p.118.

36. Hockey, S.F., *Quarr Abbey and its Lands 1132-1631* (Leicester 1970), 90. *The Charters of Quarr Abbey*, edited by S.F. Hockey (I-o-W Record Series, Vol. 3, 1991), Charter 2, page 2.

37. *Ibid.*, 91.

38. *OTR*, 6-7.

39. Stagg, D.J., *New Forest Documents AD 1244-AD 1344* (HRS III, 1979), 583, 584 (pp.211-2).

40. *Winchester College Muniments*, compiled by Sheila Himsworth, Vol II (1984) Fromond's Title, Deed Nos. 9805, 9806, 9808.

41. It is puzzling to see the term 'burgages' used to describe property outside the borough and no satisfactory explanation can account for the use of the term.

42. Exchequer K.R. Extent, 1300 (ex-info. A. Lloyd).

43. *Rotuli Litterarum Clausarum*, 1204-27, edit. T.D. Hardy (Record Comm. 1834), quoted in Warren, W.L., *King John* (1964), 123-4.

44. *Cal. Patent Rolls, Edw. I, 1301-07*, Aug. 10 and Nov. 10, 1302.

45. Jones, B.C., 'Illustrations of Lymington's Maritime Trade', *Papers of LHRS*, 18/4/1958.

46. HRO. 27M74A/DL16.

47. *The Local Port Book of Southampton 1439-40*, edited by H.S. Cobb (SRS v, 1961), li.

48. *Cal. Patent Rolls, Edw. III*, pt. 1, 286.

49. *Ibid.* pt. 2, 298.

50. Patterson, A.T., A *History of Southampton 1700-1914*, Vol. I, (SRS 11, 1966), 25, 28, quoting from *Letters Patent*, ii, 90-5.

51. Richard Warner seems to be the first to set this tradition in print, see his *Topographical Remarks on the South-Western Parts of Hampshire*, Vol 1 (1793), 33-4.

52. *Cal. Patent Rolls, Henry IV, 1399-1401*, 18 May, 1401.

53. *Ibid., Henry VI, 1453*, 8 April, 1453.

54. Jones, B.C., 'Illustrations of Lymington's Maritime Trade', *Papers of LHRS*, 18/4/1958, 2.

55. Chandler, J., *Endless Street* (Salisbury 1983), 83.

56. *The Port Book of Southampton 1509-10* (SRS xxxiii, 1991) edited by T.B. James.

57. Stagg, D.J., *op. cit.*, 201, 285.

58. Swalwe evidence from: *Cal Patent Rolls, Hen. IV, Cal. of Inquisitions Misc.*, Vol. VII, *Cal. of Close Rolls, Hen. IV*. Richard II's supporters came from traders and merchants in other towns, see, *e.g.* M. McGarvie, *The Book of Frome* (1980), 55.

59. *Cal. Patent Rolls, Rich. II, 1388-92*, 27 June, 1391.

60. *Cal. of Inq. Misc. VII, 1399-1422* (1968), entry 129.

61. *Chronique de la Traïson et Mort de Richard Deux Roy D'Engleterre* edited by B. Williams (Eng. Hist. Soc. 1846), 246.

62. *Cal. Patent Rolls, Rich. II, 1388-92*, 5 Sept. 1397.

63. *Ibid. Hen. VI*, 5 Feb. 1409.

64. *Ibid.* 5 July, 1437.

65. *Ibid.* 5 Feb. 1449.

66. *Ibid.*, 24 Feb., 1 March, and 18 April, 1459.

67. Recorded in Smith, C., *The New Forest in the Fourteenth Century: a Jurisdictional Vacuum* (Recent Research in Late Medieval Wessex, Sept. 1999), 3.

68. *Cal. of Patent Rolls*, Henry VI.

69. Stagg, D.J., *A Cal. of New Forest Documents, Fifteenth to Seventeenth Centuries* (HRS V,1983), 2-8, 22, **32, 33, 34, 45, 67, 76, 78, 161**.

70. See n.30.

71. Stagg, *op. cit.*, 9 and 35.

72. *Cal. of Charter Rolls*, Vol. I, 1226-57, 390.

73. Breamore Priory had been founded for the Augustinian Canons by Baldwin de Redvers and his uncle Hugh late in the reign of Henry II, see *VCH*, vol.II, 168. The de Redvers owned the manor of Breamore.

74. To enfeoff is to grant a fief (a land or property possession) to some individual or institution.

75. *Cal. of Charter Rolls*, 1313

76. *Christchurch Cartulary*, Brit. Lib. Tib. D.VI, Vol.II, Charter 184 (Mr Austin Willson's mss. translation).

77. HRO, Worsley Papers, 16M/48.

78. It seems possible that this 'sea gate' was at the top of Quay Hill and was the gate leading into the borough from the quay area.

79. *Cartulary of God's House, Southampton*, II, edited by J.M. Kaye (SRS 20, 1976) 251, 300, 371, 386.

80. HRO 29M82/87.

81. HRO 29M82/118.

82. Colten Developments Ltd of Lymington.

83. Accounts in *Advertiser and Times* 18 Feb, 8 April and 1 July, 1989. A close parallel is 58, French Street, Southampton. (Platt, C. *Medieval Southampton* (1973), 101-02). Also, for background, Lewis, E., Roberts, E. and Roberts, K., *Medieval Hall Houses of the Winchester Area* (Winchester, 1988).

84. Quoted in Platt, C., *The English Medieval Town* (1976), 72.

85. Quoted in Hoskins, W.G., *The Age of Plunder: The England of Henry VIII, 1500-1547* (1976), 2. These quotations do not relate specifically to Lymington but describe conditions in towns generally.

86. Lloyd, A.T., "Buckland from the mid-13th to the end of the 17th century" in *Buckland: An Anthology* compiled by Edward Marsh (Lymington 1990), 2.01.

87. Hockey, *Quarr, op. cit.*, 90.

88. *ibid.*, 2.08.

89. *Chantry Rolls*

90. Quoted in *CIL*, 65.

91. A carucate is an area of land capable of being worked by one ploughteam of eight oxen.

92. Abstracted mainly from *VCH Hampshire*, IV, 646-7. Margaret also owned land in New Lymington (HRO 29M82/50)

93. *Abstract of Feet of Fines relating to Wiltshire, 1377-1509*, edited by J.L. Kirby (WRS 41 1986), No.741.

94. *Christchurch Cartulary, op. cit.* 1st charter

95. *Ibid.*, Charter 347 (post-1270).

96. Changed to 3 July (*Alternative Service Book*, 1980).

97. Cook, G.H., *The English Mediaeval Parish Church* (1954), 32-3.

98. Cook, G.H. *The English Mediaeval Parish Church* (1970), 32.

99. HRO. 27M74/E/T215 also transcription in *OTR*,17-19. 'Bryan Fauntleroy, of Fauntleroy's Marsh, had issue Bryan and John; John married Gayne, the Lord Stourtons daughter, and went into Hampshire; he had issue, Henry Thomas and Tristram'. (Hutchins, *Dorset* IV, 180). Tristram Fauntleroy died 1538 and has a plaque in the church at Michelmersh and also to Joan, his wife.

100. An excellent background to this period and its effect on a small parish is contained in Duffy, E., *The Voices of Morebath: Reformation and Rebellion in an English Village* (Yale University Press, 2003), esp. 118ff.

CHAPTER TWO

1. Quoted in translation in St Barbe, C., *The Borough of Lymington* (compiled 1848, published in the early 1860s), 1: see also King, *OTR*, 4.

2. Information from *The Hampshire Lay Subsidy Rolls 1586*, edited by C.R. Davies (HRS IV, 1981), 1-2 and No. 345.

3. King, E. *OTR*, 29.

4. Hoskins, W.G., *The Age of Plunder: The England of*

Henry VIII 1500-47 (Longman's Social and Economic History of England, 1976), 1.

5. Sir Richard Knight of Chawton, Hants (d.1679). See Leigh, W.A. and Knight, M.G., *Chawton Manor and its Owners* (1911), 93-4.

6. This information is taken from the evidence of the Municipal Reform Commission (1835) quoted in King, *OTR*, 290-1.

7. St Barbe, C., *op. cit.*, 29.

8. Clause 35: '...there shall be standard weights also.'

9. Stamped with an official seal to show that they were accurate and had been properly approved.

10. King, *OTR*, 36. HRO 27M74/BDC2, *sub-anno* 1625.

11. HRO 51M74M/M24, Ringwood *Lawday Book* (1729-57).

12. HRO 27M74/DBC2: *The Towne Book of Lymington*, *sub-anno* 1633 and 1637.

13. As shown on the OS 1871 6 ins to 1 mile map.

14. Quoted in St Barbe, C., *op. cit*, 29; also in King, *OTR*, op. cit., 31.

15. HRO 27M74A/DBC2: *ibid.* 1614, 1631.

16. HRO 27M74/DBC202.

17. Details from *Southampton Probate Inventories 1447-1575*, edited by E. Roberts and K. Parker (SRS xxxv, 1992), pp. 57, 371, 382.

18. HRO 27M74/DBC2.

19. *OTR*, 237.

20. HRO 27M74/DBC2.

21. Quoted in *VCH Hampshire*, vol. IV, 639.

22. *ibid.*

23. HRO 27M74/DBC203; deed dated at Lymington 6 Feb. 4 Edw. IV (1465).

24. Jones, C.P., *A History of Lymington* (1930), 36.

25. *OTR*, 22.

26. Pollard, A.F., *Henry VIII* (1970 edition), 331-2, Scarisbrick, J.J., *Henry VIII* (1971), 587 and Mackie, J.D., *The Earlier Tudors 1485-1558: Oxford History of England*, vol. 7 (OUP 1972), 409.

27. See as an example the re-erected market hall from Titchfield in the Weald and Downland Museum, Singleton, Sussex. (Ref: *Weald and Downland Open Air Museum Guidebook*, edited by R. Harris (1987), 32-3).

28. HRO 27M74/DBC2, Town Book, II, *sub-anno* 1620 and 1631.

29. *Ibid.*, *sub-anno* 1656.

30 Several of these blind houses still survive in the Wessex region, *e.g* Box, Castle Cary, Kingsbury Episcopi, Shrewton and Swanage. See Bettey, J.H., *Rural Life in Wessex* (1977), 108.

31. Apprenticeship details from *A Calendar of Southampton Apprenticeship Registers 1609-1740*, compiled by A.J. Willis, edited by A.L. Merson, (SRS xii, 1968), entries 152, 195 and 220.

32. See Lloyd, A.T., *Lymington Index* (1992), Appendix F, 'Lymington Tradesmen's Tokens of 17th Century', 1-107 and 1-108 (with illustrations).

33. For background to this subject see Whiting, J.R.S., *Trade Tokens: A Social and Economic History* (1971), esp. chapters 1 and 2. For Lymington see: Wetton, J.L., *The Hampshire Seventeenth Century Traders' Tokens* (King, 1964), 17-18 and Plates 8 and 9.

34. Quoted in Holland, A.J., *Buckler's Hard: a Rural Shipbuilding Centre* (1985), 23.

35. From a deed dated November 1657 (in private hands when examined and now in the HRO). Further description on the actual operation of the salt works is given in the chapter on Georgian Lymington.

36. *Cal. of the Committee for the Advance of Money, 1642-1656*, part I, 400 (12 and 24 June, 1644).

37. *Cal. of the Committee for the Advance of Money 1642-1656*, part II, 1159. It is perhaps more likely that this may refer to Limington, near Ilchester in Somerset.

38. Godwin, G.N., *Civil War in Hampshire* (1904), 156.

39. *Ibid.*, 99.

40. HRO 27M74/DBC2.

41. *The Hampshire Hearth Tax Assessment 1665*, edited by E. Hughes and F. White (HRS 11, 1992), pp.95-7.

42. Lloyd, A.T., 'The Hearth Tax of 1673 and 1674', *NFR*, No. 15 (1978), 15-20.

43. Quoted in *OTR*, op. cit., 210.

44. Known as the Rye House Plot. TNA (PRO) SPD, Charles II, 432, No. 36i.

45. *Cal. SPD 1683*, 385. Warrant issued from Winchester.

46. *DNB*. John Tutchin was tried by Bloody Judge Jeffries at Dorchester and was sentenced to seven years' imprisonment with annual whippings. He died in 1704. Possibly a close relative to the Rev. Robert Tutchin, Lymington's first Presbyterian minister who died 1684 (see page 49).

47. Little, B., *The Monmouth Episode* (1956), 64.

48. *Cal. SPD 1685*, No.818 (9 June 1685): Entry Book 56, p.208.

49. *ibid.*, 107, PRO SP Domestic, James II, *Inland Letters*. f.8 and f.20.

50. TNA (PRO) SP44/33, p.82. See also Little, B., *op. cit.*, 193 and *OTR*, *op. cit.*, 77.

51. Pinnell, B., *Country House History around Lymington, Brockenhurst and Milford-on-Sea* (Lymington 1987), 83.

52. *Poverty in Early-Stuart Salisbury*, edited by P. Slack (WRS XXXI, 1975), 42 and 50.

53. *CIL*, 81-2, *VCH Hampshire*, 649. A charity notice board commemorating Brown's benefaction may be seen on the gallery in Minstead church.

54. Acts for Burial in Woollen: 18 & 19 Car. II, c.4 (1666), 30 Car. II, c. 3 (1678) and 32 Car. II, c. 1 (1680).

55. Lymington Burial Register: HRO 42M75/PR1.

56. *Cal. For the Committee for Compounding, Domestic, 1643-60*, part II (1890), from 'Cases'; also *CIL*, 81-2.

57. Information on churchwarden's accounts from King, E., 'Lymington Records from the Vestry Books', *Papers of the LHRS*, No. 1 (1955). For a surviving fire engine of 1723 see in the church of Great Wishford, Wilts. Fire hooks are preserved in the parish church of Bere Regis, Dorset.

58. As required under the Highway Act of Queen Mary's reign, 2 & 3 P. & M. c. 8 (1555).

59. *Lady Mary Coke: Letters and Journals 1756-74*, II, edited by J.A. Home (1970 facsimile reprint of 1889-96 edition), 386 (Sunday 16 Oct. 1768). See also *OTR*, 73-4 and *CIL*, 56-7. On briefs see: Tate, W.E. *The Parish Chest* (3rd edit. 1960), 119-124, and Clarke, B.F.L., *The Building of the Eighteenth Century Church* (1963), 96-7.

60. Douglas, T., *The History of the Baptist Church, Lymington, from 1688 to 1909* (2nd edition 1910), 12.

CHAPTER THREE

1. See St Barbe, C., *Records of the Corporation of the Borough of New-Lymington* (n.d. c.1860), 39; *History of Parliament: House of Commons 1690-1715* edited by E. Cruikshanks, S. Handley and D.W. Hayton (2002), 234-5; King, *OTR*, 105-106.

2. *OTR*, 86-7.

3. *The Later Correspondence of George III*, I, (1962), edited by A. Aspinall, 117 (letter 158).

4. *DNB*, under 'Paulet or Powlett, Charles (1661-1722)'. Note alternative spellings; the *History of Parliament* prefers Powlett.

5. Pinnel, *op. cit.*, 47.

6. Died 1766. His brother George had died in 1720.

7. Pinnell, *op. cit.*, 77ff.

8. *ibid.*, quoting from Burrard, S., *Annals of Walhampton*, 26, 30-1, 55-80. Also *OTR*, 155-7., and Jones, 89-97.

9. Valentine, A., *The British Establishment: an 18th Century Biographical Dictionary 1760-84*, Vol. I (Oklahoma, 1970), 124-5., also Pinnell, *op. cit.*, 49.

10. For list of mayors see *OTR*, 183-6 and for the later period Lloyd, *LILH*, Appendix H, 1-114.

11. Edward Gibbon 1781-4, George Rose 1788-90.

12. Information on manorial courts abstracted from *OTR*, 210-223.

13. In the following account of the poor law references to original documents were abstracted from the parish records prior to their being lost and recovered and their subsequent deposition in the Hampshire Record Office (see: James, J., 'A Lucky Escape for Lymington', *Newsletter of HAT* (Spring 1995), 36-9). Therefore it is not possible to give precise references and readers interested will have to examine the HRO files. The author has used his own photocopies, photographs and transcriptions.

14. 9 Geo. I, c. 7, 1722-3.

15. King, E., 'The First Lymington Poorhouse', *Papers of the LHRS*, (26/9/1958), 2.

16. Widnell, H.E.R., *The Beaulieu Record* (Beaulieu 1973), 67, also n.31, p.84.

17. Ibid. 72.

18. The full list is given in *A Walk*, 31-2.

19. See notes in *OTR*, 64, regarding the Great Plague. For example see also James, J., *Wimborne Minster: the History of a Country Town* (Wimborne 1982), 32-3.

20. King, *Poorhouse, op. cit.*, 2.

21. *Ibid.*,

22. *A Walk*, 32, 48-9.

23. *The Complete Letters of Lady Mary Wortley Montagu*, edited by R. Halsband, vol. 1, 1708-1720 (1965), 338-9. Also Boorman, W.H., "Smallpox Inoculation and Vaccination", *HFC&AS Newsletter*, new series 17 (Spring 1992), 29: examples from Hayward, N., *Badges and Beans* (Yetminster 1989), 66 and James, J.F, "Poor Law Administration in Hordle Parish 1786-1834" *NFR*, No. 13 (January 1974), 40. See also Fisk, D., *Dr Jenner of Berkeley* (1959), esp. pp. 188-190, and E.M. Wallace, *The First Vaccinator: Benjamin Jesty of Worth Matravers* (Worth Matravers, 1981).

24. King, *Poorhouse, op. cit.*, 2.

25. *OTR*, 113.

26. *OTR*, 3 and *A Walk* 31 and 37.

27. DCRO. PE/MBO:OV 13.

28. Reference to this in *A Walk*, 48, but King has erroneously transcribed the name as 'Rawings' instead of Hewings and the total sum as £22 instead of £11.

29. Poor Law Rate Book 1816, James Bartlett's accounts (30 Dec. 1816).

30. 126 survive in the HRO ref: 42M75/1-126.

31. HRO 42M75/PO3/3.

32. HRO 42M75/PR2.

33. HRO 42M75/PO11/4.

34. Hayward and Windridge, *Badges and Beans* (Yetminster 1989), 41.

35. Lymington Poor Law records (photocopy made before deposition in the HRO). Surname of mother too faded to read, but it is likely to be Mary Woodford whose illegitimate daughter, Mary, was baptised 27 August 1809.

36. Body, G.A., *The Administration of the Poor Law in Dorset 1760-1834* (Southampton University Ph.D. thesis, 1964, unpubl.), 157.

37. Tate, *op. cit.*, 221 (8 & 9 Wm III, c.30), *A Walk*, 48

38. *A Walk*, 35.

39. Private communication from Prof. Gordon Handcock of Newfoundland, 1/10/1973. See also Handcock, W.G. *Soe longe as there comes noe women: Origins of English Settlement in Newfoundland* (Newfoundland 1989), 196.

40. Under Gilbert's Act, 22 Geo. III, c.83 (1781-2)

parishes were allowed to unite for the purposes of providing workhouses, see Tate, *op. cit.*, 229.

41. *A Walk*, 39.

42. Quarter Sessions' order, 1 Oct. 1805.

43. St. Barbe, C., *op. cit.*, 25.

44. *CIL*, 87.

45. See Fuller, M., *West Country Friendly Societies* (Reading 1964), Appendix II, 153-5 for interesting observations on women's friendly societies.

46. Gilpin, W., 'An Account of a Society established, at Lymington, in Hampshire, for the Benefit of distressed Females', *Hampshire Repository*, Vol. II, (1800), 132-3.

47. Facsimile of the handbill reproduced in *The New Forest Book* edited by J. O'D. Mays (Burley 1989), 230.

48. Rachel Cross, widow of Captain Cross, was buried in Lymington 23 April 1752. No reference to Capt. William Cross has been found either in Boldre or Lymington.

49. HRO. 27M74A/F14, *c.*1738.

50. Quoted by Best, A.M., 'History of Lymington's Tollbridge', *A&T*, 10 May 1958.

51. Best, A.M., 'Lymington versus the Tollbridge, 1738', *Papers of the LHRS* (August 1958) and Coles, R., *Lymington and the New Forest Transport History* (Lymington 1986), 12-13.

52. Coles, *ibid.*, 13.

53. 5 Geo. III, c. 59.

54. Effectively the modern A337/A35.

55. The collections formerly on display there have been transferred to the St Barbe Museum.

56. Quoted in *OTR*, 221.

57. Account page, apparently the only one surviving, illustrated in *Buckland: an Anthology*, compiled by Ted Marsh (2nd edit. 1991), 5.05.

58. Vancouver, A., *General View of the Agriculture of Hampshire* (1810), 392.

59. For a good general account see Copeland, J., *Roads and their Traffic 1750-1850* (Newton Abbot 1968)

60. *Hampshire Antiquary and Naturalist*, vol. 2, quoted by A.T. Lloyd in *Advertiser and Times*, 1965.

61. *Sadler's Directory 1784*, Lymington entry, pp.92-6. For more detail on the turnpikes and road travel see Coles, R., *Lymington and the New Forest Transport History* (Lymington 1986).

62. Vale, E., *The Mail Coach Men of the Eighteenth Century* (1967 reprint), 251-2.

63. Garrow, D., *History of Lymington* (1825), 138-9. See also Bates, A., *Directory of Stage Coach Services 1836* (1969), 133.

64. *The Southampton Herald and Isle of Wight Gazette*, 28 July, 1823.

65. Ms. map by E. Dummer and T. Wiltshaw is illustrated in Lloyd, A.T., 'The Salterns of the Lymington Area', *Procs. HFC&AS*, xxiv (1967), plate IV.

66. *The Journeys of Celia Fiennes* edited by C. Morris (1949), 49-50.

67. Lloyd, *Salterns, op. cit.*, 89.

68. This agreement is on five large parchment sheets (unfortunately, some are very badly damaged). It is dated 30 December 1743. The document is privately owned.

69. See useful information on French salt supply in 'The Salt Trade of Guerande (Le Croisic)', *Soms. & Dorset Notes and Queries*, xxxvi, pt. 364 (September 2006), 70-5.

70. Davies, G.J., 'The Supply of Salt for the Newfoundland Trade', *ibid.*, xxxi, pt. 313 (March 1981), 114.

71. Hearn, J.R., 'Hampshire and Isle of Wight shipping visiting the "Liberty of the Water of the Thamer" in 1760-61', *HFC&AS Newsletter*, I, No. 4 (Nov. 1966), 52. Briewell is probably a misspelling for Pilewell.

72. *Salisbury & Winchester Journal*, Monday 18 May 1789. This not Johann Glauber (1604-70) the chemist who discovered Glauber Salts.

73. James Baker of Lymington reported to Daniel Defoe that two salterns belonging to Mr Perkins were almost ruined in the great storm of November 1703 (Defoe, D., *The Storm* (Penguin edition 2005), 128.

74. *OTR*, 167 and note.

75. *OTR*, 165 gives a figure of 5,000 tons.

76. Garrow, *op. cit.*, quoted in Lloyd, *Salterns, op. cit.*, 96.

77. Lloyd, *Salterns, ibid.*, 97. His paper is valuable in giving much more detailed information and should be referred to by those interested.

78. Jones, *op. cit*, 171.

79. Defoe, D., *A Tour Through the Whole Island of Great Britain*, I, 1962 edition with introduction by G.D.H. Cole and D.C. Browning, 206.

80. 'Journeys of Thomas Baskerville', HMC *Portland* II (1893), 287.

81. *Cal. of Treasury Books* XXVIII, 300 and *Reference Book* IX, 179. See also Heygate, A.C.G., 'Keyhaven', *M-o-S Occ. Mag.*, Vol. 5, No. 3 (Sept. 1938), 17.

82. *Cal. of Treasury Books*, XXVIII, *Out Letters (General)*, XXI, 184.

83. The title given to the officer superintending the landing of coastwise trade.

84. *Hampshire Repository*, I (1799), 127.

85. Quoted in James, J., *Hurst Castle: an Illustrated History* (Wimborne 1986), 41.

86. Quoted from Customs House records by Lloyd, A.T., 'Local History Snippets', *Advertiser & Times*, 1966.

87. HRO 42M75/PR3. He was buried 29 July 1781, aged 25. Also quoted in *OTR*, 267 and *CIL*, 43.

88. *The Hampshire Repository*, II (1799), 30. Buried at Lymington 11 July 1799, aged 56 (HRO 42M75/PR3).

89. Morley, G., *Smuggling in Hampshire and Dorset* (Newbury 1983), 22.

90. *ibid.*, 58-9.

91. Cullingford, C., *A History of Poole* (Chichester 1988), 147.

92. Southampton Petty Customs Books, quoted in Jones, B.C., 'Illustrations of Lymington's Maritime Trade', *Papers of LHRS* 18/4/1958, 5.

93. Handcock, private communication.

94. *ibid.*

95. *Sadler's Directory 1784*: Lymington entry, 92-3, 96.

96. Hearn, J.R., 'Hampshire and Isle of Wight shipping' *op. cit.*

97. *The Western Gazette* '200 Years Ago', 16 May, 1980.

98. *The Western Gazette*, '200 Years Ago', 17 Jan., 1986

99. King, *A Walk*, 17.

100. William Towsey quoted in *A Walk*, 21.

101. *Salisbury & Winchester Journal*, 1 February, 1819, 4.

102. Lord Liverpool, Canning and the other ministers were in favour of recognising the new republics but George III was against. He only agreed after they threatened to resign. (Halévy, E., *History of the English People in the Nineteenth Century: Vol. II, The Liberal Awakening, 1815-1830* (1961 edition), 184.

103. *Salisbury and Winchester Journal*, 6 January, 1823, 4, col.3.

104. *ibid.*, 18 January, 1819.

105. Letter amongst Lymington Poor Law records rescued from the rubbish pit at Efford (now in HRO). Unclassified at time of transcription. The date (1771) given for its foundation may be incorrect in view of Boucher's description made in 1789. Verification has not proved possible.

106. HRO. 26M79/PO24-PO29

107. *Rowlandson's Drawings for a Tour in a Post Chaise*, Introduction and Notes by R.R. Wark (San Marino, Calif. 1963), illus. 30.

108. Details from *Sadler's Directory 1784* and abstracted from HRO 66M88/167, 169, 170, 172.

109. His bride was Elizabeth Jones, a spinster of Lymington (HRO 42M75/PR9).

110. King, E., 'The Story of an Old Business – King's', *Papers of LHRS* (25/9/1960). Also 'Kings Booksellers and Printers' *Advertiser & Times*, 22 August and 3 October 1987.

111. Pigot & Co. Directory 1824.

112. *Diary of Colonel Peter Hawker*, edited by Payne-Gallwey 1893), i, 310, 26 July 1827. Muzio Clementi (1752-1832).

113. HRO 27M74A/DBC206 (doc. unfit for production) quoted in *CIL*, 84. See also Hole, R.H., 'The History of the Lymington Schools', *Papers of LHRS* (5/2/1960), *OTR*, 81-2, Jones, 119-120.

114. It probably dates to about the 1770s.

115. *Parson and Parish in Eighteenth Century Hampshire: Replies to Bishops' Visitations* edited by W.R. Ward (Hampshire Record Series, 13, 1995), No. 136, page 84. Samuel Belbin is not recorded in Douglas's *History of the Baptist Church* in Lymington.

116. Quoted in *OTR*, 117.

117. *OTR*, 139n., 248.

118. For further information see Gilpin, W., *Memoirs of Josias Rogers, RN* (1808) and Warner, R., *Literary Recollections*, vol. 1 (1830), 223-244.

119. For background see Mason, A.S., 'Summer Camps for Soldiers 1778-1782', *The Local Historian*, Vol. 29, No. 4 (Nov. 1999), 212ff, and Western, J.R., *The English Militia in the Eighteenth Century* (1965).

120. Abstracted from: Verney, L., *Records of the Infantry Militia Battalions of the County of Southampton from AD 1757 to 1894* and Lt.-Col. J. Mouat Hunt, *Records of the Artillery Militia Regiments of the County of Southampton from AD 1853 to 1894* (London, Longmans, Green & Co. 1894). These two works bound as a single volume.

121. TNA (PRO) WO13/4361.

122. *OTR*, 139.

123. A curious anomaly arises on 31 March 1797 when a daughter, Anne Mary Laura, of *Philip* de Plessis and Anne Buisson de la Vigne is born at Lymington and recorded in the baptismal register there.

124. *Comyn's New Forest*, edited by Jude James (Ringwood 1982), SHI 14, p. 136, see also PIL 41, p.109 and note.

125. *The Later Correspondence of George III* edited by A. Aspinall, vol. II 1793-1797 (1968), 1258, p.354.

126. Francis Rawdon Hastings, 2nd Earl of Moira (1754-1826), a distinguished and experienced soldier.

127. A record of their arrival is made by the Rev. Ellis Jones in the Lymington burial register, 22 Jan. 1794.

128. *OTR*, 142. King gives a detailed and illuminating account 143-4 and 244-251. Figures from *OTR* and *A New Dictionary of British History* edited by S.H. Steinberg (1964), 299.

129. *The Later Correspondence of George III*, *op. cit.*, 1263, p.356.

130. *ibid.*, 1289, p.385. One of the regiments was the 42nd 'destined for an expedition to the coast of France to assist the Royalists there', Lym. Parish Burial Register, 1794.

131. Boldre Marriage Registers.

132. Nichols, A., *Wellington's Mongrel Regiment: A History of the Chasseurs Britannique Regiment 1801-1814* (2005). It contains a number of references to Lymington.

133. Abstracted from Boldre and Lymington Marriage and Burial Registers see *OTR*, 248 for list of other military forces based at or near Lymington.

134. *OTR*, 146.

135. Lymington Burial Register, HRO 42M75/ PR3 and

/PR12

136. Photocopy of the Ringwood examination given to the author by Mr Ted Baker of Ringwood.

137. Full text in *A Walk*, 50.

138. TNA (PRO) WO13/4361.

CHAPTER FOUR

1. For example, the impact of Utilitarianism (Jeremy Bentham) which was applied to Poor Law and prison administration.

2. Lymington is fortunate in having a list of heads of family for both the censuses of 1801 and 1811 (HRO 42M75/PZ10a and 42M75/PZ10b.)

3. Provisions of the Court of Probate Act 1857.

4. 51 and 52 Vict, c.41.

5. The Reform Act, 1832 (2 Will IV, c.45)

6. Jones, 141-2.

7. The issues surrounding reform are far too complex to be dealt with here. All that can be provided is a summary.

8. The anti-slavery movement was running parallel with the issue of Reform. It was mainly the Whigs and Radicals who supported the abolition of slavery, though the actual details are complex. Although the slave trade had been abolished in 1807 the full emancipation of slaves was not enforced until 1833, a year after the passage of the Reform Act.

9. The 'nine' comprised a committee which formed the principal support for reform. Many of the members were political radicals.

10. Entry in the *Dictionary of National Biography*.

11. John Fleming (d. 1844), a Tory, of Stoneham Park, Southampton.

12. Alias Newtown Park. Wellington was amongst those most strongly opposed to parliamentary reform.

13. This refers to Sir Harry Neale who in a broadsheet declared himself independent of the other candidates.

14. The 1832 poll book is in the collections of the St Barbe Museum, Lymington.

15. Letter dated 23 May, 1832, postmarked Lymington addressed to Lord Radnor, London, made available through the kindness of Mrs Margaret Smith of East Boldre.

16. DCRO. D/WLC/E176 (capitalisation as in the original catalogue).

17. Candidates who would oppose the grant made by Sir Robert Peel to the Maynooth Roman Catholic seminary in Ireland. (see, e.g., Gash, N., *Sir Robert Peel: The Life of Sir Robert Peel after 1830* (1972) or any good 19th century history).

18. DCRO. D/WLC/C297.

19. Son of William Alexander Mackinnon, who had earlier served as a Conservative MP for Lymington but had changed sides and become a Liberal.

20. Patterson, A.T., *A History of Southampton*, I, (SRS 11, 1966),159.

21. HRO. 27M74/DBC7 and Vincent, J. and Stenton, M. (editors) *McCalmont's Parliamentary Poll Book: British Election Results 1832-1918* (8th edition, Harvester Press, 1971). Mackinnon had in fact crossed the floor to the disgust of the Lymington Conservatives.

22. 48 & 49 Vict., c.23.

23. 5 & 6 Will. IV, c.76.

24. *OTR*, *op. cit.*, 290. Text of commissioner's report given in full, 290-299.

25. Now in the St Barbe Museum collections.

26. HRO 27M74A/DBC227. See description in Jones, 178-9.

27. HRO. 27M74A/DBC216.

28. His father, James Brown (1768-1835), had served as town clerk to the old corporation.

29. Edward King's manuscript note book in private hands.

30. The gas column was moved in 1958 and re-erected by the clubhouse after the Lymington Historical Record Society had raised £70 to preserve it.

31. Police information from: HRO. 27M74A/DBC373-378 and Jones, 155-7, Geddes, A.G., 'Public Life in Lymington a Century Ago', *Papers of the LHRS* (April 1963).

32. 4 & 5 Will IV, c.76.

33. *First Annual Report of the Poor Law Commissioners* (1835), 399

34. Cannon, J., *Lymington Infirmary: From the Poor Law to the N.H.S.* (1992), 26. Some other material on the workhouse is abstracted from this source.

35. 1851 census. (TNA HO107/1666/47-51)

36. 11 & 12 Vict. c.63.

37. Quoted by Geddes, *op. cit.*, 2.

38. HRO. 27M74/DL1, under 30 April, 1867.

39. Quoted by Geddes.

40. Quoted in Coles, R., *The Story of Lymington* (1983), 41.

41. *William Allingham's Diary*, edited by H. Allingham and D. Radford (1967 reprint), 139. 'Ned' is Edward (later Sir) Burne-Jones, the Pre-Raphaelite artist. He and his family joined Allingham in Lymington on 15 August.

42. Jones, 181.

43. *Ibid*.

44. Raban, J., *Coasting* (1987), 164.

45. Whitaker, W., *The Water Supply of Hampshire* (Memoirs of the Geological Survey, HMSO, 1910), 41.

46. Information on dentists from advertisements in *The Poole and Bournemouth Herald and Lymington and South Hants Chronicle*, 5 July, 1877 and 1861 and 1881 censuses.

47. *Salisbury & Winchester Journal*, 13 February 1858 but with the boy's name misspelled. Buried Lymington churchyard on Sunday, 14 February 1858.

48. *Ibid.*, 17 July 1858.

49. Most information on the railway abstracted from Paye, P., *The Lymington Branch* (1979) and Coles, R., *Lymington and the New Forest Transport History* (1986), 57-60; see also Hill, K., *From Forest to Ferry: the Story of the Brockenhurst-Lymington Branch Line* (Lymington, St Barbe, 2004).

50. Quoted in Coles, *ibid.*, 119.

51. Agreement in private hands: the author has a photocopy. See also O'Brien, F., *Early Solent Steamers* (1973), 169ff.

52. '150 years of Lymington-Yarmouth Ferries', *Advertiser and Times*, 14 June, 1980.

53. *ibid.* and Coles, *Transport History*, 123.

54. Chitty, J., *The River is within us: A Maritime History of Lymington* (1983), 62. There is a stone above Totland Bay commemorating Marconi's early work in wireless telegraphy. In '150 years of Lymington-Yarmouth Ferries', *Advertiser and Times*, 14 June, 1980, the ship involved is named as the *Solent*.

55. *The Western Gazette*, '100 Years Ago', 13 July, 1984 and Maggs, C.G., 'The Lymington Railway - 125th Anniversary' *The New Forest Post*, 26 May, 1988, 9.

56. *Salisbury & Winchester Journal*, 17 July 1886.

57. James, J., *Pylewell, Lymington and the Weld Family* (LHRS 30 March 1979), 2 and Berkeley, J., *Lulworth and the Welds* (Gillingham 1971), 166 and 206.

58. Quoted in Berkeley, J., *Lulworth and the Welds* (1971), 248, from the *Memorials of the Royal Yacht Squadron*.

59. DCRO. D10/C167. See James, J., 'Pylewell, Lymington and the Weld Family' *Papers of the LHRS*, March 1979, 8-10 and Weld, C., *The Weld Family's Connection with Lymington* (unpubl. mss.), 12-15. Trades and professions, where known, have been added.

60. Jones, 159-166 gives a valuable account.

61. Rashley & Co. Ltd., Contract and Estimates Book, 1862-1873 held in the offices of the company.

62. *The Diary of Col. Peter Hawker*, edited by R. Payne-Gallwey (1971 reprint), 13 Feb. 1823, 262. See also 24 Sept. 1823, 269.

63. *Salisbury and Winchester Journal*, 1 February, 1819; Hawker's letter dated 27 January.

64. Was a substantial landowner having inherited wealth from estates in Jamaica. He was a member of the RYS from 1825-47. He lived in Grove House for a short period.

65. *OTR*, 277-8.

66. Page 314. The 1871 census stated that he employed, '75 men and boys'.

67. George Henry Watkins, shipbuilder, later took over Inman's yard, trading as Watkins & Co.

68. *The Western Gazette*, '100 Years Ago', 17 October, 1981.

69. *William Allingham's Diary*, *op. cit.*, 120.

70. Jones, 162.

71. The Customs House closed permanently in June 2000 (report *A&T*, 17 June 2000).

72. Quoted in Jones, 189.

73. Baptised in Lymington church, 20 May 1824, son of Edward and Ann Hicks.

74. Probably 128/129, tenanted by Charles Hampton.

75. At this time the Petty Sessions were held every Saturday.

76. The painting, entitled 'Before the Magistrates' measures 31" x 64" and is reproduced in colour in *George Elgar Hicks: Painter of Victorian Life* being a catalogue of an exhibition at the Geffrye Museum and the Southampton Art Gallery, 1 Oct. 1982 to 22 Feb. 1993 (published by ILEA, 1982).

77. *Diary of Col. Peter Hawker, II*, *op. cit.*, 315 (12 Jan 1850).

78. Married in Lymington, 14 June 1845.

79. *The Thomas Rackett Papers, 17th-19th centuries*, edited by H.S.L. Dewar (DRS No. 3, 1965), 54.

80. The Henry Hapgood Letters in a private collection.

81. HRO. 6M80/F/A3.

82. *The Lymington Chronicle*, 12 July, 1872.

83. Cole, A., 'Recollections of Milford', *Milford on Sea Record Society Occasional Magazine*, Vol. 2, No. 5 (Nov. 1920), 25-6.

84. Hunt and Co's *Directory*, 1851, 58.

85. *Salisbury and Winchester Journal*, 14 Oct. 1776.

86. *The Hampshire Repository*, Vol. 2 (1801), 259-263.

87. Letter published in *The Lymington and Isle of Wight Chronicle*, 26 November, 1869, curiously enough dated from Cornwallis West's home at Ruthin Castle, 22 November

88. *S & W Journal*, 28 Nov. 1856.

89. Henry Hapgood's letters, private collection, dated Lymington 10 May, 1850.

90. Bostock, C.H. (Chairman), '*Lymington Yesterday*' (Transcript of recordings of old residents, 28/10/1955).

91. HRO 42M75/PD1. William Gatrell may be an ancestor of 'Mr Gatrell'.

92. For background to these riots see: Afton, B., 'A Want of Good Feeling, a Reassessment of the Economic and Political Causes of the Rural Unrest in Hampshire, 1830', *Procs. HFC&AS*, 43 (1987), 237-54.

93. Pinnell, *Country House History, op. cit.*, 25.

94. Quoted in *ibid*. The Rev. Ellis Jones and the Rev. Peyton Blakiston were both curates of Lymington parish.

95. DCRO. D10/E172 (Royal Exchange Insurance No. 401151).

96. HRO. 27M74/DBC369 and DBC372 and Jones, 99.

97. 'How Lymington High Street has Changed', *Advertiser and Times*, 28 January, 1939. Coles, *Lymington High*

Street, op. cit., records that the new buildings were given their nickname because 'they were never taken' also quoted in *A Walk*, 10.

98. Grove, R.A., *Views of the Principal Seats in the Neighbourhood of Lymington* (Lymington 1832).

99. From the original 1832 prospectus in the author's collection.

100. He trained under Auguste Pugin, father of the great A.W. Pugin, and became Hon. Diocesan Architect for Bath and Wells.

101. An Account of the Journeys undertaken by the Rev. Richard and Mrs Boucher, 1788-89' edited by M. Barratt in *History Studies*, Vol. 1, No. 1 (May 1968), 39-50

102. Quoted in Coles, *The Story of Lymington*, 52.

103. *A Walk*, 79.

104. Following Richard Martin's Act of 1822 to prevent cruel and improper treatment of cattle (the first such legislation designed to legally protect animals) the Society for the Prevention of Cruelty to Animals was formed and given the prefix 'Royal' by Queen Victoria in 1840.

105. Known only as the Lymington Theatre.

106. *The Hampshire Telegraph*, 28 November 1825 quoted in Jones-Evans, E., 'Lymington's Theatres', *The Hampshire Magazine*, vol. 8, No.1 (November 1967), 24 (this is a well-researched and useful article).

107. *Ibid.*

108. I am indebted to the late Eric Jones-Evans, *op. cit.* for most of the information on the theatres.

109. Hapgood letters, *op. cit.*, 10 Feb. 1848.

110. *Salisbury and Winchester Journal*, 10 January 1885.

111. Hapgood letters, *op. cit.*

112. Quoted in 'Replacement at last for Lymington's 156 year old school', *Advertiser and Times*, 16 February, 1991.

113. *The Lymington Chronicle*, 12 July, 1872.

114. Barratt, *op. cit.*

115. HRO. 55M72/T20 "A newly erected bathing house near Waterford..."

116. Reproduced in *Rowlandson's Drawings for a Tour in a Post Chaise*, edited by R.R. Wark (1963), illus. 32.

117. Letter signed by S. Hawes, dated October 1840 quoted by Alan Roy in the *Advertiser and Times*, 17 February 2001

118. Figures quoted in 'Lymington Market value goes up 84 times', *Advertiser and Times*, 20 January, 1990.

119. The books on Lymington's cricket and football history (detailed in the bibliography) by Norman Gannaway should be consulted for their comprehensive coverage and interesting details.

120. Down, B.J., *Lymington in old picture postcards* (1985), illus. 50.

121. *The Hampshire Chronicle*, 21 July, 1820.

122. See Street, R.T.C., *Victorian High-Wheelers: The social life of the bicycle where Dorset meets Hampshire* (1979), 6, 25 and other references to Lymington.

123. *OTR*, 126-7.

124. This articulate and satirical letter appeared in *The Lymington Chronicle*, 22 January 1869.

125. Gannaway, N., *A History of Lymington Football Club 1876-1984* (1984), 36

126. See *A & T*, report, 'Can anyone solve cannon mystery?', 6 Jan 2001.

127. Figures from the 1851 census of education.

128. William Ingham Whitaker, 1866-1936 and his son (bearing the same name), 1910-88. For background to this wealthy family see Trevelyan, R., *Princes under the Volcano* (1972).

129. *William Allingham's Diary, op. cit.*, 109, 126. See also Chedzoy, *William Barnes: a Life of the Dorset Poet* (1985), 158-9 for Barnes as a lecturer. Barnes was aged 64 at the time of this visit.

130. Patmore, D., *The Life and Times of Coventry Patmore* (1949), 204 and Robert Coles, *The Story of Lymington*, 55. Robert Hole in his 'A Boyhood's Memories of Lymington', *Papers of the LHRS*, 17/1/1958, 6, incorrectly states that 'he lived at 63, High Street from 1891 till his death in 1896'.

131. Young, D.S., *The Story of Bournemouth* (Robert Hale 1957), 213-215.

132. Oldfield, J. R., ' Private Schools and Academies in Eighteenth Century Hampshire' (Appendix and References), *Proceedings of the Hampshire Field Club & Archaeological Society*, Vol. 45, (1989), 153-5.

133. Quoted in King, E., *A Walk through Lymington* (1st edition 1972), 14 (2nd edition 1990), 16 (photocopy in HRO).

134. *Salisbury & Winchester Journal*, 16 October, 1885.

135. The elder, Sidney Gerald Burrard, became the 7th Baronet in 1933, on the death of his cousin.

136. *A Walk*, op. cit., 88.

137. William Murdock took over this school in about 1895 and remained there until his death in 1903.

138. King, R., *Hand-book for the town of Lymington* (Lymington 1851).

139. Bostock, C.H. (Chairman), 'Lymington Yesterday' (Typewritten transcript of recordings of old residents, 28/10/1955).

140. There is a fine biographical sketch of Dan Bran in Chitty, *The River is Within Us*, 88-89.

141. Quoted in Douglass, D.A., *The Story of the Lymington United Reformed Church* (n.d., c.1983), 14.

142. For Congregationalists, *ibid.*, 18 and for the Baptists, Douglas, T., *The History of the Baptist Church, Lymington* (1910). 41-2 and 48, summarised in Down, B.J., *Lymington Baptist Church* (1988), 14.

143. *Comyn's New Forest* edited by J. James (1982), entry UND 1, 145.

144. From details in the 1851 Religious Census.

145. This sect was founded by Edward Irving, a Scottish Presbyterian minister until 1833. It was never largely supported and it is interesting that Lymington should have had a chapel.

146. Ash, E.G. 'The Dawning of Catholic Emancipation in Lymington', *Papers of the LHRS*, 6 Feb. 1959. See also *Parson and Parish in Eighteenth Century Hampshire: Replies to Bishop's Visitations*, ed. W.R. Ward, 84, which gives the number of 'Papists' as 10.

147. See Cannon, J., *Two Hundred Illustrious Years: the story of the Catholic Parish of Lymington* (Lymington, n.d. but 1999) for fuller background.

148. The R.C. *Parish Newsletter*, Aug./Sept. 1974. Hansom (1803-82) is remembered as the inventor or the cab that bears his name.

149. *CIL*, 19.

150. Researched by the late William Fletcher, FSA and briefly noted in the guide to *The Parish Church of St Thomas, Lymington* (n.d., c.1990).

151. A note to this effect is in the parish baptismal register, 25 Oct 1821 though *CIL*, 36-7, gives area as ½ acre on p. 92.

152. Grove, *op. cit.*, 2.

153. Quoted in *CIL*, 45. The story cannot but be contrasted with that related by Fanny Burney when the mayor of Weymouth was introduced to Queen Charlotte 'Colonel Gwynn, who stood by whispered, "You must kneel, sir!". He found, however, that he took no notice of this hint, but kissed the Queen's hand erect. As he passed him, in his way back, the Colonel said: "You should have knelt, sir!". "Sir", answered the poor Mayor, "I cannot". "Everybody does, sir", "Sir, —I have a wooden leg!". [*The Diary of Fanny Burney*, edited by L. Gibbs (1940), 255.]

154. *CIL*, 15-17 relates the details.

155. *The Poole and Bournemouth Herald and Lymington and South Hants Chronicle*, 5, July, 1877.

156. *CIL*, 24-6,. Jones, 79.

157. From a copy of the returns made by the enumerator, Henry Hapgood, and kept with his private papers. Photocopy in author's collection. This was the only religious census ever held. See also, *The Religious Census of Hampshire 1851*, edited by John A. Vickers (1993), 60ff. where there are differences in recorded numbers and greater detail.

158. *C in L*, 91.

159. *C in L*, 93-5.

160. Cole, A., 'Recollections of Milford', *op. cit.*, 24-5.

161. There is a full and descriptive account in *The Lymington Chronicle*, Thursday, 27 January 1881.

CHAPTER FIVE

1. *The Lymington Chronicle*, 2 January 1902 [HRO 27M74/DBC 181.]

2. For the Solent Tunnel see Turton, F., *A Solent Tunnel? The History of the Solent Tunnel Scheme* (Revised edition, Southampton 1953) or useful summary in Hill, K., *From Forest to Ferry op. cit.*, 38ff.

3. Holme Mead is the spelling in the original documents. Sometimes the property is known as Home Mead.

4. William Henry Romaine-Walker (1854-1940) designed other local work, most notably Rhinefield House (1888-90) and the White House (1903-07), Milford-on-Sea, for the Walker-Munros.

5. *CinL*, 67ff. Born 1876 at Yateley, son of a C of E clergyman. MA, Oxford. He married in 1909.

6. 'Church sold for £160,000', *A&T*, 26 Jan. 2002 and 'Woodside church history unearthed', *A&T*, 17 August 2002.

7. Howlett, J., *The Guv'nor: The Autobiography of John Howlett* as told to Iris Woodford, (John Howlett, 1973), 67

8. Edith Dent, widow of Villiers Francis Dent, four times mayor of Lymington, and mother of H.H.M. Dent, had bought Buckland Farm House (sometimes called Buckland Manor) from Keppel Pulteney in 1896, see *Buckland* 3.36.

9. *The Guv'nor, op. cit.*, 89. All personal information on John Howlett is obtained from this source.

10. For this interesting story see Pearce, D. and Hodges, D.I., *Wellworthy: The First Fifty Years* (1969), 29-36.

11. Ibid., 45.

12. Quoted in Chitty, *op. cit.*, 38.

13. 'End of the Line for Wellworthy', *Advertiser and Times*, 7 October, 1989.

14. *The Guv'nor, op. cit.*, 309.

15. *Ibid.*, 170.

16. OBE = Officer of the Order of the British Empire.

17. *OTR*, 172-3.

18. Member of the Eyre family of the Warrens, Bramshaw, born 1913, New Forest MP from 1945-65, died 1978.

19. *Advertiser & Times* reports, August 1963.

20. *Labour Organiser*, April 1965, 74.

21. *The Guv'nor, op. cit*, 173-4.

22. Information on Percy Blunt from *Advertiser and Times*, 1 June, 1991 and 4 January, 1992.

23. Valuable and interesting background to this topic in Cockram, J. and Williams, R., *Lymington War Memorial* (privately published, 2005)

24. Report of the St John Ambulance Association, 1916 submitted by J.A. Harris, Hon. Secretary.

25. Gadd, E.W., *Hampshire Evacuees* (1982), 24 October 1940, 23.

26. *Ibid.*, 3 January 1941, 24.

27. Cockram and Williams, *op. cit.*, 381-383.

28. Dr Basil Thornton (1912-99) makes reference to another bomb falling in the grounds of Fairfield which did no damage (HRO AV379/1/S1 audio tape).

29. HRO 27M74/DBC257 and DBC260 and the recollections of the late Mrs Floss House of Pennington.

30. Coles, *Transport, op. cit.*, states that a short-lived service operated in 1904, (p.90), but that Lymington Borough Council did not grant a licence for steam buses until 13 July, 1905 (p.71).

31. Hole, R.H., 'A Boyhood's Memories of Lymington', *Papers of the LHRS*, 17/1/1958, 4.

32. Obit. of Albert Stride, *Advertiser and Times*, 16 February, 1985.

33. Coles, *Transport, op. cit*, 98.

34. Bostock, *Lymington Yesterday, op cit*. Mrs Sherrier's recollections. According to Robert Hole, 'Boyhood Memories', the first car belonged to Dr Rennie of Linden House.

35. *Advertiser & Times*, 21 May 1932.

36. For example see report 'Lymington Parking Problems', *Advertiser and Times*, 10 April, 1993.

37. Information from '150 years of Lymington-Yarmouth Ferries', *Advertiser & Times*, 14 June 1980 and Coles, *Transport, op. cit.*, 128-131

38. 'How Lymington High Street has changed', *Advertiser and Times*, 28 January, 1939.

39. *Lymington & South Hants Chronicle*, 22 February 1900.

40. Hole, 'Boyhood Memories', *op. cit.*, 1.

41. *Lynlec News*, edited by B. Bennett and R. Jackman, vol. 5, No. 12 (n.d., *c.*1968)

42. Hole, 'Boyhood Memories', *op. cit.*

43. Howlett, *The Guv'nor, op. cit.*, 217-19.

44. From Miss Buckeridge's published talk to the LHRS, February, 1967, from which much of the foregoing information is derived.

45. Local Government Act 1929.

46. Dame Cicely Saunders (1918-2005).

47. Hasselt, Marc van, *A History of Oakhaven Hospice* (2003). 'Oakhaven founder honoured', *A&T*, 23 October 1999 and 21 January 2006.

48. Details from: Slater, A.L., 'Lymington Corporation in the Nineteenth Century', *Papers of the LHRS*, 6 April 1959, 12-13: Down, B.J., *Lymington in Old Picture Postcards* (1985), 12, 32 and 64 and Down, B.J., *Lymington—a Pictorial Past* (1991), 43.

49. Bostock, *Lymington Yesterday, op. cit.* (1955).

50. 'Sharp fall in sales forces electrical store to close', *New Forest Post*, 2 March 2006.

51. 'When Woolies came to Lymington', *A & T*, 26 Oct 2002.

52. Later Morrisons who then sold out to Waitrose.

53. 'The Cathedral' and other poems (1864), *Songs of Lymington* (1867) and *Songs in the Shade* (1881)

54. Ravenscroft, W., 'Henry Doman and his Poems', *M-o-S Occ. Mag.*, Vol. 2, No. 3, (March 1917), 6-7.

55. Details reported by Andrew Ross in *The New Forest Post*, 21 May, 1987.

56. Report in the *Advertiser & Times*, 3 June 1989.

57. *A&T*, 1 April 2006 and 17 June 2006.

58. Logan V.K.C., 'Some Notes about Lymington River and Yachting' *Papers of the LHRS*, September 1968, 2. The pram was a 12-foot, lug sail, clinker built vessel made by Dan Bran and the Berthon Boat Co.

59. A leading figure in the promotion and support of the regatta was Charles Thomas King (1857-1914), bookseller and printer.

60. Chitty, J., *The River is within Us* (Lymington 1983). A rich source for information on maritime Lymington.

61. Chitty, *ibid.*, 126.

62. *Ibid.*

63. Interesting material on this topic and the problems it aroused is covered in Drummond, M., *Conflicts in an Estuary* (Ilex Press, n.d. *c.*1971)

64. Raban, *op. cit.*, 167.

65. Letter, 'Memories of Lymington', *Advertiser & Times*, 21 January 1989.

66. See obituaries in *The Times*, 15/12/1990 and the *Advertiser and Times* 8/12/1990.

67. Down, B.J., *Lymington: a Pictorial Past* (1991), 70.

68. *Advertiser and Times*, 14 May, 1932.

69. '50 Years Ago' quoted in the *A&T*, 21 Feb 1998.

70. Jonathan Raban's father, the Rev. Peter Raban, was vicar of Pennington 1959-66.

71. Raban, op. cit., 166.

72. *The Times*, 29 October, 1992, 9; *Advertiser and Times*, 7 November, 1992.

73. Letter from Gordon Young in the *Advertiser & Times*, 17 April 1993.

74. *Advertiser and Times*, 10 October, 1992.

75. *The Lymington and Isle of Wight Chronicle*, 26 November 1869.

76. Most information from Jones, *History of Lymington* (1930), 190-2.

77. *Ibid.*, 191.

78. Letter in *A & T*, 14 Sept. 2002.

79. Hole, R.H., 'The History of the Lymington Schools', *Papers of the LHRS*, 5/2/1960, 8; and Gatrell, R., 'Sea Scouting in Lymington: the early days', *Hampshire Magazine*, Vo. 35, No. 1, Nov. 1994, 47-50.

80. Down, B.J., *One Man's Vision: The History of Lymington Community Association* (Lymington 1996) provides a valuable source for this subject.

81. Thanks largely to two generous legacies worth £½m bequeathed by Mrs Daphne Fuller and Miss Joyce

McLellan. (*A&T*, 1 April 2006)

82. Information abstracted from *Half our Present*, a survey produced by Priestlands County Secondary School in 1967.

83. The figure given in the Key Stage 3 performance table.

84. Later Hordle Walhampton School following a merger in 1996.

85. A very detailed account appears in Pinnell, B., *op. cit.*, 82-115. See also Wheatley, D., *Saturdays with Bricks*

(1971).

86. James, J., *Lymington: A History and a Celebration* (2005), 57.

8. 7 Pinckney, R., 'A Look Around Lymington', *Advertiser and Times*, 25/10/1952 (also as 'Some Old Houses in Lymington', *Papers of the LHRS, 1952*).

88. Figures abstracted from the census profile provided by the New Forest District Council.

Bibliography

Published papers of the Lymington Historical Record Society (those relating or referring to Lymington only. Date of lecture in brackets.)

Ash, E.G., *The Dawning of Catholic Emancipation in Lymington* (6/2/1959)

Beagley, J.W., *The Manor of Lymington* (15/3/1957)

Best, A.M., *Family Affairs in Queen Anne's Reign* (25/11/1955)

Best, A.M., *Lymington versus the Tollbridge 1738* (14/2/1958)

Bruce, H., *The Salterns* (17/10/1958)

Cowley, S.W., *The History of the Baptists in Lymington* (14/11/1958)

Geddes, A.G., *Public Life in Lymington a Century Ago* (19/4/1963)

Haig, K.B., *The St Barbe Family* (1953)

Hockey, S.F., *The Links Between Quarr Abbey and the Lymington District* (n.d)

Hole, R.H., *A Boyhood's Memories of Lymington* (17/1/1958)

Hole, R.H., *The History of the Lymington Schools* (5/2/1960)

James, J., *Pylewell, Lymington, and the Weld Family* (30/3/1979)

Jolly, R.H., *The Lymington Congregational Story* (11/12/1959)

Jones, B.C., *Illustrations of Lymington's Maritime Trade* (18/4/1958)

King, E., *Lymington Records from the Vestry Books* (25/2/1955)

King, E., *The First Lymington Poorhouse* (26/9/1958)

King, E., *The Story of an Old Business - King's* (25/9/1960)

Knight, A., *The Lymington Railway Centenary* (14/3/1958)

Lloyd, A.T., *Medieval Place Names of the Borough Area* (24/2/1956)

Lloyd, A.T., *Local Place-Names: Their Interest and Meaning* (6/3/1959)

Lloyd, A.T., *Lymington's History from sources in London* (-/9/1963)

Lloyd, A.T., *The Salterns of Lymington, Milford and Hordle* (-/9/1964)

Logan, V.K.C., *Some Notes about Lymington River and Yachting* (1968)

Pinckney, R., *Some Old Houses in Lymington* (1952)

Pinckney, R.A., *Lymington Parish Church* (-/1/1957)

Slater, A.L., *An Eighteenth Century Post Bag* (n.d)

Slater, A.L., *Lymington Corporation in the Nineteenth Century* (6/4/1959)

Welch, E., *Admiralty Courts, 1199-1835* (19/2/1965)

Whitaker, W.I., *The History of Pylewell* (17/11/1961)

Willmer, H., *The Hustings in Lymington* (23/3/1956)

Books and booklets on or about Lymington (including biographies)

Allwood, R., *George Elgar Hicks* (ILEA Exhibition Catalogue, 1982) [Lymington born artist.]

Barrey, H.C., *Prehistoric Lymington* (1855)

Beeching, F.J. (compiler), *Official Guide: Lymington, New Milton, Milford-on-Sea and Barton-on-Sea*, (Borough of Lymington, 1937-38) 40pp. illus. booklet with advertisements.

Birks, M., *Lymington and the French Revolution: The Quiberon Expedition 1795* (Lymington Museum, Trust leaflet, No. 1, September 1995)

Birks, M., *National School to St Barbe Museum* (Lymington Museum Trust leaflet, No. 2, October 1995)

Blackburn, E., *The Saga of Quiberon and the Emigrés of Lymington, June-July 1795* (Lymington, Buckland Trust, 1995)

Blakiston, P., *A Sermon preached in the Parish Church of Lymington on the occasion of the death of the Rev. Ellis Jones* (printed by J. Martin, Lymington, 1833)

Blakiston, P., *A Farewell Sermon preached in Lymington Church* (26 May 1833 and printed by J. Martin, Lymington)

Bostock, C & Hapgood, E., *Notes on the Parish Church, Lymington* (King, Lymington 1912)

Bridger, A. (editor), *Index to 1891 Census*, vol. 11, *Lymington*, parts 1, 2 and 3 (HGS 1997)

Brown, A., *Lymington – The Sound of Success* (Nuneaton 1988)

Burrard, S., *Annals of Walhampton* (1874)

Cannon, J., *Lymington Infirmary: from Poor Law to NHS* (Privately published 1992)

Cannon, J., *Two Hundred Illustrious Years: The Story of*

the Catholic Parish of Lymington (no publication details [1999])

Chitty, J., *The River Within Us: A Maritime History of Lymington* (Lymington 1983)

Cliffe, J., *History of the Congregational Church in Lymington 1700-1900* (1901)

Close-Brooks, J., *Buckland Rings and Ampress Camp* (St Barbe Museum & Art Gallery leaflet, No.5, December 2000). A5, 8pp leaflet, illus.

Cockram, J. and Williams, R., *Lymington War Memorial* (Published by the authors for the Royal British Legion, 2005)

Coles, R. *The Story of Lymington* (Newbury 1983)

Coles, R., *Lymington High Street, Then and Now* (Ringwood 1984), St Barbe Museum reprint 2002

Coles, R., *Picture Postcards of Lymington and the New Forest* (Lymington 1985)

Coles, R., *Lymington and the New Forest: Transport History* (Lymington 1986)

Coles, R., *Local Photographers of Lymington and the New Forest* (Lymington 1990)

Douglas, T., *History of the Baptist Church* (Lymington 1910)

Douglass, D.A., *The Story of Lymington United Reformed Church* (Lymington 1983)

Down, B.J., *Lymington in Old Picture Postcards* (Zaltbommel 1985)

Down, B.J., *Lymington: Steeped in History* (Ringwood 1989)

Down, B.J., *Lymington Baptist Church 1688-1988* (Lymington 1984)

Down, B.J., *Lymington: A Pictorial Past* (Southampton 1991)

Down, B.J., *Lymington Town Sailing Club – the first fifty years* (Privately publ. n.d. [1996]). 72pp. A5 booklet with advertisements.

Down, B.J., *One Man's Vision: The History of Lymington Community Association* (Lymington Community Association, 1996). 48pp A4 booklet, with advertisements.

Down, B.J., *125 Years: The House of Elliott* (no publisher details [Dec. 1997]). 32 pp, illus.

Down, B.J., *Lymington in Old Picture Postcards* (European Library, Zaltbommel, The Netherlands, 5th edition, 1999)

Down, B.J., *Lymington & Pennington Town Guide* (The Brit. Publ. Co., Ltd., 2001)

Down, B., *Lymington and Pennington 'Then and Now'* series (Tempus Publishing, Stroud 2003)

Drummond, M., *Conflicts in an Estuary: A Study of Lymington River* (Ilex Press, n.d., c.1972)

Ford, D.E., *A Sermon occasioned by the lamented death of John Nike. Esq* (R. King, Lymington 1827)

Gannaway, N., *175 Years of Lymington Cricket Club 1807-1982* (Eon Graphics, Highcliffe 1982)

Gannaway, N., *History of Lymington Football Club, 1876-1984* (Eon Graphics, Highcliffe 1984)

Gannaway, N., *The Barfield: One Hundred and Fifty Years of Cricket at Lymington Sports Ground, 1836-1986* (Eon Graphics, Highcliffe 1986)

Gannaway, N., *A History of Lawrence Boys' Club, Lymington, 1928-1988* (Highcliffe, privately published, n.d. [1988])

Garrow, D., *History of Lymington and its immediate vicinity, etc.* (Simpkin and Marshall, 1825)

Grigsby, J., *Lymington: the History and Today's Guide* (Southampton, Paul Cave n.d. c.1975)

Grigsby, J., *This was Lymington* (Southampton, Paul Cave n.d., c. 1976)

Grove, R.A., *Views of the Principal Seats and Marine and Landscape Scenery in the Neighbourhood of , Lymington, drawn on stone by L. Haghe* (Lymington 1832)

Hill, K., *From Forest to Ferry: The story of the Brockenhurst-Lymington Branch Line* (St Barbe, Lymington, 2004)

Hobby, C., *An Album of Old Lymington and Milford-on-Sea* (Southampton, Ensign Press, 1989)

Howlett, J., *The Guv'nor: the Autobiography of John Howlett* (as told to Iris Woodford, privately published 1973)

James, J., *The Salt Industry of Lymington and the Solent Coast* (Lymington Museum Trust leaflet No. 3, 1996). A5, 6pp. folder, illus.

James, J., *Lymington: A History and a Celebration* (Francis Frith/Ottakers 2005)

Jones, C.P., *History of Lymington* (King, Lymington 1930)

Keen, M., *Lymington National School* (unpublished typescript, 1968)

King, E., *Old Times Revisited, Lymington, Hants* (London, Hamilton, Adams and Co. and Lymington, King, 1879)

[King, E.], *Round Lymington and through the New Forest* (n.d. c.1873)

King, E., *Old Times Revisited, Lymington, Hants* (New edition, enlarged format, Chas T. King, Lymington 1900)

King, E., *A Walk through Lymington* (Lymington 1972)

King, E., *A Walk through Lymington*, (revised and extended edition by D. and J. Irvine, Southampton, 1990)

[King, R.], *A New Guide to Lymington* (R. King, Lymington, 1828) ['By a Resident', alias Richard King]

King, R., *A Handbook for the Town of Lymington the New Forest and the surrounding Neighbourhood &c.*, with map and plates (R. King, Lymington, 1845)

King, R., *The Handbook for the Town of Lymington, &c.* (R. King, Lymington 1853)

Lloyd, A.T., *Lymington Index* (Private publ. 1962)

Lloyd, A.T., *The Salterns of Lymington, Milford and Hordle* (Privately publ. 1966)

Lloyd, A.T., *Lymington Index of Local History* (2nd enlarged edition, Buckland Trust, Lymington 1992)

Lymington Corporation, *Official Illustrated Guide to Lymington* (A.E. Woodford, Lymington, n.d. [probably mid 1920s])

Lymington Borough, The Silver Jubilee of King George V: Souvenir-Programme (1935).36 pp. booklet with portraits of mayor and mayoress.

Lymington Borough Council, *Borough of Lymington: New Milton, Barton on Sea, Milford on Sea, Official Guide 1971-1972* (Gloucester, The British Publ. Co., n.d. [1972])

Lymington and Pennington Town Council, *Town Guide* (Gloucester, The British Publ. Co., n.d. c.1984), with folding street map.

Mate (publisher), *Mate's Illustrated Lymington Guide* (issued under the auspices of the Town Improvement Association, publ: W. Mate and Sons, Bournemouth and Lymington, n.d., c.1913.). Booklet with advertisements. [See also list of trade directories, *infra*.]

Mate (publisher) *Lymington Guide* (issued under the auspices of the Town Improvement Association, publ: W. Mate and Sons, Bournemouth and Lymington, 2nd edition, 1915). 68pp., booklet (different format to above.)

Maturin, B., *Disendowment and Disestablishment of the Church* (speech delivered by Rev. B. Maturin, in the Assembly Rooms, Lymington, 25 Dec. 1885 and printed and published by King Bros of Lymington)

Michell, H.C., *A Sermon preached in Lymington Church, 23 Feb. 1840, for Sir Harry Burrard Neale* (Printed and published by R. King, Lymington, 1840)

[Oake, R.], *Pen and Pencil Sketches of Lymington and Ten Miles Round* (Lymington, F.L. Watson, n.d., c.1860.)

Paye, P., *The Lymington Branch* (The Oakwood Press 1979)

Pearce, D & Hodges, D.I., *Wellworthy: the first Fifty Years* (Lymington 1969, Qto publication)

Pearce, D. & Hodge, D.I., *Wellworthy: the first Fifty Years* (Lymington 1969, A4 publication)

Pink, B.J., *Wartime Exploits of Coastal Forces Craft built at Berthon Boat Company, Lymington, 1939-1945* (St Barbe Museum, 2005)

Pinnell, B., *Country House History around Lymington, Brockenhurst and Milford-on-Sea* (1st edition published by the author 1987, 2nd edition St Barbe Museum, Lymington 2002)

Rackley, A. and Adams, J., *Investigations of a Timber Structure in the Lymington River* (Hampshire, and Wight Trust for Maritime Archaeology, 1994)

St Barbe, C., *Records of New Lymington* (compiled 1848, published c.1861)

Speed, H.F., *Incidents in the Life of a Berthon Dinghy: A Series of Rough Pen and Ink Sketches* (privately published, printed by King, Lymington, 1890)

Taylor, J.C., *The Lymington Submersibles of 1804* (Lymington Soc. Occasional Paper 1991)

Taylor, J.C., *Lymington's Wavy Walls* (Lymington Soc. Occasional Paper No. 2, 1991)

Towndrow, J., *Moore and Blatch: A Brief History* (Cedar Press, Southampton, 1990)

Warner, R., *A Companion in a Tour Round Lymington* (Southampton, 1789)

Wheatley, D., *Saturdays with Bricks (and other days under shell-fire)* (Hutchinson 1961)

White, H.L., *The Old Gravestones of Lymington Churchyard* (Bournemouth 1979)

Wilson, E., *A Few Observations on the Port of Lymington* (1855)

Wilson, E., *A Few Observations on the Practicability of Improving the Port of Lymington in connection with the Projected Railway* (Hamilton Adams, 1885)

Books with significant Lymington material

The Annual Hampshire Repository Vol.I (1799), Vol.II (1801)

Bearman, R. (editor), *Charters of the Redvers Family and the Earldom of Devon 1090-1217* (Devon & Cornwall Record Society, New Series, Vol. 37, 1994) [see index for references]

Berkeley, J., *Lulworth and the Welds* (Gillingham, The Blackmore Press, 1971). [Lymington references, esp. 237-254.]

Brown, N., *Dissenting Forbears* (Chichester 1988), mainly pp. 25-41. [David Everard Ford and family]

Coles, R., *History of Communications in South West Hampshire, Vol. 1, The Development of the Postal Service and Transport* (Lym. & District Historical Society 1996)

Coles, R., *History of Communications in South West Hampshire, Vol. 2, Village Post Offices* (Lym. & District Historical Society 1997)

Coles, R., *History of Communications in South West Hampshire, Vol. 3, Postal and other Communications* (Lym. & District Historical Society n.d. c.1998)

Coles, R., *Messuages and Mansions around Lymington and the New Forest* (Published by the author, 1998)

Defoe, D., *The Storm*, edited by Richard Hamblyn (Penguin Classics 2005), pp.127-8.

Fiennes, C., *The Journeys of Celia Fiennes*, edited by Christopher Morris (The Cresset Press, 1949), pp. 49-50

Hockey, S.F., (editor) *The Beaulieu Cartulary* (Southampton Record Series, 17, 1974) [see index for references]

Hockey, S.F. (editor), *The Charters of Quarr Abbey* (I-o-W Record Series, Vol. 3, 1991) [see index for references]

Hughes, E., *Studies in Administration and Finance, 1558-1825: with Special Reference to the History of Salt Taxation in England* (Manchester University Press 1934, reprint Porcupine Press, Philadelphia 1980) [many refs, see Index]

Hughes, M., *The Small Towns of Hampshire: The Archaeological and Historical Implications of Development* (Hampshire Archaeological Committee, Jan. 1976). Lymington pp.83-8.

Kidd, W. *Picturesque Companion to the Watering Places* (n.d.), engravings by G.W. Bonner, pp. 66-71.

Little, B., *The Monmouth Episode* (1956), see Index for various Lymington references.

Merewether, H.A. and Stephen, A.J., *A History of Boroughs and Municipal Corporations*, 3 vols. (1835, reprinted by Harvester Press 1972). Lymington, p. 1368.

New Forest Magazine (1887-1975). Lymington features in monthly articles from the later nineteenth century into the post-World War I period – however there are gaps and the amount of detail is erratic.]

Nichols, A., *Wellington's Mongrel Regiment: A History of the Chasseurs Britanniques Regiment 1801-1814* (Spellmount, Staplehurst 2005), see Index for Lymington refs.

Patmore, D., *Coventry Patmore: his Life and Times* (Constable, 1949) [mainly pp. 203-216.]

Raban, J., *Coasting* (Picador edition 1987) [mainly pp. 164-9.]

Vancouver, C., *General View of the Agriculture of Hampshire including the Isle of Wight.* (London, Richard Phillips, 1810). [Salterns described, pp. 419-423.]

Warner, R., *Topographical Remarks relating to the South-Western parts of Hampshire* (1793), volume I, 1-43.

Warner, R., *Literary Recollections* (2 vols, London: Longman, Rees, Orme, Brown and Green, 1830), pp.35ff.

Welch, E., *The Admiralty Court Book of Southampton 1566-85* (1968), various references.

Wetton, J.L. (editor), *The Hampshire Seventeenth Century Traders' Tokens* (Kings of Lymington, 1964)

White, W., *History, Gazetteer and Directory of the County of Hampshire* (1st edition 1859, 2nd edition 1878)

The History of Parliament: The House of Commons in various volumes contains detailed information on the parliamentary borough and biographies of the MPs who represented Lymington. The series is incomplete and on-going.

Articles and Papers on Lymington

Agg Large, J.S.P., 'The Salterns Linger On', *Hampshire Magazine*, Vol. 11, No. 6 (April, 1971), 27-8.

Brook-Hart, D., *Some Notes about Antique Prints* (Old Custom House, Lymington, n.d. *c*.1972) [printed by Kings of Lymington]. 8pp booklet in glossy card cover, illus.

Constant, A., 'High Days of the Hampshire Salt Trade', *Hampshire Magazine*, Vol. 14, No. 8 (June 1974), p.57.

Country Life, 'Lymington: A Little Town in Jeopardy' *Country Life*, 20 June,1936

Garbett, H., 'Lymington Borough', *VCH Hampshire and the Isle of Wight*, Vol. IV (1912), 639-49

Gatrell, J., 'Sea Scouting in Lymington: the early days', *Hampshire Magazine*, vol. 35, no. 1 (Nov. 1994), 47-50

Hayward-Broomfield, W., 'Lymington school days after the First World War', *Hampshire Magazine*, vol. 26, no. 6 (Apr. 1986)

Hewitt, E.M. and Vellacott, C.H., 'Salt' (Industries section), *VCH Hampshire and the Isle of Wight*, Vol. V (1912), 469-72.

Horne, J., 'Gas Lighting in Lymington', *Hampshire Industrial Archaeological Society Journal* No. 15 (2007), 30-2.

James, J., 'A Lucky Escape for Lymington', *Newsletter of Hampshire Archives Trust* (Spring 1995), 36-9.

Jones-Evans, E., 'Lymington's Theatres', *Hampshire Magazine*, vol. 8. no. 1. (Nov. 1967)

Little, B., 'The Ancient Port of Lymington', *Country Life*, 4 Aug. 1960

Lloyd, A.T., 'The Early Officials of Old Lymington and of the Borough of New Lymington, and a , Reference to its First Two Charters', *HFC&AS New Forest Report* No. 13 (Jan. 1974), 30-2.

March, J., 'Centenary Plus of a Family Business', *Hampshire Magazine*, Vol. 17, No 7 (May 1977) 47-57. [Elliotts].

Moody, S.J., 'Grove Gardens Excavation, Lymington', *The Avon Valley Archaeological Society Newsletter, No. 11* (Sept. 1997), 3-5. With plan and section.

Ravenscroft, W., 'Old Lymington Salterns', *Procs. HFC&AS*, Vol. VII, part 1 (1914), pp.81-5.

Rice, F.A., 'The Rices of Lymington', *Hampshire Magazine*, vol. 10, no. 1 (Nov. 1969), 45-6.

Riley, R.C., 'The Lymington Railway Line', *Railway Magazine*, February, 1956.

Warner, O., 'Admiral Burrard's Red Book', *Country Life*, 18 June, 1948, pp.1239-1240.

Wellworthy Topics (house journal of Wellworthy Ltd, edited by D.I. Hodges, established in 1960 and published quarterly into the 1980s) [contains many articles relevant to Lymington and the New Forest.]

Acts of Parliament

The Lymington Railway Act, 1856. 19 & 20 Vict. c. 71.
Lymington River Act, 1865. 28 & 29 Vict. c. 228.
An Act for authorizing the Lymington Railway Company to acquire the Ferry across the Lymington River, etc. 21 July, 1859. 22 & 23 Vict. c. 15.
An Act for incorporating "The Lymington Harbour and Docks Company", etc. 23 June, 1864. 27 & 28 Vict. c. 120.
Lymington Harbour and Docks (Extension of Time) Act, 1872. 35 & 36 Vict. c. 165. Lymington Harbour and Docks (Extension of Time) Act, 1875. 38 & 39 Vict. c. 56.
Local Government Board's Provisional Orders Confirmation (No. 9) Act, 1889. Borough of Lymington. *52 & 53 Vict. c. 112.*
Pier and Harbour Orders Confirmation (No. 1) Act, 1913. Lymington River and Harbour. 3 & 4 Geo. V. c. 146.
Lymington Rural District Council Act, 1921. 11 & 12 Geo. V. c. 29.
Pier and Harbour Order (Keyhaven) Confirmation Act, 1936.
Pier and Harbour Order (Lymington) Confirmation Act, 1951. 14 & 15 Geo. VI. c. 25.

Trade Directories

Note: *Hampshire Directories* by a variety of publishers from 1784 to 1939 contain sections on Lymington. However, Mate, King and Kent, respectively, published specific trade directories for Lymington. These are the ones listed here.
1913 W. Mate & Sons
1914 W. Mate & Sons
1915 W. Mate & Sons
1931 Chas. T. King
1939 Chas. T. King
[1955] Kent Service Ltd.*
[1958] Kent Service Ltd.*

*These directories are not dated, but dates are deduced from internal evidence.

Newspapers

The Salisbury and Winchester Journal and the *Hampshire Chronicle* were the principal local newspapers until the founding of the *Lymington Chronicle and South Hants Chronicle* on 11 November 1858.
The New Milton Advertiser bought out the *Lymington Chronicle* in 1934 and then published the *Lymington Times* which continues to the present time.
Free newspapers include Bright's *Lymington Courier* (fl. mid-1860s), Henry Doman's *The Lymington Monthly Illustrated Journal* (fl. 1870s) and C.T. King's *The Popular Advertiser* which ran monthly from November 1891 to about 1914. *The New Forest Post*, first published in 1981 continues to the present time.

Books of hymns, poetry and literary works and fiction written about Lymington or by Lymingtonians and/or printed and published in Lymington

Anon., *The Book of the Pageant* (Lymington, n.d. [28 June 1933]). Organizers: The Lady Lily Greene and Mrs Gott, OBE. List of events and performers.
Collins, W., *The Rationalist* (Heinemann, 1993)
Collins, W., *The Marriage of Souls* (Weidenfeld & Nicholson, 1999) [salterns feature largely]
Doman, H., *The Cathedral and other Poems* (1864)
Doman, H., *Songs of Lymington* (1867)
Doman, H., *Songs in the Shade* (Lymington 1881)
Ford, D.E., *Hymns chiefly on the Parables of Christ* (Westley and Davis, London 1828) [Printed by Richard King of Lymington]
Glamorgan, T.H., *Poems and Songs* (Lymington, R. King, 1843)
Rutherfurd, E., *The Forest* (Century, 2000), esp. pp. 169-220

Index

Because of its frequent occurrence in the text the name Lymington is not included.